Well Trained

by

David Packer

Triangle

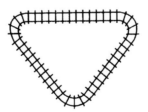

Publishing

Copyright © David Packer 2003
First published 2003 by Triangle Publishing.
British Library Cataloguing Data.
Packer D.
Well Trained.
ISBN 0-9529333-8-1
Printed in England by
The Amadeus Press,
Cleckheaton.
Text by David Packer
Maps by A.Palmer.
Compiled and edited for publication
by D.J.Sweeney.
Cover design by Scene, Print & Design Ltd.,
Leigh, Lancs.
Designed and published by
Triangle Publishing,
509, Wigan Road,
Leigh, Lancs. WN7 5HN.
Tel: 01942/677919
www.trianglepublishing.co.uk

Front cover. A pair of ex-LMS Stanier engines, class '5' No.45204 and 'Jubilee' No.45558 *Manitoba,* depart from Manchester Exchange with the 08.55 Newcastle-Liverpool Lime Street express about 1960.

Photo, Jim Carter.

Rear cover, top. Birmingham New Street on 3rd August 1957. Ex-LMS 'Jubilee' 4-6-0 No. 45623 *Palestine* has just taken over from 'Crab' 2-6-0 No.42754 at the head of the 10.35am Bournemouth-Manchester Victoria   *Photo, Michael Mensing.*

Rear cover, bottom. Stanier Class '5 'No.45079 leads 'Jubilee' No.45558 '*Manitoba'* in a smoky departure from Leeds City station about 1960 working a Newcastle-Liverpool Lime Street express.

Photo, Jim Carter.

Plate 1. Ex-LMSR 'Jubilee' class 4-6-0 No.45619 *Nigeria* at Bristol Temple Meads station, awaiting departure at the head of the 7.20pm 'Mail' to Newcastle-on-Tyne. The author's first railway journeys were on this train from Birmingham to Darlington.
Photo, R. F. Leonard,The Kidderminster Railway Museum Trust Collection.

CONTENTS

INTRODUCTION

I make no apologies for wallowing in nostalgia. I know there are many who dislike looking back and I would imagine that psychologists could argue that thinking too much of times past reveals a little of a person's present state of mind and happiness. Let them! I was fortunate in having a happy childhood and trains were very much a part of my life, but there are many things that make me happy today. So why look back? Because life was different then and the happiness experienced at that time was of a child with an undeveloped mind exposed to different influences, one of which was the steam train. And the steam train has disappeared from everyday life. This book is not intended to be too technical but more of a light-hearted excursion through the twentieth century concentrating, in particular, on the last fifty years as seen through the eyes of a railway enthusiast. I hope that some fond memories are evoked.

Locomotives, trains and railway journeys over the years have made a big impression on me. During my childhood the steam engines that were familiar to me were the 'Jubilees' and 'Royal Scots' of the London Midland Region, 'A3s', 'V2s', 'D49s', 'A5s' and 'A8s' of the Eastern Region and the Moguls and pannier tanks of the Western Region. The trains I remember were the expresses between Liverpool and Newcastle, the Darlington-Saltburn trains and the Chester-Barmouth services, while the most memorable journeys were along the East Coast Main Line between York and Darlington, the passage through the industrial heartland of Teesside, east of Darlington, and the Llangollen-Cynwyd section of the Western Region's route to Bala and Barmouth. Though still vivid in my mind the actual number of journeys was relatively small compared with, say, the hundreds of times I commuted from Brooklands to Manchester Oxford Road on the old electric multiple units (EMUs), designed by the LMS for the MSJ&AR, where they were the standard motive power until 1971. By then I was travelling to all parts of England, Scotland and Wales behind a wide range of diesel and electric locomotives.

What follows is not just about railways and trains, however. It is also about life the way it used to be and about the changes that have taken place. From the innocent, secure world of the nineteen-fifties to the worldly-wise time at the end of the twentieth century; the end of a millennium. Was there ever a better period for a child to develop than in the post-war decade of security, togetherness and respect with all the technological advantages and improvements over previous decades. At first, television and the motor car added pleasures to this era. Television opened our eyes to the outside world, put us immediately in touch with important people and events, and gave us visual entertainment in our sitting rooms. The motor car allowed us to visit places that were so much more difficult to see when dependent on public transport. Then things changed and I accept this may be partly because I began to view the world with more adult eyes. However, owing to a combination of a more relaxed censorship regime and the media's desire to push existing boundaries as far as possible, standards and attitudes changed. It helped bring about a more open society but did that mean a better one? In so far as it helped to abolish many old injustices the answer has to be yes but it also brought about a new set of social problems, caused partly by a breakdown of the old, mainly unwritten rules of life. Television made us more insular but the car has also contributed to this change of behaviour. Driving was once a pleasure but that heyday has already gone and it is largely the convenience that remains. It is possible that the information technology revolution will come to the rescue and save us from the predicament of excessive congestion through making it possible for a growing number of people to work from home, thereby reducing car journeys and also helping to cut down crime and impacting on the health of the nation in a positive way.

While the motor car increased our mobility railways also played their part in allowing us to travel much greater distances. Looking at three generations of my family one can see an example of how developments in transport as well as improved standards of living have facilitated such changes. My paternal grandfather never travelled more than two hundred miles from his home in his life and relied on public transport, a bicycle and his feet. My father bought his first car when he was nearly forty and my parents took their first foreign package holiday when they were nearly fifty. I had acquired my first car and had my first package holiday by the time I was twenty-one. The pace of change can sometimes appear frightening and one reason why second homes are purchased in the country is to allow a return to a more natural rhythm of life. Fortunately, there are still places off the beaten track in, say, quiet valleys on the mainland and on the islands off Scotland where the way of life remains relatively unchanged and evokes a world that, to many of us, is a distant memory. This is one of the reasons why I find some of the stations on the preserved steam railways so appealing with their timeless qualities but, now that I have returned to the subject of railways, perhaps this is an appropriate point to start the book in earnest.

For those readers who do not consider themselves to be railway buffs the appendices contain explanations of the abbreviations and further background information on railways and locomotives.

Plate 2. Ex-LMSR class '5' No.44964, departs from platform 7 at Birmingham New Street station with the 8.05am to Newcastle-on-Tyne on 29th June 1957.

Photo, Michael Mensing.

ACKNOWLEDGEMENTS

In preparing this book I would like to thank my father for his help in reviewing the text and providing suggestions and corrections. In some ways the writing was the easiest part as I was only too aware that my own photographic collection was woefully inadequate to support the text. Consequently I am very grateful to a number of people. Firstly, I would like to thank the staff at *Steam Railway* for initially putting me in touch with photographers; it is a drawback when you don't know anyone! They were very forthcoming with help and that was appreciated. Once I had made contact with one photographer other names were suggested and I soon found that I was receiving help from various sources. Tom Heavyside's friendly willingness to help and put me in touch with other photographers proved to be invaluable. Likewise the help of J.D. (Doug) Darby has been of vital assistance and I would like to thank him for the many happy hours I have spent at his home studying his well-organized collection of photographs, especially those that relate to the nineteen-fifties in the south Manchester area. Peter Fitton too, who lives only a mile or so away from me, has been very generous with his time and it is only when I looked at some of his superb photographs that I realise how deficient mine were. David Stratton, Raymond Hughes and Tony Oldfield have also welcomed me into their homes to look at their collections and this has been truly appreciated.

There are a number of photographers whom I have not had the pleasure of meeting but who have also provided me with crucial assistance. Michael Mensing, Ron Gee, David Chatfield, Don Rendell, Jim Carter, Gerry Bent and Gavin Morrison have all supplied photographs (and in many cases, meticulous caption detail) which I am proud to include in this book. Neville Stead has been of great help with scenes in the north-east; we have spoken many times on the phone and, on each occasion, I have marvelled at his enthusiasm, his memory and, of course, his photographs and those in his collection. To all these photographers I really am extremely grateful.

A big thank you is due to Rex Conway, Derek Jones, David Johnson, Nigel Packer, Dennis Sweeney, the Stephenson Locomotive Society and Audie Baker of the Kidderminster Railway Museum for their help in offering material from their collections. I also wish to acknowledge the help provided by Ed Bartholomew of the National Railway Museum at York, Birmingham Central Library, Leeds Central Library, Manchester Central Library, Basil Jeuda, John King of King's in Saltburn and John Lever for their help.

My thanks go out to Norman Spilsbury, Alan Gilbert, Richard Casserley, Roger Carpenter, Hugh Ballantyne, Paul Chancellor, John Whiteley, Barry Mounsey, Ron Whiteley at Birmingham Railway Museum, David Walton and Andrew McFarlane of the Altrincham Electrics Railway Preservation Society for their help in tracing photographs.

I should like to pay a special tribute to Jim Peden, who went out of his way to help with one or two specific shots and apologized for any delays as a result of recent ill-health. I did not know how ill he really was and sadly he died while this book was in preparation. His wife courageously informed me of her bereavement in the weeks that followed and I wish to express my gratitude to her for offering assistance.

Finally, and I think this applies to virtually all the photographers mentioned, I wish to acknowledge the dedication and enthusiasm of those contributors who, whether they devoted a few months or a lifetime of effort, have helped to provide a wonderful legacy of pictures for all enthusiasts to enjoy. Some of these photographers are now elderly and, indeed, I was hesitant about making approaches to some of them but I have been staggered at their continuing enthusiasm. The conclusion I have come to is that an interest in railways has got to be of good therapeutic value.

1.THE BIRMINGHAM CONNECTION

I was born in Birmingham in 1948 at the General Hospital in Loveday Street, a stone-throw away from the Great Western's Snow Hill station and not much further away from that major intersection of the LMS, New Street station; almost within sight of trains and certainly within hearing distance. Indeed, it is a feature of my life that wherever I have lived and at almost all the regular holiday haunts, especially those of my childhood, I have been able to see or at least hear trains. In the words of Siegfried Sassoon, "the train's quite like an old familiar friend".

Sassoon's train reassured him of peace-time and it was into such a period that I was born a generation or two later. It had been a hard-won peace and few families were left unscathed by the turmoils of the first half of the twentieth century. On my father's side, my great-uncle Arthur was killed during the Great War and from my mother's family the life of another great-uncle was claimed, murdered during one of Stalin's purges.

Our side of the Packer family had been the village blacksmiths of Childrey in Berkshire for the best part of two hundred years, carrying on their business from Charles Cottage which still stands today. My great-grandfather, William, moved to Bristol as a young man and became a buyer of butter. He lived comfortably with his wife and seven children until he discovered whisky at the age of forty. He was dead within two years and the family was quickly consigned to poverty. My grandfather, also a William, was a teenager at the time. He had been born in 1886 when Gladstone was prime minister, left school at the tender age of twelve, and now, with his brother Charlie, was sent to Childrey in Berkshire to be looked after by their uncle, the last of the village blacksmiths. They found work at the smithy and supplemented their earnings by labouring on farms before eventually gravitating to Birmingham where work was plentiful and the motor industry was in its infancy. My grandfather found work as an engineer at the Austin Motor Company in Longbridge, not long after the company was established there in 1905. His mother moved to Birmingham with her other children including Dolly, who became a secretary, and Margaret, who entered a furniture business where she would later become a partner. Neither sister married, possibly as a result of the tragic events that had overtaken their father.

During the First World War, the Austin Works was heavily involved in armament production and my grandfather remained there during the War, thus avoiding the traumas of the trenches. He was, nevertheless, required to wear a khaki armband to show that he was in a reserved occupation as some women were known to give white feathers to men of military age in civilian clothing. His brother, Alec, was a machine gunner who survived the hostilities but another brother, Arthur, was killed in action. In the summer of 1917 my grandfather married Lucy Maltby. This was at a time when the Women's Social and Political Union (the 'Suffragettes') was actively trying to secure voting rights for women. During that year such rights had been obtained for women over thirty but my grandmother still had no entitlement to vote at the time of her marriage. Their first home was in Harborne living next door to Lucy's brother, Len, who worked for the London & North Western Railway at Curzon Street Goods Depot. It was here, at Harborne, where my father was born just three months before the end of the Great War.

By 1921 the family had moved to Erdington, my grandfather joining Dunlop as a pipe fitter. Although Erdington was in L&NW territory the family loyalties were with the Great Western Railway and summer holiday destinations at Paignton, Aberystwyth, Boscombe and Ilfracombe usually involved some GWR travel. At Ilfracombe, Dolly had opened a ladies' dress shop, having forsaken her secretarial job, and my father recalled one intriguing journey, courtesy of a Great Western train to Bristol and paddle steamer across the Bristol Channel to Ilfracombe. His earliest railway memories, however, were of being taken to see the almost-new *Caerphilly Castle* at the British Empire Exhibition at Wembley in 1924 and catching a glimpse of the unique GWR Pacific, *The Great Bear*, during its brief life before conversion to a 'Castle' class locomotive.

On leaving the local primary school my father went to King Edward V1 School at Aston, close to Villa Park where he was taken three or four times a year to see Aston Villa play. At the end of his schooldays he joined Dunlop in 1936 (the year of Edward VIII's abdication), working in the laboratory for the princely sum of fifteen shillings (seventy-five pence) a week! At that time there was very limited financial help for students and with insufficient funds at home to pay for a university education my father decided to study for an external degree at London University while still working at Dunlop. Ironically, his father had now lost his job at the company owing to an 'efficiency' purge but later found employment at the Hercules Cycle Company at Aston Cross, where he remained until his retirement in 1953.

In the years preceding the Second World War the family regularly walked at weekends, sometimes in the Lickey Hills but, more usually, a little further afield, travelling via tram and train to Wood End, Danzey, Solihull or Knowle and walking between stations before returning to Erdington. Three incidents from this period have often been recalled in family conversations over the years. On one walk my father's brother, Dennis, was carrying a bottle of lemonade when a stop was made for refreshments at a tea shop in Tanworth in Arden. Presumably the contents of the bottle had been seriously disturbed prior to entering the shop as, immediately the cap was released, a force of Krakatoan proportions exploded upon the scene of hitherto quiet domesticity, covering the family and adjacent wall in the sweet liquid. This was followed by a volunteered cleaning-up operation and a rather shortened refreshment break!

On another occasion my grandfather became the centre of attention in tea rooms (hopefully not the same one) when the boiled egg he had cracked open parted company with the holder, rolled off the plate, bounced off his outstretched leg, which he stuck out in a vain attempt to check the progress of the elliptical body, and proceeded to trace a course in yolk across the dark-brown polished linoleum floor. There was silence in the immediate aftermath as eyes that were initially focused on my grandfather were met by a menacing stare. He was a powerful, stockily-built man. Nothing was said but, once again, cleaning of the affected area was volunteered, as one did in those days. After all, it was the honourable thing to do.

The third escapade was an impromptu game of cricket following a lunch break during a walk near Tanworth in Arden. On a warm summer's day the men of the family were enjoying their version of that most English of sports when my grandfather, tempted by an invitingly-flighted ball bowled a little off-line, prepared for an almighty blow with his inverted walking stick, which had proved very useful as a make-do bat, and missed but connected instead with a large cow-pat which, it is claimed, was distributed over a large area of Umberslade Park!

All too soon this pattern of life with its memorable interludes was disturbed once again by the threat of war and in April 1939 the Government announced that conscription into the forces would begin in July. This was the first time that there had been conscription in peace-time in Britain and my father joined the Signals TA unit, moving to Catterick Camp near Richmond, Yorkshire in July 1939. In September he met my mother but, all too soon, they were separated (as were so many couples during this period) when he was transferred to the reserve as a temporary measure and returned to work at Dunlop. It was not until April 1943 when he returned to the army for training with the Royal Signals at Catterick, and here he renewed his friendship with my mother while training as a radio mechanic. In January 1944 they were married in Saltburn, the best man being Len Hyde, a family friend who lived just around the corner from my grandfather in Erdington. His parents had apparently separated and he found comfort and friendship with the family. With the upheaval of war it had been a while since my father had seen Len but he commented many years later how much he had aged in such a short time. Len was in the Pathfinder Force, formed in 1942 to locate targets for other bombers, and it takes little imagination to appreciate the stress this must have placed on all but the strongest constitutions and spirits. Unfortunately, just over two months after the wedding, on the night of 30th March 1944, Flight Lieutenant Hyde's Lancaster was shot down in the Nuremberg raid and there were no survivors.

In October 1944, following a three-week period of training at a transit camp at Worsted in Norfolk, my father was sent abroad, travelling by troop train to Glasgow and transferring to a ship, the *Eastern Prince*, which became part of a convoy heading for Naples. His ultimate destination was a small hill-top town known as Castelfidardo, near Ancona, where he was a wireless mechanic. He remained here until July 1945, after the War had finished, and was then posted to Gibraltar for eighteen months.

The demobilization process was a massive operation involving over a million soldiers and a million munitions workers. It was based on the principle of releasing first those who had been in service the longest but there was also sufficient political uncertainty to require troops in any event after 1945. Indeed, fifty years later, the disclosure that provisional plans had been discussed for an attack on Russia entered the public domain.

Plate 3. Ex-LMSR 'Jubilee' class 4-6-0 No.45649 *Hawkins* stands at Birmingham New Street station's platform 9 with the 5.20pm Derby-Worcester slow train on 7th September 1961. *Photo, Michael Mensing.*

Consequently it was February 1947, during a very severe winter, when my father was demobilized, returning to the Fort Dunlop site, which can still be seen to the east of the M6 motorway south of Erdington.

By the time he returned his mother had died. She had been ill for some time with cancer but because she was a Christian Scientist my grandfather was requested not to call a doctor. This caused much resentment on her side of the family who felt that my grandfather should have overruled her. However, my mother was released from the ATS at his request to help look after her in the weeks before she died in 1945. My parents lived at my grandfather's house in Oval Road during the post-war years. There were undoubtedly privations caused by rationing at this time but there was an overwhelming feeling of relief that the war had been won, freedom had been achieved and life was there to be enjoyed. However, it was also time to take stock. My father

decided to study for a degree in Chemistry at Birmingham University in September 1947 and the following year, another product of chemistry, I was born into an England that was changing. A Labour Government had created a welfare state and a national health service as well as nationalizing the railways, ports, civil aviation, coal, electricity, gas, steel and atomic energy. At the same time the first stages in the dismantling of the British Empire had already begun, India and Burma gaining their independence by 1948.

During that year of the London Olympics there were also major developments on the railways. Nationalization had merged the four principal independent companies, the LMS, LNER, GWR and the Southern Railway to form British Railways. From an enthusiast's point of view this involved a lot of number-changing except for the former Great Western engines which retained their four-figure numbers on

9

Plate 4. Looking west at ex-LMSR class '4P' 4-4-0 No.41095, alongside Birmingham New Street's platform 7 at the head of the 1.45pm to Cromer, Norwich and Yarmouth on 16th May 1957. Although only a five-coach train, separate coaches served the various East Anglian destinations. In the background is the lattice-framed footbridge.   *Photo, Michael Mensing.*

brass plates (presumably on cost grounds). Locomotive liveries were standardized with green being used for express locomotives and black for all others although there were deviations such as the Western Region practice of adopting green on a variety of locomotive types including tank engines. There was also a brief experimentation with blue for some express types.

In 1948 the most notable of the locomotive exchanges took place. This involved the selection of various classes of engines, drawn from the four pre-Nationalization companies, which competed with each other on twelve principal routes around the country in order to compare performance and efficiency. For trainspotters of the time the sight of 'foreign' locomotives on home territory must have been welcomed enthusiastically and, together with the new Ian Allan

locospotters books, would undoubtedly have helped win over a new generation of enthusiasts.

My birth date fell during the period of the exchanges and my first train journeys occurred later that year as a traveller on the Bristol-Newcastle Mail! We still lived with my grandfather in his large terraced house close to Gravelly Hill, immediately north-east of what is now 'Spaghetti Junction' on the M6, while my mother's family lived in Saltburn-by-the-Sea on the north-east coast. Consequently, at fairly regular intervals, we travelled the two hundred or more miles between Birmingham New Street and Saltburn using the mail train which, naturally, had limited passenger accommodation. The New Street station of my childhood was substantially reconstructed in 1965/6 in preparation for electrification but its location remained the same, set deep in a cutting below the city centre, with tunnels at either end. Regardless of the opinions about the present station I believe that the old New Street had a more awe-inspiring presence with its LNWR and Midland sections, its curved roof and detailed lattice work both in the roof supports and on the internal footbridge, and its setting, combining to give the feeling that here was one of the great 'cathedrals' of the steam age.

Perhaps this early image of a large railway station, mainly in the dim light of the evening, wreathed in swirling and rising steam and smoke that accompanied the characteristic distorted echo of the public announcements and the sound of moving trains played its part, subconciously, in shaping my interest in trains. It was certainly a stirring image which I would later marvel at in other 'cathedrals' such as Manchester Exchange, Leeds City, York and Darlington. The 'Mail' spent the best part of an hour at New Street although most travellers would probably only have been aware of its departure time. It was the family practice to board the train soon after its arrival in order for me to be settled and I dare say that we would have enjoyed the benefit of a compartment to ourselves on occasions as a result of the circumstances. This would have been particularly welcomed as this was always an overnight journey. Hauled usually by, say, a Bristol-based Stanier-designed

Plate 5. Again looking west, ex-LMSR class '5' 4-6-0 No.45221, having arrived at Birmingham New Street station's platform 7 with the northbound 'Pines Express', is in the process of being detached on 18th February 1961.

Photo, Michael Mensing.

11

'Jubilee' the train was worked via Derby and Sheffield to York where Eastern Region motive power took over. It is quite likely that in this early post-Nationalization period some of the locomotives would still have been sporting the old numbers and livery as the process of re-numbering much of the stock of 20,000 engines would have taken some considerable time. One can only speculate but, of greater certainty, was the chance of a large Pacific at the head of the 'Mail' from York. Often, an 'A1' or 'A2', such as York-based *Cock o' the North*, once the pride of Sir Nigel Gresley and the most powerful express locomotive in the land until its rebuilding by Thompson, would restart the train across the Vale of York still in the early hours of the morning. Overnight travel is rarely sleep-inducing but a change of trains at this time can be even more disturbing. However, this was required as the train swung to the left and rolled up alongside the northbound through platform of Darlington Bank Top station (as it used to be called) at some time after 3.30am, about five hours after leaving Birmingham.

There followed a wait of nearly one hour before the connecting train, the first of the day for Saltburn, set off from the branch platforms at the southern end of the station. The sea-side terminus was reached a little after 6am and from the station it was, conveniently, less than a five-minute walk to my maternal grandparents. On a bright summer morning this must have been a pleasant experience, inhaling the crisp sea air, before the smoke from the trains and houses had taken hold, and the extensive views across the North Sea would have added to this gratifying feeling. On a damp or cold dark winter morning, however, I feel sure that the experience would have been very different!

The journey from Birmingham to Saltburn was made on a regular basis until 1951. By this time my father had graduated and the family had expanded in the previous year providing me with a brother, Nigel. But I had already discovered my surroundings, a long narrow garden stretching from the rear of the house, and had the company of a very accommodating mongrel dog, Micky, who patiently accepted the unsophisticated handling by a young child. I occasionally used him as a 'table' to place objects upon as he lay on his side to oblige. Micky was a constant companion until Nigel was old enough to play with meaningfully but, by then, we had moved on.

Plate 6. York-based ex-LNER 'A2/2' Pacific No.60501 *Cock o' the North* seen at York in the 1950s. This Thompson rebuild of Gresley's magnificent 'P2' 2-8-2 engine, bearing the same name, was one of two of the six rebuilds shedded at York and, as such, employed on the 'Mail' train from time to time. It was also one of the first ex-LNER Pacifics to be withdrawn from service (in 1960).   *Photo, The Stephenson Locomotive Society.*

2. THE SALTBURN BRANCH

It was to Saltburn where my mother's family moved a few years before I was born and where my grandmother spent most of the remaining years of her life until she was no longer able to cope with the three-storey terraced house in Emerald Street. But this settled period in her life belies a complex and harrowing past (shared by millions of others in Europe) which began in 1893 when Olga Kniaziewskaya was born in Tarnograd, a small town about seventy miles north-west of Lvov (now in the Ukraine) and about fifty miles south of Lublin in Poland. Tarnograd lay in a region known as Galicia which had, at one time, been independent and, at another time, become part of Poland but, in the years before the First World War, this region was part of the Austro-Hungarian Empire. The official language was Polish although nearly half the population was Ukrainian in Galicia at the outbreak of war in 1914.

Galicia became one of the battlefields of the War when the Russian army defeated the Austrians at the Battle of Lemberg (the German name for Lvov) in September 1914, bringing the area under Russian control, but in May 1915 the German army pushed the Russians back and took control of the territory until the end of the conflict. With the benefit of modern television reporting we have become familiar with the everyday stresses and tragedies of life in war zones and it would have been no different for my grandmother who, by this time, had started work as a teacher. Then, one day, German soldiers knocked at the door and took her away. They told her she was to be detained for a while. She asked if she could take her case with some belongings but they refused her request and, without any possessions, she left home never to see her parents again. She did not speak much in later years about this time but one can only imagine the distress she must have suffered, worrying about the devastation felt by her parents, concerned for her own safety, and then subjected to the conditions that had to be endured on the railway journey to an internment camp at Katzenau in Austria. It was not uncommon to transport large groups of people, at this time, in covered wagons with little if anything that could be described as toilet facilities!

It was at Katzenau where my grandmother met my grandfather, Thomas Walker, who was born in Middlesbrough in 1892. He trained as a teacher of languages and it was his desire to improve his linguistic skills that brought him to Germany and Austria in 1913. He had not returned to England by the outbreak of War and was consequently interned for the duration of the conflict. My grandmother claimed that she was taught English in the camp by the brother of the Irish writer, James Joyce. John Stanislaus Joyce was, like my grandfather, a British subject interned at Katzenau in 1915 and, partly through having a common language, they became friends. Perhaps it was through him that my grandparents met but it was probably quite likely that my grandfather's quick grasp of languages would have been of great assistance to my grandmother. She would also have appreciated his skills at the piano as, like the camp commandant, he was an accomplished pianist.

They married at Katzenau Camp in 1917 shortly before my grandmother was released. She moved initially to neutral Switzerland where she worked for the postal services in Berne, her fluency in German being very useful. However, it was agreed that she should make her way to England and stay with his parents in Marske where, in time, they would be re-united. She duly arrived in England in April 1919 and was treated with kindness by her new parents-in-law but she must have reflected many times on the changes that had caused her to be taken from her homeland and settle in a small town on the north-east coast of England, across the other side of Europe, with only a limited ability to communicate in English.

In one sense my grandparents were fortunate because they had, at least, a home to return to after the turmoil of the previous four years. My great-grandfather owned Longbeck House, which was in fact two semi-detached houses, near Marske-by-the-sea. Of his three children, Hilda lived at home while their younger son, Herbert, lived in the other half of the house with his wife Dolly. However, they had found a home of their own by the end of the War, leaving a vacancy for my grandparents to conveniently fill and where my mother was born in October 1919. At this time they still used German as their common language and, indeed, this continued for much of their life together even though they frequently conversed in other languages. In fact, Italian would shortly come into everyday use after my grandfather received notification by a former camp colleague, with whom he had kept in contact, of a post which would draw on his knowledge of languages. The position was at the Banca di Napoli in Genoa as a foreign correspondent and early in 1921 the family returned to the continent to settle there.

My grandfather had now found a job where he could make full use of his linguistic skills and among the customers he was able to assist during his years at the bank was Marlene Dietrich, the most famous European entertainer at the time. My mother and her younger brother, Boris, were sent to La Scuola Swizzera-Italiana where French, Italian and German were spoken. The school was mainly for foreign nationals and taught a full range of subjects while specializing in languages, but the long summer holidays of three months was the highlight of the year for the children who would spend the first half of their holiday visiting the beach each day to sunbathe and swim. The second part of the vacation was regularly spent on a fruit farm owned by a friend of my grandfather, near Cuneo in the hills close to the French border. The children helped to pick fruit but were also allowed to eat as much as they wanted and duly helped themselves to the plentiful supply of peaches, apricots, cherries and grapes. Only an extended visit to England in 1927, to see their grandparents, interrupted this regular pattern of holidays.

These were happy and carefree times also enjoyed by a third child, Nadyejda, born in 1930, but it was not long before storm clouds gathered once again after Mussolini rose to power in Italy and Hitler was in the process of turning Germany into a powerful military force. After the First World War Italy suffered unemployment and violent strikes causing the Government to resign. Mussolini was asked by the King to form a new Government in October 1922 and, from then, gradually concentrated power in his own hands. The King remained the figurehead but the Fascist Grand Council was now the supreme body of which Mussolini, or Il Duce (the leader) as he became known, was the head. All opposition parties were dissolved and criticism of the Government was silenced but, although his tactics began to cause alarm among sections of the Italian population, his Party breathed new life into the country with agriculture, railways and industry generally benefiting and unemployment substantially reduced by a massive re-armament programme. Little wonder then that he was such a popular figure especially with the young at this time. Like Hitler he was able to whip up an audience or crowds into a frenzy of patriotic fervour

as my mother saw for herself when Mussolini came to Genoa and she stood among the crowds as he drove through Piazza Manin, near to her home.

However, by this time, Boris had already been sent to England as there was pressure on him to join the Blackshirts, a Fascist militia, separate from the army. My grandfather was determined to ensure that he was not going to be recruited and made arrangements for him to be sent to Longbeck House where, from 1934, he had to adjust very quickly to a new language and the English way of life. The writing was on the wall for the rest of the family in Italy when Mussolini invaded Abyssinia in 1936 as part of a programme of colonial expansion. Britain and France objected to this action and applied sanctions, thus stirring up anti-British sentiment. From an Italian viewpoint this seemed perhaps understandable as it was bearing the brunt of hostility from two nations who had themselves acquired substantial empires.

As far as the Walker family was concerned, however, their years spent in Italy counted for nothing and their British surname drew unwelcome attention, sufficient to force my grandfather to lose his job at the bank. It was now clear that his family had to leave Italy and he was the first to return to England in order to organize living accommodation and hopefully find a job while my grandmother was left with her two daughters and the task of selling the flat in Via Cabella as quickly as possible. Consequently, their home was sold cheaply and many of the larger possessions were left behind as they bade farewell to Genoa and Italy in 1938.

Their new home was, once again, one side of Longbeck House in Marske where the whole family was re-united; my grandfather and his family on one side and his widowed father and sister on the other. The family even featured in a Daily Mirror article of October 1940 which referred to the family of five as a 'League of Nations' speaking six tongues. My grandparents still spoke German between themselves; my mother and her brother, Boris, spoke Italian and English; while Nadia, at nine, was still mainly speaking Italian. At other times French, Russian and Polish were used. By the time the article had appeared, however, the family had, once again, split up with my mother having joined the Auxiliary Territorial Service (A.T.S.) in July 1939 and Boris joining the Navy in 1940.

My mother's Aunty Hilda had introduced her to a local girl, Molly, and it was she who planted the idea that they join the A.T.S. There was a lot of patriotism at the time

Plate 7. Ex-LNER 'A5' Pacific tank engine No.69842 at the head of a local passenger train in Darlington Bank Top's south bay. Although this class was designed for the Great Central Railway a further batch was constructed for work in the north-east in 1925. Both Saltburn and Richmond services used these bay platforms. *Photo, Neville Stead.*

Plate 8. Ex-NER 'A8' Pacific tank engine No.69894 ready for departure from Darlington with a local train on 27th March 1954. Designed by Sir Vincent Raven these engines were one of three classes of tank engines to handle Saltburn services prior to dieselisation. *Photo, J.D.Darby.*

Plate 9. A third view of Darlington Bank Top station with ex-LNER 'L1' 2-6-4 tank engine No.67742 at the head of a Saltburn train of articulated stock (coaches with shared bogies) that was frequently employed on these services.

Photo, The Stephenson Locomotive Society.

Plate 10. Ex-NER 'A8' Pacific tank engine No.69866 at the junction station of Eaglescliffe with a Saltburn train.

Photo, R.Payne, Neville Stead Collection.

especially among the young and my mother agreed to join. The irony was that whereas my mother passed her medical, Molly failed! It appears that my grandfather was not very pleased with this outcome, perhaps because he hoped in vain for some stability in the family following the succession of unsettling experiences and, maybe because he felt that his daughter should be at home in the same way that his sister Hilda had remained at home with her parents. My grandmother, on the other hand, wanted her daughter to experience something of what she had been through, and so it was that Catterick Camp accepted another new recruit who was able to put shorthand and typing skills to good use working for various people including Herbert Sutcliffe, the famous Yorkshire and England cricketer who was also stationed there. Within three months my mother and father had met. At Christmas 1939 he visited Longbeck House and

becoming a Chief Petty Officer before returning to the north-east in 1946. In the meantime my parents were married in Saltburn in January 1944 shortly before my father, too, was posted overseas. Stability returned only after demobilization and, thankfully, I first appeared at this time but, unfortunately, my grandfather died in 1952 when I was four and I have no personal memories of him. The grand piano in the front room, the mounds of sheet music and the guitar from Innsbruck hidden away in one of the wardrobes were all testimonies to his musical activities and, in the bookcase, were some of his language books which remained there until the house in Emerald Street was sold.

Late in the nineteen-fifties my grandmother received some consolation for the turmoil in her life when she was contacted, via the Red Cross, by her brother's son, Boris. He was now living in Lvov, by then in the USSR

Plate 11 The approach to Thornaby marked the beginning of a heavy industrial environment. Ex-NER 'Q6' 0-8-0 No.63368 is seen with a train of wagons that includes a number of older wooden-bodied vehicles. *Photo, Neville Stead.*

discovered for himself the different languages spoken when, for example, while he was talking to his future father-in-law, my grandmother walked in and the conversation changed to a German dialogue and when my mother entered the room the family spoke in Italian!

In 1942 my great-grandfather died and Longbeck House was sold. At that time it still depended on candles for lighting! My grandparents moved to Saltburn with Nadia but, with the two other children in the Armed Forces, my grandfather decided to follow his son into the Navy, volunteering in 1943. He spent much of his time on administrative duties at a base in Mombasa, Kenya,

(while Lublin and Tarnograd were in Poland), and was able, to a limited extent, to update her on what had happened since she left Tarnograd. He explained that her brother became the owner of a brick manufacturing company near Tarnograd until he was murdered during one of Stalin's purges. Boris was eleven at the time and he and his sisters, Vera and Nadia (it was quite a coincidence that my grandmother's children were also Boris, Vera and Nadia even though contact had been lost before the children had been born) were brought up by their grandparents, who had also died by the time that my grandmother had been traced.

Plate 12. Middlesbrough station as ex-LNER 'B1' 4-6-0 No.61237 *Geoffrey H. Kitson* enters from the west with an excursion train in the 1950s.

Photo, Neville Stead.

Plate 13. At Middlesbrough, ex-NER 'J26' 0-6-0 No.65752 passes through the station with a mixture of wooden-bodied wagons and modern hoppers. All the 'J26s' were based on either side of the Tees and all but two were allocated either to Newport or Middlesbrough at the beginning of the 1950s.

Photo, G.Pierson, Neville Stead Collection.

Plate 14. A view from the east end of Middlesbrough station towards the docks with, from left to right, ex-NER 'J71' 0-6-0 shunters Nos.8312 & 68260, and ex-NER 'A8' 4-6-2 tank No.69890, photographed on 14th September 1950.

Photo, J.D.Darby.

Plate 15. On a fine summer's evening in the 1950s, ex-NER 'A8' Pacific tank engine No.69871 passes Middlesbrough from the east. The cranes of Middlesbrough docks can be seen in the background.   *Photo, G.Pierson, Neville Stead Collection.*

Plate 16. Having left the industrial landscape behind, ex-NER 'A8' Pacific tank engine No.69891 prepares to depart Redcar Central station with a train of articulated stock for Saltburn. Only the eastbound platform had the benefit of one of the North Eastern Railway's typical train sheds.

Photo, G.Pierson, Neville Stead Collection.

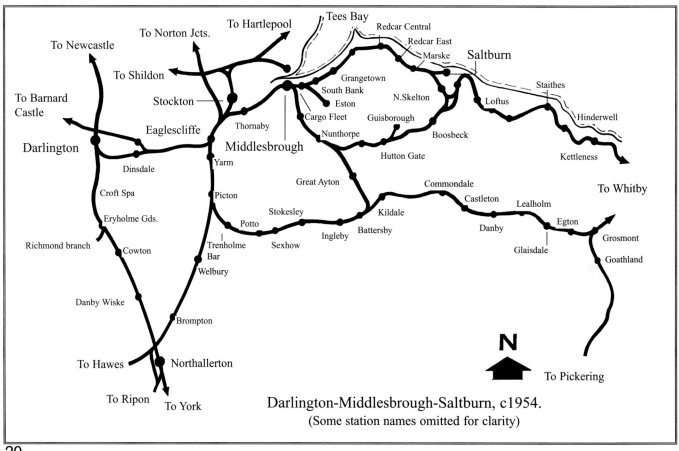

Darlington-Middlesbrough-Saltburn, c1954.
(Some station names omitted for clarity)

3.FROM THE CHERRY TREE

In 1950 my father joined the Rubber Chemicals Department of I.C.I. at Blackley, north of Manchester, as a graduate chemist and the family moved to Sale, just south of the river Mersey, which marked the boundary between Cheshire and what was then Lancashire. Our house in Overton Crescent was on an estate built in the nineteen-thirties and the nearest shops and public transport were situated on the main A56 trunk road, a distance of about one mile. This meant some inconvenience in the days when private cars were uncommon, although this was accepted as part of life. People seemed to be more tolerant to hardships in those days. It was the same, of course, for most people and I believe there was still, in those early post-war years, a basic appreciation and enjoyment of life that is particularly evident in the aftermath of war.

We lived in a medium-sized, semi-detached house occupying a corner plot on the estate having the benefit of a mature garden of generous proportions for the size of house. In front there was a formal lawn with borders in which I hardly ever set foot. It was the public side of the house. A thick, tall privet hedge formed the boundary to the side, on Overton Crescent, and together with similar hedges along the remaining boundaries, made most of the garden very private. Behind the front hedge there was a large lawn (later reduced in size to make way for a garage) where my brother and I concentrated our activities. From here a small orchard led to the back garden where there was a third lawn and a large greenhouse with vegetable plots and a dirty pond about three-feet deep. The greenhouse was eventually demolished and the pond emptied to reveal a couple of Dinky toys at the bottom! Another lawn replaced the greenhouse and the rest of the garden was punctuated by some well-established trees including three elms, two cherry trees and a rowan. It was a perfect haven in which to indulge our childhood fantasies. For instance, old curtains and blankets, a pedal car (resembling a convertible Austin Somerset) and some chairs would often be used as a framework for a den. This was more

Plate 21. Ex-Lancashire & Yorkshire Railway class '2P' 2-4-2 tank engine No.50705, designed by Aspinall, is seen at Sale station working the 7.18pm Manchester London Road-Warrington Bank Quay Low Level service on 14th August 1956. The train would leave the electric line at Timperley Junction.

Photo, D.Chatfield.

exciting than using a tent or Wendy house. At other times we would 'camp' out for an hour or so behind the coal bunker at the bottom of the garden taking a torch and a bowl of Corn Flakes to show that we meant it! There were many nooks and crannies to utilize when playing cowboys and Indians and plenty of paving to use as railway tracks while pulling an assortment of brooms, representing coaching stock, and garden implements that were better suited to noisier goods trains! The verandah, attached to the side of the house, provided the perfect terminus for the 'trains' to arrive and depart.

As I grew older I became aware of the sound of trains in the distance. It was mainly the clanking of goods trains but also the more rhythmic sound of passenger trains, perhaps a mile away, and when it was quiet and the wind in the right direction even the electric trains on the Manchester to Altrincham line could be heard accelerating between Brooklands and Timperley stations. There were other sounds too such as sinister factory sirens (perhaps I had been told that the sound was similar to an air-raid siren) at various times of the day, probably from the industrial area of Broadheath, and the sounds of ships as they approached Irlam locks on the Manchester Ship Canal, but more than anything else I listened out for the trains. And then one day, just by chance (for that is how most childhood discoveries are made), while looking through the front bedroom window towards some undeveloped land and across the farmland beyond, I noticed what looked like the level formation of a railway line. I did not need to wait long before a train passed across about half-a-mile of track that was visible between the houses and situated to the west of West Timperley station, on the former Cheshire Lines Committee railway between Stockport Tiviot Dale and Glazebrook Junction (where the line joined

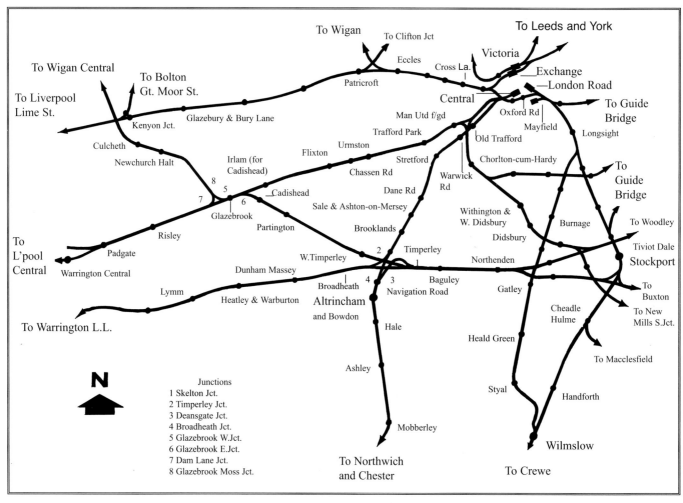

Railways in the South Manchester area c1957.
(Some station names omitted for clarity)

Plate 22. At the southern end of the Manchester South Junction & Altrincham Railway's electrified line, two ex-Manchester, Sheffield & Lincolnshire Railway 'N5' 0-6-2 tank engines Nos.9274 & 69281 are seen at Altrincham on 12th March 1949. The engine on the right is about to depart with a Chester service while No.9274 is deputising for the more usual electric trains on a Sunday when maintenance was taking place.   *Photo, J.D.Darby.*

the main line from Manchester Central to Warrington and Liverpool Central). The railway was probably about half-a-mile from the bedroom window but it was not difficult to identify locomotive types, in time. Those of L.M.S. origin, and with which I was already familiar, were comparatively easy to spot such as Fowler class '4' 0-6-0s and class '5' 2-6-0s, Stanier class '8F' 2-8-0s and tank engines of both 2-6-2 and 2-6-4 varieties. Likewise the 'W.D'. class '8' 2-8-0s were instantly recognizable but there were types that made appearances from time to time which I could tell were different but still I could not identify. It was not until I was given a copy of H.C.Casserley's *Observer Book of Railway Locomotives*, which I studied avidly, that recognition became easier and I then knew that I was looking at L.N.E.R. classes such as 'B1' 4-6-0s, 'K3' 2-6-0s, 'J39' 0-6-0s, 'D11' 4-4-0s and, less frequently, 'J10s' and 'J11s'. There really was plenty of variety along this interesting line which acted as a feeder route for trains, especially freights and excursions, crossing Manchester. It was eventually realised that in the summer months, and particularly on Saturdays, one could expect to see a steady stream of passenger trains often with L.N.E.R. locomotives, probably from South Yorkshire, Nottinghamshire and Derbyshire. Almost

certainly, many of these excursions would have been heading for Blackpool and Southport, just a few short years before mass ownership of the motor car would bring rail-borne holiday extras to an end.

One day I noticed that the plot of land which permitted this distant view of trains was being built upon and, before long, a new house had been erected, blocking the view across the fields towards this line and, indeed, a further almost parallel line between Stockport and Warrington of L.N.W.R. origin, where a faint outline of trains and smoke could be seen. This part of Sale, on the edges of Carrington Moss, was to become a major landbank for new housing until the nineteen-eighties. Housebuilding got underway in the mid nineteen-fifties, after I had started primary school, and, gradually, the fields of grazing cattle around the corner in Woodhouse Lane, that I would pass on my way to infant classes, gave way to building sites. While it was not in my nature to venture into such places on my own I knew a boy who did and his name was Clive Turpin, my first friend at school. When I was old enough to walk home from school unaccompanied we would sometimes stray on to the site and mix water and sand together or wander into the unfinished houses.When I was first allowed to have tea at Clive's house it was also like wandering into

Plate 23. This undated view of a train entering Princes Dock evokes memories of the author's trip to Liverpool as a child to see the burning remains of the liner *Empress of Canada* in Gladstone Dock in January 1953. A bird's eye view of the ship could be obtained from Liverpool's Overhead Railway, known locally as the 'Docker's Umbrella', which closed in 1956.
Photo, D.Sweeney Collection.

an unfinished building only their house was twenty years old! There was no wallpaper anywhere that I remember but a lot of free expression with pictures, words and sums forming an unusual pattern on the walls, even in the lounge!

My first day at Woodheys Primary School in September 1953 had been noteworthy in that I ran back home at lunchtime only to be taken to a toyshop, Pembertons, where I was given a new Dinky toy to comfort me, I assume, before being returned to school by my parents. Unfortunately, still in a stressed condition, I slapped the teacher on the face, was given a smack on the hand and eventually settled down! One of the first things all children had to do was to tie up their shoelaces and, once this was accomplished, the serious business of reading and writing began, starting with 'Janet and John' books. Being able to read must be one of the great achievements in everyone's life. It builds confidence and independence, like walking for the first time or passing one's driving test. Having acquired the basic skills I naturally reached for my Reverend Awdry's *Thomas the Tank Engine* series of books which had previously been read to me. Admittedly, these books, which were still fairly new at that time, were mainly composed of pictures and one could understand the story without reference to the words but, no matter, I was able to put to good use this new-found independence. I don't know how old I was when I stopped reading them as a child but I do recall that when, as an adult, I turned their pages in a bookshop out

of curiosity, many of the pictures and stories were remembered with affection, especially the mishaps - Gordon in the ditch, James covered with tar, Henry splashed with white paint and Thomas in a large hole caused by mining subsidence.

By this time my brother and I had acquired our first train sets - my earliest recollection of Christmas. They were Hornby 'O' gauge clockwork trains, one of them being a green express engine and tender with two or three coaches while my brother was given a red tank engine. These would have been the highlight of that particular Christmas but, like a lot of toys for children, anything that required some preparation or assembly soon lost its appeal and I feel sure that in my case the brooms and garden implements were soon back in action along the 'main line'.

It was in the early nineteen-fifties that I can recall my first trips in a car; into Cheshire once in a neighbour's Morris 8 convertible and out into the Yorkshire Dales with the family of one of my father's colleagues. To this day I do not know how four adults and four children were capable of fitting into a Ford Popular which at that time had only three gears - there was no room for a fourth! It was our first visit to Wensleydale and the Craven District of Yorkshire and, while I remember nothing of the attractive countryside, I do recall the unusual sight of a large number of army tanks lying idle in fields, seemingly abandoned. I can only assume that they were surplus to requirements after the war and that there was insufficient space at the nearest camp at

Catterick to store them. Another reminder of the country's recent past were the two air-raid shelters situated a few yards from our school playground. Although strictly off limits I am sure that most children, including me, peeped through the openings to look inside.The shelters were still there in 1960, when I left school, possibly in case of any Cold War hostilities.

Our holidays at that time were mainly to Saltburn and Cynwyd in North Wales with occasional weekend trips to see my grandfather in Birmingham but there was a day trip by train that made quite an impact on me. It was to Liverpool to see the remains of a Canadian Pacific liner, the *Empress of Canada*, that had caught fire in Gladstone Dock, north of the city on 25th January 1953. At that time the Liverpool Overhead Railway afforded a bird's-eye view of all the docks from Toxteth to Seaforth but the smouldering remains of this ship was a sad sight indeed. It was only four more years before the 'Docker's Umbrella', as the railway was affectionately known by Liverpudlians, closed owing to the high cost

of replacing the decking. On 31st December 1956 the last trains ran above the docks.

1956 was a landmark year as we became the proud owners of our first television. In the same year the Independent Television Authority was set up and, for the first time, two channels were available. There was also plenty for children to watch. Until then *Listen with Mother* on the Home Service (now Radio 4) was the only contact I had with programmes broadcast for children whereas television introduced us to *Picture Book* on Mondays, *Andy Pandy* on Tuesdays, *Bill and Ben The Flowerpot Men* on Wednesdays, *Rag, Tag and Bobtail* (a hedgehog, mouse and a rabbit) on Thursdays and *The Woodentops* (with the legendary Spotty Dog) on Fridays. Most of this output was probably of little educational value but it was entertaining, despite the very basic settings, and my brother and I duly lapped it up, graduating in time to a daily diet of American programmes for slightly older children such as *Lassie, Brave Eagle, Rin Tin Tin, Hopalong Cassidy* and *Roy*

Plate 24. Ex-LMSR Stanier 2-6-2 tank No.40203, one of the few large-boilered examples of the class, passes another passenger train as it arrives at Cheadle station with the 6.23pm Stockport Tiviot Dale-Liverpool Central train on 11th June 1957. It will follow the CLC route to Warrington via West Timperley and pass along the section visible from the author's home to the west of West Timperley.
Photo, Ron Gee.

Plate 25. Seen passing Cheadle station with the 6.25pm Mottram-Dee Marsh freight on 4th June 1957 is one of the ex-GCR '04/7' 2-8-0s No.63805. This train would diverge from the route taken by 40203 *(see plate 24)* at Skelton Junction and follow the LNWR route through Broadheath, to the west of which trains were faintly visible from the author's home. *Photo, Ron Gee.*

Plate 26. At Baguley station on 7th October 1950, ex-Midland Railway 4-4-0 class '2P' No.40464 arrives with the 3.23pm Stockport-Glazebrook local train. The locomotive is a Fowler rebuild of a Johnson design introduced in 1912 for the Midland Railway. Other engines of the same class Nos.40322-40326 were built for the S&DJR, 1914-21, and taken into LMS stock in 1930. *Photo, J.D.Darby.*

Rogers. They were mainly 'Westerns' that perpetuated the myth that the cowboy was the 'goody' and the Indian the 'baddy' and it would be many years before I understood the truth. There were programmes of educational value such as *Zoo Time*, introduced by Desmond Morris, that helped the viewer understand more about the animals in London Zoo. Animals were ideal subjects for television, and naturalists such as Amanda and Michaela Dennis and Jacques Cousteau opened up the animal kingdom on the land and in the sea to the armchair viewer. The early programmes of David

Attenborough explored not only animals in different parts of the world but people in remote areas, some of whom had never had previous contact with the outside world. I well remember the occasion when Attenborough spoke to the camera to explain that the crew needed to exercise great care as the tribe they were hoping to meet were still practising cannibalism! The production techniques may have been basic and the picture quality poor but such programmes allowed the viewer to see remote parts of the world in a more atmospheric way than the best nature book could achieve.

Plate 27. Hughes 'Crab' 2-6-0 No.42886 arrives at Baguley station with a Blackpool excursion on 21st September 1952. This train would take the route via Glazebrook, Lowton St. Marys and Bickershaw & Abram, joining the Whelley route at Amberswood, thereby avoiding the congested central area around Wigan North Western and, by way of a bonus, traverse some pleasant countryside to the east of Wigan before connecting with the WCML at Standish Junction for Preston and Blackpool. In the summer months a seemingly endless procession of these excursions could be seen from the author's bedroom window.

Photo, J.D.Darby.

1956 was a significant year for another reason. It marked the beginning and first tentative steps of youth culture in Britain as we know it today, when popular music simply became 'pop' music, and when teenage icons such as James Dean and Elvis Presley had a great impact on young people. Popular music in the post-war years was still dominated by, mainly American, song stylists such as Frank Sinatra, Nat King Cole, Frankie Laine and Perry Como. The quality of the song was still of great importance and the sales of sheet music significant. The first charts to be compiled in Britain to monitor record sales were published in 1952 and it was not long before popular British acts such as Dickie Valentine and Alma Cogan, singing mainly cover versions of American tunes, were making regular appearances in the charts. The first sign of change in this country came with the release of Bill Haley's *Rock Around the Clock* and the film *Blackboard Jungle*, which featured the song. The new music created a lot of excitement, some of which became uncontrolled and transformed itself into physical violence, especially in

theatres where the film was showing and at venues played by Bill Haley on his subsequent visit to Britain. But it was the unprecedented world-wide success of a much younger Elvis Presley that quickly changed the face of popular music and soon the B.B.C. created a music programme for younger people called *Six Five Special*. Until that time our main source of music at home had been the Third Programme (later Radio 3) with some lighter music on *Housewife's Choice* and *Family Favourites*. In retrospect, I am surprised that we were allowed to watch the *Six Five Special* as its musical content was so different but, it may have been due to its coinciding with our Saturday tea-time. There was a bonus for me in that the opening credits featured footage of the 'Coronation Scot' at high speed (almost certainly the record-breaking run of 1937) but the programme itself, an informal gathering of studio audience, singers and musicians around presenters Pete Murray and Josephine Douglas, gave us our first glimpse of the new rock 'n' roll music and of Tommy Steele, who for a short time was the leading British act.

Jazz and skiffle also featured regularly and, if I was to associate any song with the programme, it would be skiffle's biggest hit *Freight Train* by Chas McDevitt's Skiffle Group and Nancy Whiskey. It was one of the first songs I can recall singing at home.

As there were only two channels at this time an appearance on television was quite a noteworthy event so it came as quite a surprise followed by some excitement when my father told us that he was going to appear live on B.B.C. television. The programme concerned was the short-lived *What's New* which featured a new song, book, or technical development, for instance, in a magazine format and was introduced by a popular presenter of the time, MacDonald Hobley. In an otherwise carefully-scripted programme my father was left to demonstrate the properties of a foam called polyurethane that was still in its early stages of development. Into a beaker he poured a liquid which immediately expanded until it hardened just at the point where it would have spilled over the edges of the beaker. The purpose of the experiment was to show that the liquid foam could expand into a large, light mass with good insulating properties and to that extent it was a success. In time it would become a huge commercial success too. Meanwhile, at home, Mum had invited various friends to watch the programme with us, to share the excitement of watching his only television appearance. *What's New* was produced in Manchester and the studio was a converted church in Withington, south of Manchester city centre. Once the programme had finished it was back to earth again for my father and

a bus journey back to Sale but, as he was walking home from the bus stop, he was greeted by a distant neighbour, busy in his front garden, who looked up and asked "Haven't I just seen you on T.V.?" demonstrating how television could bring instant recognition.

Before too long even steam trains would have their own programme in the form of the much-loved *Railway Roundabout* series introduced by Patrick Whitehouse and John Adams. While television opened up my world and gave me a measure of independence, another developing activity brought me an illusory feeling of freedom—tree climbing. The garden was blessed with many trees, some of which were easy to climb and others more difficult, but providing me with an incentive and an opportunity to gradually hone my climbing skills and reach the uppermost branches. The apple trees presented few obstacles to reaching near to the tops although not quite as high as one of the boys next-door reached on one occasion. For some reason David and Peter, who did not normally play in our garden, were spending the day with us and they arrived complete with their garden swing which was a bonus for us as the nearest swings were in a park about two miles away. We took turns and then while one of us was on the swing the others would kick a football on the lawn. It was while three of us were tackling each other for the ball that we noticed the swing moving through an arc but without Peter. After briefly searching the garden without success, a cracking twig drew our attention to the top of one of the apple trees where he sat in a state of shock and with a few grazes! He had reached the top

Plate 28. Ex-Manchester, Sheffield & Lincolnshire Railway 'J10' 0-6-0 No.65178 is seen in the exchange sidings at Skelton Junction on 22nd May 1953. The line from Stockport split into three at this junction with separate routes to Glazebrook and Liverpool via the CLC to Warrington; Liverpool and the Wirral via the LNWR; and to Altrincham, Northwich and Chester via the MSJ&AR and the CLC. In the distance is an ex-MS&LR 'N5' tank engine No.69317, awaiting departure for Heaton Mersey with a local goods train.
Photo, D.Chatfield.

Plate 29. Another of the Hughes 2-6-0s, No.42775, is seen crossing the Bridgewater Canal south of Timperley station, on the cross-country route between Glazebrook and Stockport, with a Liverpool Central-Stockport Tiviot Dale train on 2nd October 1954.
Photo, D.Chatfield.

Plate 30 Having just negotiated Glazebrook West Junction, ex-GCR 'J11' 0-6-0 No.64376 is seen approaching Glazebrook on 25th March 1950 with the 10.10am Warrington Central-Stockport Tiviot Dale service.
Photo, J.D.Darby.

without passing 'Go' while I was happy to set my sights a little lower up a cherry tree.

For years this tree had been used as one of a pair of goalposts and, because of its ideal width, made a very suitable wicket when we played cricket. A thick horizontal branch, about six feet from the ground, provided me with the incentive I needed and many times I would jump up, first touching, then gripping and finally holding on to the branch from which, by swinging my legs up to a fork, I could gain access to the centre of the tree and, from there, on to the many branches that helped make it such a lovely sight in

spring when fully laden with blossom. As the tree was quite large it was easy to look over the hedges and survey the scene on the other side. My attention was quickly drawn to the plot of land where the house had been built and I discovered that the obscured view from the bedroom window had once again opened up from this new angle. It was not so comfortable a viewing point but whenever I was in the garden and heard a train or on a summer Saturday I had the means, once again, of watching trains from a distance. The cherry tree became a firm favourite of mine for several years until I had a bicycle and was able to take a closer look at the railway.

4. CYNWYD

For just a few years of my childhood the peaceful setting of Cynwyd in North Wales became a regular holiday destination. The village is situated in the heart of attractive Welsh countryside, south west of Corwen and in the shadow of the Berwyn Mountains immediately to the east, with fine views westwards across the Dee valley to hills such as Foel Goch. My great-Aunty Margaret had retired as a partner in a furniture business in Birmingham after the War and had acquired an attractive bungalow, Bryn Gwynt, on the southern edge of the village on the Bala road. It was set in a large garden, the back of which sloped on the edge of the valley, and provided a young child with a

wonderful location to play and explore and, coincidentally, an excellent view of the railway at the bottom of the valley.

The journey was much shorter than to Saltburn and always undertaken at holiday periods as there was no Sunday service. It entailed changing trains once or twice depending on the time of day that we travelled but usually began with a taxi to Altrincham where the train from Manchester Central (now the G-Mex Centre) to Chester Northgate (demolished and replaced by a sports complex) made its first stop. This line, like the one I could see from our house in Sale, was owned by the Cheshire Lines Committee which became part of the

Plate 31. Under the impressive arched roof of Manchester Central station, ex-GCR 'D11' 4-4-0 No.62666 *Zeebrugge* is seen in sparkling condition in the 1950s. Sometimes referred to as 'Large Directors' the 'D11s' were regularly employed on both Liverpool and Chester services during this period. The station building still survives as the G -Mex Centre where exhibitions and concerts are held. *Photo, Neville Stead .*

32

Great Central Railway which, in turn, was absorbed into the London and North Eastern Railway at the Grouping in 1923. This explained why, deep in Midland Region territory, the locomotives in charge of our trains were ex-G.C.R. types, typically 'D10' and 'D11' 4-4-0s, designed as express passenger engines for the Great Central but now whiling away their final years on secondary passenger duties. Their origins probably explained why they bore names and two, in particular, that I recall were *Princess Mary* and *Zeebrugge*. Other G.C.R. types such as the 'C13' 4-4-2 tank engines and 'N5' 0-6-2 tanks also handled Chester trains until the mid nineteen-fifties.

The first half of the journey to Chester was mainly through the rolling farmland of Cheshire calling first at Hale station with its attractive Midland-influenced glass-and-iron canopies. Many of the succeeding stations such as Ashley and Mobberley were small, of brick with barge-boarding around the gables and small canopies to give passengers some measure of protection. Knutsford was the only town of any size, before our approach to Northwich and a change of scenery. Fields gave way to an industrial landscape dominated by the large I.C.I. chemical complex, which was serviced by a regular procession of limestone trains, originating in Derbyshire and following our route through Altrincham to Northwich. Here the sidings ushered the approach to the station with the engine shed on its left and an array of mainly freight locomotives in the shed yard. Resuming the journey south, a triangular junction marked the point where the Middlewich and Sandbach line veered off to the left while we crossed the Weaver Navigation and the river Dane on a substantial viaduct. From there it was possible to look down on the boat yards and the cargo boats that had made their way to this most inland port on the Weaver. About a mile or two further on we crossed the West Coast Main Line, which was in a cutting below at Hartford, and before long the scenery was changing again as the train entered Delamere Forest, with its picturesque station on the edge of the forest. In this part of Cheshire the underlying red sandstone was more in evidence and both Delamere and the next station at Mouldsworth were built using this rock. Soon we were approaching Chester, and its terminus, about one and a quarter hours after leaving Altrincham. Chester Northgate had two main platforms with four lines in between under a double span roof, supported in the middle by columns. The small engine shed stood just to one side of the station and here one could see a mixture of L.M.S. and older L.N.E.R. types of locomotives. I can recall nothing else about the station but do remember the occasional lengthy walk with our belongings to Chester General to continue our journey into Wales.

Chester General was a popular location for trainspotters and with good reason for it served both Midland and Western Region trains including expresses from London. Indeed, one curiosity about this station was that while trains from Euston arrived from the east, the express trains from Paddington approached from the west! Our train was now Western Region and would be hauled by a variety of locomotive types depending on the destination. If our train was bound for London or the Midlands there would usually be a 'Hall', 'Grange', 'County', or 'Castle' class 4-6-0 at the front and we would change trains at either Wrexham or Ruabon, but if we travelled on a direct train for Barmouth then motive power was more than likely going to be a G.W.R. 2-6-0 or 'Manor' class 4-6-0. The seventeen-mile journey to Ruabon took us up the formidable Gresford Bank, one of the steepest gradients on the Western Region, and if we were on the Barmouth train then a stop was usually made at Gresford Halt, half way up the bank, adding to the engine's task. On one occasion while the train was briefly at rest here I remember being told of the mining disaster at the nearby colliery about twenty years earlier in 1934 when more than 250 miners lost their lives. A touching monument incorporating colliery wheels can be seen in the village of Gresford recording the tragedy. Sometimes we would change trains at Wrexham General with its staggered platforms and where, on one occasion, I was taken along to the front end to inspect the engine, *Drysllwyn Castle*, but whether we changed at Wrexham or Ruabon, the final stage of the journey was usually on an auto-train for Bala, invariably hauled by a G.W.R. pannier tank. These trains were a novelty for me, the first thing I noticed being the doors that opened inwards and the different seating arrangement, but the most striking aspect of these trains was the position of the locomotive, which sometimes would be pushing from the rear or be even sandwiched in between the coaches.

Soon our train would be heading into the Dee valley and entering the long platforms of Llangollen station situated in a narrow valley, in between steep-sided hills, with the attractive wide river alongside and below the station. There was almost a Swiss feel to this place

Plate 32. Another ex-GCR 'D11' 4-4-0, No.62664 *Princess Mary,* at the head of a Chester Northgate train near Dane Road on 19th May 1956. Between Sale and Old Trafford the line was four tracks.
Photo, D.Chatfield.

Plate 33. Until the mid-fifties, ex-GCR 'C13' tank engines could also be seen on the Chester trains. Here we see one of the regulars at the time, No.67436, passing the author's local station, Brooklands, with the 6.39pm service to Chester Northgate on 26th May 1950.
Photo, J.D.Darby.

which continued as the train skirted around the edge of the hillside, high above the river, to Berwyn on the now single-track section with passing loops. The line was subject to steep gradients and sharp curves along this section and the sound from the engine left no one in doubt that it was working hard but, by the time we had reached the next stop at Glyndyfrdwy we were much closer to the valley floor and, beyond Carrog, the railway had previously been flooded by the river. At Corwen there was a junction with the Midland Region line from Rhyl and Denbigh. I don't recall seeing any passenger trains with L.M.S. motive power (in any event services had been withdrawn by 1953) but there

would sometimes be a Midland '3F' 0-6-0 in the goods yards beyond the station. Freight trains used these yards until the sixties and the extensive sidings testified to the volume of traffic that was once handled here.

The train now had little more than two miles to go to our destination, with the river Dee not far away on our right. Within five minutes it would draw into the single platform at Cynwyd with its neat single-storey station building under a hipped roof of slate and small canopy. A chocolate-and-cream nameboard on the platform proclaimed the name of the station whose boundary was marked by iron railings, behind which was a bay goods line and livestock pen. Completing the scene was a goods warehouse through which the siding passed to gain access to the main line. It was a model of peace and tranquillity for much of the day, and so it would have been shortly after we alighted from the train with our cases and made our way up the station approach as the shrill whistle sounded and slowly our train drew out of the station, picking up speed on its way to the next stop at Llandrillo. I would listen to the train as the sound of it became fainter until, by the time we had reached the centre of the village, it would be slowing down again for Llandrillo.

From the main road junction in the village it was only a further two hundred yards along the Bala road to my great-aunt's bungalow which we would usually reach about mid afternoon. Bryn Gwynt was essentially black and white in appearance with whitewashed rendered walls and the surrounds to the windows and doors and the barge-boarding in black and white. The finials at the top of the gables provided further embellishment while the roof itself was covered in diamond-shaped slates. At the front of the bungalow a large hedge offered privacy to the garden, which had neat flower borders and a path leading around the property. One source of interest at the front was a large drum into which a drainpipe deposited water. In summer, in particular, it provided plenty of ammunition for water fights which were

generally frowned upon especially as Margaret was a member of the strict religious sect, the Plymouth Brethren. Her sister Dolly and brother Frank were also members and their adherence to this movement almost certainly dates from their father's discovery of whisky and its appalling consequences. To the side of the property was a large shed which held a variety of garden implements, including a formidable roller that nearly caused my brother some grief when he was spotted attempting to move it behind him down the sloping lawn! Whenever I walked into the shed I was made immediately aware of the distinctive smell of creosote which, to this day, reminds me of the bungalow.

It was the well-laid-out back garden with its large borders that provided the greatest attraction. Five steps from the rear porch led on to the firm lawn where we first learnt to putt and where we would play until a passing train in the valley below would capture our attention. When it came to playing trains, however, I was on my own. Instead of the broom and the garden implements at home I used the golf clubs that were stored in the umbrella stand in the hall, near the rear porch, and because there was lots of space in the garden I had more scope to unleash 'express' trains on unsuspecting adults. I now realise that this may have been a little alarming for the older members of the

Plate 34. Seen just south of Timperley station with the 6.40pm train for Chester on 10th May 1952, is ex-GCR 'D11' No.62667 *Somme*. The line curving away to the left is the LNWR branch that climbed round to Broadheath and was used by services from Manchester London Road to Warrington and Liverpool Lime Street.

Photo, Ron Gee.

Plate 35. Until 1956 the ex-GCR 'D10' 4-4-0s were in regular use on the Chester trains. Here we see No.62659 *Worsley-Taylor* about to depart Altrincham for Chester Northgate. Introduced in 1913 and also termed 'Director' class, these locomotives were very similar to the 'D11s' except that they had cut away cabs. *Photo, Raymond Hughes.*

family, in particular, when I dashed round a corner of the building with the trailing 'coaches' flying round at a tangent! Surprisingly there were no accidents despite the absence of automatic train control! Of course, all this was accompanied by appropriate sounds such as 'ch ch ch ch' for a moving train and the 'sh' for steam. Representation in loud or soft tones added a further degree of sophistication and when my train was 'blowing off' in the station it could really get quite messy!

Behind the lawn a little path made its way through the border to a fence in the valley side, marking the boundary of the property, and from which we were discouraged owing to the steepness of the bank on the other side. From here there was a more extensive view of the hills across the valley where we would often walk with parents or visiting relatives. Cynwyd was popular with the Packer family, most of whom lived in Birmingham at this time. Frank and Dolly, who like Margaret, never married, were regular visitors and always brought their dog, Peter, a Manchester Terrier,

who would accompany us on our walks and prove his usefulness by tugging on the lead and helping me up the nearby hills such as Gaerwen, to the west of the village. We would often walk down to the solid stone bridge, with its triangular refuges overlooking the Dee, passing Cynwyd station on the way. From here there were good riverside walks on both sides and a suspension bridge that could be crossed to make a round trip. Alternatively, we would walk along the Bala road (much quieter then) passing farms and those platforms that were occasionally situated at the roadside for the steel milk churns awaiting collection. Conveniently, this walk kept us within sight of the railway and it would always be a bonus to see the red and cream or plain maroon coaches of the time hauled by a G.W.R. 2-6-0 or a pannier tank perhaps. Occasionally we would just be taken down to the station to relax on the bench in the sunshine and await the passage of the next train, maybe an auto-train, the Barmouth-Chester passenger service, an express passing through Cynwyd or a humble pick-up freight. Sometimes the train would be a mixture of coaches and one or two wagons and on a summer Saturday there was a good chance of seeing an unexpected through train. There was ample opportunity for number-taking but at Cynwyd I had not progressed to an Ian Allan locospotters book and any lists I made at the time probably did not last long but, in that setting, number-taking was not so important. It was the atmosphere that counted, a quiet pastoral scene of which the train was a part, that old familiar friend.

I have heard a lot of railway enthusiasts refer to the nineteen-fifties as a golden period for watching steam trains. I suspect that many of them were children at the time and trainspotting represented uncomplicated times of little responsibility and plenty of holidays to indulge in their favourite hobby. I believe that there was something else, perhaps unique, about this very brief period. It was immediately after a world war which we and other allies had won, bringing the promise of security for the future. There was a feeling of togetherness, partly because of what people had been through and before it would be irrevocably affected by the coming of the television and motor car, en masse, to turn people into a more insular lifestyle. This feeling of togetherness had a beneficial effect on family life and on children in particular, but I feel sure that full employment and job security were also significant factors.

Plate 36. Ex-GCR 'D10' 4-4-0 No.62656 *Sir Clement Royds* makes progress through the pleasant Cheshire countryside between Hale and Ashley with a Chester train on 11th September 1954.

Photo, D.Chatfield.

Plate 37. Another ex-GCR type, 'C13' 4-4-2 tank engine No.67436, enters Mobberley station with a Manchester-Chester train also on 11th September 1954.

Photo, D.Chatfield.

Plate 38. This superb study of life in the 1950s captures an altogether more sedate pace of living when we did not run around like headless chickens. Furthermore, there is not a foreign car in sight, the names of the motor vehicles in view recalling the former British car industry- Rover, Hillman, Morris, Daimler etc. Another sign of the changing times is that the number plates would probably be worth more than the vehicles themselves are now. The gated level crossing, the lamp standards and traffic signs all help to evoke the period as a bus and pedestrians wait patiently for the train to pass and the crossing gates to open. Ex-GCR 'D11' 4-4-0 No.62662 *Prince of Wales* departs Hale station with a Chester train. *Photo, Doug Rendell.*

Plate 39. An overview of Northwich station and adjacent shed on 15th June 1958. A parcels train, with a rebuilt 'Patriot' class '7P' at the head, is ready to depart towards Manchester while at the depot on the right there are ex-LMSR 2-8-0s, a GCR 'O4' 2-8-0, Midland Railway '3F' 0-6-0s and an ex-MS&LR 'J10' 0-6-0 No.65169 in store. *Photo, D.Chatfield.*

Theories apart, life for this young railway enthusiast was very happy but all holidays had to come to an end and, before too long, we would be waving my great-aunt goodbye and making our way to the station for the return journey to Sale. On just one occasion our travel arrangements took an unexpected turn when in the Whitsun holiday of 1955 the 65,000 members of A.S.L.E.F. decided to strike bringing the railways to a standstill for seventeen days from 28th May. Travelling back home at the end of a holiday by a series of buses was certainly inconvenient but the union action was to rebound on them as it is recorded that, during the strike, there was an enormous increase in road traffic.

Plate 40. A train from Manchester Central is seen after arrival at Chester Northgate behind ex-LMSR Fowler 2-6-4 tank engine No.42308 on 13th June 1959, shortly before displacement by DMUs. This was the first locomotive of its class to be withdrawn.

Photo, D.Chatfield.

Plate 41. Typical of the motive power to be seen at Chester on express trains for Shrewsbury, Birmingham and the south during the 1950s and 1960s is this ex-GWR 'Castle' class 4-6-0 No.7012 *Barry Castle* seen at Chester General on 8th May 1963.

Photo, B.G.Barlow, JimPeden Collection.

This was a critical moment especially for railfreight haulage as most customers who transferred from rail to road, as a short-term expedient, did not return, hastening the decline in rail-borne traffic.

1955 was noted for its long warm summer but it would be the last we would spend at Cynwyd. In June 1956 we received a telegram at home which stated that my great-aunt had died. There was a little sadness at the time but life went on and, as one era closed another began when television arrived in our home. In any event there were only a few short years before the line would become another statistic in Doctor Beeching's long list of closures. Services were withdrawn in November 1964 without the line ever witnessing regular diesel trains and, although they were reinstated because of problems in providing alternative bus services, nature intervened when floods destroyed the track near Llandderfel on 12th December 1964.

Plate 42. Another class of locomotive seen on the Great Western route to Barmouth was the ex-GWR '2251' class 0-6-0s. On 12th August 1952, No.2209 is seen at Llangollen with an up stopping train.
Photo, V. R. Webster, The Kidderminster Railway Museum Trust Collection.

Plate 43. The ex-GWR pannier tanks were in charge of the Wrexham-Bala trains. Here, ex-GWR class '7400' pannier tank No.7442 is seen approaching Llangollen station with a local service in 1959.
Photo, Rex Conway Steam Collection.

40

Plate 44. Journey's end for the author was Cynwyd station, just beyond Corwen. Ex-GWR '2251' class 0-6-0 No.3206 is about to depart with a local service in 1952. This particular example is attached to one of the larger, former GCR tenders, transferred from withdrawn ex-ROD 2-8-0s.

Photo, Eric Packer.

Plate 45. A meeting of two of the types of locomotives to be seen on the Ruabon-Barmouth Line. At Dolgelley station ex-GWR '4300' class 2-6-0, No.6303, awaits the arrival of ex-GWR 'Manor' class 4-6-0 No.7807 *Compton Manor* with a train for the Cambrian coast, before proceeding towards Ruabon on 30th July 1955, a few weeks after the damaging ASLEF strike of that year.

Photo, V. R. Webster, The Kidderminster Railway Museum Trust Collection.

Plate 46. At Bala Junction station ex-GWR 2-6-0 No.6380 calls with a passenger train for Pwllheli on 26th August 1959. A Bala Town shuttle service waits in the background to run into the station.

Photo, V. R. Webster, The Kidderminster Railway Museum Trust Collection.

Plate 47. Last stage of the journey back home. Ex-GCR 'C13' 4-4-2 tank engine No.67433 at Chester Northgate station with the 5.24pm to Manchester Central on 4th September 1954. A leisure centre now stands on the site of this station.

Photo, Raymond Hughes.

5. THE AIR IS SO BRACING

The famous London North Eastern Railway poster used these words when promoting the benefits of Skegness but they could have applied equally to Saltburn, the only place where my school cap, fitting so tightly around my head, was blown off as a strong north-easterly wind found its Achilles Heel, the peak at the front. Our visits to this sedate coastal resort became more civilized with the move to Sale. There were no more mail trains and the journey time was considerably reduced, making it possible for us to reach our destination, perched high on a cliff above the North Sea, by early Saturday afternoon and benefit from a weekend by the sea. As I reached school age the visits became longer in duration and mainly in the holidays but, with a few exceptions, the journey routine remained unchanged.

The day would start with either a taxi ride directly to the station, or the 48 bus, as it was then known, to St. Mary's Gate at the north end of Manchester's Deansgate where, like the rest of the city centre, all the buildings had been blackened by a century or more of soot and dirt. From here it was just a short walk to Manchester Exchange station which, though opposite the cathedral, was actually situated on the other side of the river Irwell in Salford (are there any other examples in Britain or anywhere for that matter of two separate cities next to each other ?). The journey was fascinating for a young child interested in steam trains and Exchange station was an ideal place to fire that enthusiasm. It was a large, dark station with overall roof comprising three arches, though the entrance to its concourse was unprepossessing, partly due to the bomb damage suffered in the last war. Naturally, this did not matter to me as within this huge structure was the promise of steam trains in an awesome setting. Passing through the barriers attention was first drawn to the terminus on the left, where trains departed for the North Wales coast. Our way, though, was ahead and over the lattice-framed footbridge that crossed the through lines between platform three and our departure platform, usually number five. This served a single line just within the outer wall of the large train shed. The train we regularly caught originated at Liverpool Lime Street as the 9am to Newcastle and, shortly after 9.45am, the express would slowly approach between platform and side screen with a green locomotive at the front, almost always a 'Royal Scot' (including on the odd occasion one of the few unrebuilt examples) or a rebuilt 'Patriot'. The coaches were a mixture of Gresley-designed wooden-bodied vehicles and LMS or BR stock, all in red and cream initially but, by the mid nineteen-fifties, an increasing proportion of maroon coaches.

Within seconds of setting off, the train would be passing through the much larger Victoria station with its seventeen platforms which, at that time, handled over six hundred departures and arrivals on weekdays. There was originally only one station here shared by the Lancashire and Yorkshire Railway and the London and North Western Railway but, because of traffic congestion, the LNWR decided to build its own station at Manchester Exchange in 1884 when Victoria came under sole ownership of the L&YR. Beyond the larger station lay the formidable gradient of Miles Platting bank, often requiring the assistance of a banking locomotive such as the veteran L&YR 0-6-0s. The train passed through the eastern suburbs of the city where there was often a view of a goods train in sidings or awaiting a right of way at junctions before our first stop at Stalybridge. Within minutes of leaving this mill town we would enter the seemingly endless tunnel at Standedge, one of the longest in the country at over three miles, and taking us under the Pennine moors towards the Yorkshire towns of Huddersfield and Dewsbury. Within the hour the train would be making its way above the roofline of Leeds and meeting or crossing tracks from all directions before becoming engulfed in the cavernous gloom of Leeds City station. In one sense the dark interior, broken by shafts of sunlight through gaps in the building, provided me with even greater interest than Exchange station because here was a meeting place for engines of both the Midland and Eastern Regions and where trains such as the 'Thames Clyde Express' changed locomotives. Indeed, our train not only changed engines but would now be handled by an Eastern Region class and change directions too!

It was at Leeds City that I first experienced the frightening effects of standing close to a locomotive when it released a powerful and noisy jet of steam. The engine-change permitted us to spend a few minutes on the platform and as I watched the 'Royal Scot' locomotive uncouple at the front end, the driver released steam in the cylinders by opening the drain cocks causing the huge machine, 65-feet long and nearly 140 tons in weight, to take on the appearance of a dragon! It certainly made me very wary of standing too close to an engine. While the uncoupling was taking place at the front there would often be a brace of locomotives attaching to our train at the other end to resume the journey to the north-east. Usually a Gresley 'A3' Pacific (*Sunstar*, *Harvester*, *Gainsborough* and *Trigo* were regulars) or 'V2' 2-6-2, and a Gresley 4-4-0 'Hunt' class, as pilot engine, would combine forces to tackle the steeply-graded route as far as Harrogate. The train initially retraced its steps south of Leeds City before veering to the right and heading through the northern suburbs. Once through the two-mile long Bramhope Tunnel the Pennines were, at last, left behind and we were now in attractive Yorkshire countryside. Just a few minutes after negotiating one major engineering feature along this line the train would be crossing another, Crimple Viaduct, on the approach to Harrogate. The viaduct stands high above the valley of Crimple Beck and was approached virtually at a right-

angle, the train running alongside one side of the valley and then swinging round sharply to the left to cross this imposing structure, offering an excellent view of the locomotives if we were seated in a suitable position.

At Harrogate the pilot engine would uncouple and our journey would resume, calling at Ripon and then joining the East Coast Main Line at Northallerton, where there was a chance for the Gresley locomotive to get really into its stride over the best part of fifteen miles to the next stop. If we were near the front of the train it was the ideal time to savour the three-cylinder exhaust beat of an A3 Pacific at speed but all too soon we would be crossing the River Tees and slowing down for Darlington Bank Top station which was reached before 1pm. Here was another of my favourite stations with its very large platform area, incorporating north and south bays under a substantial single-span roof. The through lines ran on either side of the main platforms and these were contained within the brick side screens that formed the boundary walls of the train shed. Beyond the eastern boundary of the station were many more lines including those for non-stop expresses and the sidings, where

Plate 48. The brewery looms large in the background as rebuilt ex-LMSR 'Royal Scot' 4-6-0 No.46153 *The Royal Dragoon* approaches Manchester Exchange station on 29th June 1953 with the 9am Liverpool-Newcastle.   *Photo, Ron Gee.*

Plate 49. Almost immediately after departing from Exchange station, a heavy Newcastle express, hauled by unrebuilt ex-LMSR 'Royal Scot' 4-6-0 No. 46137 *The Prince of Wales's Volunteers (South Lancashire)*, storms through on the centre road at Manchester Victoria station in order to climb the steep bank to Miles Platting. An ex-LYR 0-6-0 stands to the right of the 'Scot' to offer banking assistance to many of the trains including the service to Newcastle. 46137, an Edge Hill engine at the time, was the last of its class to be rebuilt in 1955. *Photo, Neville Stead Collection.*

there would invariably be an assortment of close-coupled wagons. There was almost always a scene of activity and excitement as we stepped off the express and headed for the bay platform at the south end of the station passing, on our way, a high plinth near the buffer stops of the southern bay upon which stood two historic locomotives. One was *Locomotion No.1* that hauled the first train along the Stockton and Darlington Railway in 1825 and the other was *Derwent*, a later design that also worked on that historic railway. Here was a reminder that our journey connected the two areas of England that are forever associated with the birth of railways. In 1975 the two engines were transferred to relative obscurity at North Road Museum beside the first station north of Darlington on the Bishop Auckland branch line.

Meanwhile, in the south bay our next train awaited. Bound for Saltburn it stopped at all stations and was usually hauled by an ex-GCR class 'A5' 4-6-2 tank or ex-NER class 'A8' 4-6-2 tank engine but sometimes the

motive power would be one of the more modern LNER counterparts, the powerful 'L1' 2-6-4 tank engines at the head of a rake of, usually, non-corridor coaches. As the train made its way out of the station I would always press my head to the window to catch sight of a locomotive, a tank engine again, at the head of any Richmond train that happened to be in the opposite bay platform. Now venturing on to the East Coast Main Line, once again in the opposite direction from our previous train, we would soon branch off and head thirty miles eastwards for the coast, leaving the industry of Darlington behind and entering open countryside. Usually we would have passed a train from Saltburn by the time we had arrived at the first stop, Dinsdale, set in a cutting. On our way again, attention would soon focus on the aerodrome at Middleton St. George, used by bombers during the last war and which has since developed into the busy regional Teesside Airport. In this vicinity there was a halt that we never stopped at, presumably because it was for workmen only. It was called Allen's West and it was from about this point that we followed the exact course of the original Stockton and Darlington Railway as far as Eaglescliffe. Excitement would increase as lines converged from the right, indicating the approach to Eaglescliffe Junction with its large island platform, where we would usually meet another train from Saltburn. A number of cross-country expresses from Bristol, Wales and Liverpool used the coastal route to Newcastle and it was here where they crossed our path. Naturally I always hoped to see one of these trains, especially as we ran parallel with the Newcastle route for well over a mile before parting company, but I can only recall once being overtaken by an express bound for the north-east with a class 'A2' Pacific, No. 60515 *Sun Stream*, at the head.

By the time the lines had diverged we were now approaching an industrial area like no other that I could imagine existed. For the next half hour we would pass through the heart of a seething monster of heavy industry producing, for ten continuous miles, a mixture of black, brown, red and yellow smoke as well as steam and flame. In these environmentally-conscious times it is difficult to convey how all-pervading was the sight and smell of the unrestrained smoke in this industrial area before, first, the Clean Air Acts and then the more modern environmental legislation transformed the quality of the atmosphere. All branches of the iron and steel, shipbuilding and chemical industries lined each side of the railway together with sidings, wagons and goods trains hauled by NER 'J25', 'J26' and 'J27' 0-6-0s, 'Q6' 0-8-0s and War Department 2-8-0s, going about their business like worker ants, while smaller tank engines such as NER 'J71', 'J72' and 'J77' 0-6-0s would potter about on shunting duties. It was almost as fascinating to watch the industry and buildings of all shapes and sizes as it was to study the locomotives on view. There were so many numbers to take down and written so quickly that, when there was a chance to look at the notepad, all one could read was a mass of unintelligible hieroglyphics!

Before reaching Thornaby we encountered the first steel works on the right while, on the left, beyond the junction with a spur from Stockton, were diverging lines following the course of the Stockton and Darlington Railway towards their terminus at coal staithes by the River Tees. Beyond Thornaby the train picked its way between the industrial sites and the masses of sidings. Ahead, on the left, the Newport road bridge came into view. Built in 1934 it was the first vertical lifting bridge, providing clearance for shipping, and its steel towers on either side of the river were, and indeed are still, a clear landmark. Looming up, and also on the left before passing level with the bridge, was Newport motive

Plate 50. A closer look at one of the ex-LYR 0-6-0 bankers seen 'Wall Side' at Manchester Victoria on 2nd April 1960. This example is a work-stained No.52271, one of a class introduced by Aspinall in 1889. Behind 52271 is a passenger train at Platform 12.
Photo, Peter Fitton.

Plate 51. Another busy scene at Manchester Victoria with 52271 on the left and ex-LMSR, Fowler-designed, 0-8-0 No.49618 bringing its westbound freight to a halt in order to release the brakes. *Photo, Peter Fitton.*

power depot, surrounded by its large allocation of mainly freight locomotives including the unmistakable shape of the bulky NER class 'T1' 4-8-0 tank engines designed for shunting in marshalling yards. The familiar clang clang of wagons being shunted was very much in evidence here, and also in the sidings throughout this industrial area, adding to the cacophony of industrial sounds. Passing another iron works on the approach to Middlesbrough I was able to obtain my first view of the transporter bridge, one of three that then existed in the country. Built in 1911 it comprises two tall towers and, high above the river, a bridge section from which was suspended, via cables, a gated section of road in a cage moving across the river by means of a wheeled platform on the bridge. It is now the only one of its kind as the others at Newport, Gwent and at Runcorn in Cheshire were dismantled many years ago.

Beyond Middlesbrough, the largest of the intermediate stations, the Whitby line veered off to the right where there was also a brief view of the engine shed but, on the left, the ships berthed at the docks alongside the railway competed for my attention. As a child I did not associate

the name of the next station, Cargo Fleet, with the shipping industry. It just sounded intriguing, like Wells Fargo, and its grim setting only served to accentuate the sense of mystery. Similarly, Southbank and Grangetown were dirty-looking stations set in the heart of industrial complexes that could not provide a greater contrast with the wayside country stations with hanging baskets and milk churns. I imagined that only muscular steelworkers and dockers in overalls and open shirts would use these stations which, at night, with their dim lighting and dark shadows on the platforms and subways, would be places to avoid. At Grangetown, where we would pass another train from Saltburn, the massive blast furnaces of another steel works appeared on our right. The train was passing through an almost surreal landscape of chimneys, towers, masts, covered elevators or walkways for materials or workers, pipes and bridges that spanned the line and, without letting up, the steel gave way to chemicals as the huge ICI complex at Wilton that produced nylon appeared. Further on the left, amidst a barren wasteland, stood yet another iron and steelworks near Warrenby while, on the right,

Plate 52. The Newcastle train arrived in Leeds City station about an hour after departing Manchester. It then changed locomotives and direction and one of the regulars on the Leeds-Newcastle portion of the journey was ex-LNER 'A3' Pacific No.60074 *Harvester*, seen here at the west end of Leeds City after arrival with the 9.55am service from Newcastle on 15th June 1960.

Photo, Gavin Morrison.

greenery re-appeared as the Cleveland Hills came into sight, a reminder that it was from these hills that iron ore was extracted leading to the establishment of an iron and steel industry on Teesside.

Now, though, as the railway swung to our right, all industry was being left behind and the residential area of Redcar entered. The long excursion platform on the left signalled the approach to Redcar Central station with its overall roof covering station buildings, platform and a single line for the Saltburn-bound trains. On leaving the station the level crossing was negotiated and houses appeared on either side to the next stop at Redcar East with its wooden platforms. Picking up speed once again the train returned to open countryside for the first time since Eaglescliffe and, at last, the sea was visible. Our penultimate stop was at Marske, which had the atmosphere of a wayside country station, and after a brief pause, when we would sometimes draw up alongside another train from Saltburn, it was not long before we were rounding the last bend on the approach to Saltburn with Hunt Cliff dominant beyond the town.

A clatter of points indicated the junction with the coastal line to Staithes and Whitby that diverged to the right, climbing inland and skirting round Saltburn via a substantial viaduct over Skelton Beck towards Hunt Cliff. On the left masses of caravans appeared at the large caravan site extending from the railway down to the wooded gorge beyond and then, on the same side, lines of railway coaches mainly stored in the sidings for use on summer excursions would be seen, occasionally with a tank engine at the head waiting to draw them into the station. Attention was often focused, by this time, on Saltburn shed to the right noting the usual 'A5' or 'A8' tank engine outside awaiting its next duty. As the train clattered over the points and crossed over the road leading to the upper promenade, the signalbox and excursion platform appeared on the left while, on the right, were the bay platforms with their tangerine totem signs proclaiming our destination. The notepad would now be put away as cases and belongings were gathered together, the train drawing into the 'through' platform underneath the small overall roof, typical of many

North Eastern stations, with its brick sidescreen to the left and station buildings to the right. There would be a subdued squeak as the brakes were applied for the last time and a hiss of steam while the echoing sound of doors being opened and then slammed shut would bounce off the surrounding walls and roof of the station. Steam would gently issue from the tank engine at the front of the train as all the passengers converged on the booking hall, whose hollow-sounding, wood-boarded floor led us to the station's portico and out onto Station Square.

The 'through' platform was most unusual in that it continued beyond the station buildings and up to the rear entrance of the Zetland Hotel on the upper promenade. Passengers could conveniently walk directly from the train into the hotel via the back door. Our journey was also a short walk, turning left outside the station and first left again at the edge of the Square through the subway, taking us underneath the extended platform and run-round loop, to Milton Street, which ran parallel with the railway on the seaward side. After turning left we would walk two hundred yards to where the iron railings formed the boundary with the excursion platform and then turn right down Emerald Street with the North Sea directly in front of us and the station behind. As far as I was concerned this was what a holiday was all about - sun, sea and steam! The distinctive smell of coal smoke, not only from the engines but also from the houses (especially in the winter months) continued until, first, the Clean Air Act had been passed and then steam engines were replaced by diesel trains.Until then one had to stand much closer to the promenade to sample the more invigorating sea air.

Saltburn was a product of the railway. The line from Darlington was extended to Saltburn as a result of pressures from industrialists on Teesside who wanted to live in a pleasant environment and travel by train to

Plate 53. Often, the heavier Newcastle trains were piloted over the steeply-graded section as far as Harrogate and it was common to see an 'A3' or 'V2' attached to a 'D49', the usual pilot engine. At Monkton Moor near Ripon, ex-LNER 'A3' Pacific No.60074 *Harvester* and ex-LNER 'D49' 4-4-0 No.62753 *The Belvoir* are seen on a northbound Newcastle express.

Photo, J.W.Hague, Neville Stead Collection.

49

work. The station was completed in 1861, as the dates on the subway bridge testified, and fanning out from there to the upper promenade, skirting the high cliffs overlooking the sea, was a series of streets with rows of substantial terraced houses. These were called the 'Jewel' streets and my grandmother's house at 25 Emerald Street was a typical three-storey property with small front garden and a rear yard overshadowed by the towering brickwork of the surrounding houses. The window above the front door once bore the painted name 'Tockwith' but over the years this faded and disappeared. The internal entrance door had large stained-glass panels in reds and yellows, surrounding a centre panel composed of ground-glass patterns. The effect created when sunlight passed through the glass was particularly pleasing but the hall, with its red-and-blue tiled floor, was generally dark. Directly off the hall on the right was the front lounge, the lightest room on the ground floor, with a massive mirror occupying the whole of the chimney breast above the cast-iron fire surround complete with its inset Paisley-patterned tiles. Adding to this grand setting and in a central position on the mantlepiece stood an imposing clock with a casing of black Whitby jet including the several fluted Doric columns on either side of the clock face. At first glance it bore a superficial resemblance to the Euston Arch! A handle situated at the side of the fireplace alerted maids in the morning room during Victorian and Edwardian times and, though it was very tempting to use, I must have showed considerable restraint as I recall causing mild annoyance on only a couple of occasions. Two other items of interest in the room were a large revolving bookcase with some photograph albums, including pictures of the prisoner-of-war camp where my grandparents were interned, and a grand piano which was not often used except when my mother occasionally, and rather flamboyantly, played Neapolitan tunes accompanied by the sound of her clicking fingernails on the keyboard. She liked the big chords but sometimes had difficulty in getting to grips with them. The resultant sound of those fingernails, reflecting the panic in trying to ensure that the right notes were struck and maintaining continuity, reminded me of a short, sharp hailstorm on the keys! My father also sat at the piano and played, though more furtively. The room was only regularly used on a Sunday evening when friends or relations of my grandmother called for a chat and a drink. Her brother-in-law, Herbert, and his wife Dolly from Marton, near Middlesbrough, were

regular visitors and the room was particularly inviting when there was a well-established fire.

Beyond the lounge was the staircase on the right and, at the far end of the hall, the cellar entrance and the rear lounge. In later years this living room was used more often as my grandmother appreciated the convenience of transferring the coal from the cellar to the adjacent room. Beyond the hall was the morning room with, beside the door, four bells which indicated to the maids the location of the summons, but the source of greatest interest to me was the large black cast-iron range occupying a significant amount of space. On the front of the range, and also in cast iron, was a model of *Locomotion No.1* with, if memory serves me correctly, two wagons. Incorporated into the range to celebrate the arrival of the railway in Saltburn it was certainly the focal point of the room as far as I was concerned but, some time in the nineteen-fifties, it was replaced by a typical small tiled fireplace of that period. Although lacking in character it undeniably made the room appear more spacious and bright. Beyond the morning room was the scullery with its Belfast sink and ancient gas stove.

Elsewhere in the house the main front bedroom was of interest as, from its bay windows, there was an excellent view up the road towards the station allowing me to check on train movements. As this was my grandmother's room it was regarded as out of bounds so stealth was practised in this part of the house and also up the creaking bare steps leading to the attic. In those top rooms lay a treasure trove of memories and curiosities, including old clothing and hats, pictures, books and little objects such as old coins, badges and buttons. Stored in a bedroom cupboard and also of interest was an acoustic guitar made in Innsbruck and used by my grandfather while in Katzenau Camp. I often strummed it quietly with the thumb but it was never possible to tune properly as the neck had been damaged, probably through upright storage over many years.

The rear yard was a scene of much activity in which many railway fantasies were played out. Brooms and long sticks were collected and stored as make-believe trains in imaginary sidings before being 'hauled' around the yard by me, in my guise as a steam engine. Such movements would usually be inspired by a visit to the station, often as a result of an errand such as the purchase of milk, a newspaper or ten Senior Service cigarettes (for Mrs Walker please!). It was on just such

Plate 54. An ex-LNER 'A5' Pacific tank engine No.69840 awaits departure from Darlington with a Saltburn train in the mid-1950s. A wooden-bodied Gresley brake coach is attached to the engine.   *Photo, The Stephenson Locomotive Society.*

Plate 55. Thornaby station as ex-NER 'Q6' 0-8-0 No.63349 passes with a coal train for the steel works on Teesside.
Photo, Neville Stead.

Plate 56. One of the ex-LNER 'V3' 2-6-2 tank engines No.67684 is seen at Middlesbrough, probably having arrived with a train from Newcastle via the coast. Occasionally this class could be seen in Saltburn but they were more usually employed on the services to Newcastle via Sunderland.

Photo, The Stephenson Locomotive Society.

Plate 57. Ex-NER 'A8' 4-6-2 tank engine No.69870 arrives at the grim surroundings of South Bank station with a train for Darlington.
Photo, J.F.Sedgwick.

an errand that, by remarkable coincidence, I bumped into a boy from my class at school. He, too, had a grandmother in this part of the world. One of my favourite shops was Hamilton's on Milton Street which, apart from selling newspapers, also displayed buckets and spades and 'goodies' that only seemed to be available at seaside shops. There was another shop on the same street which had a substantial pillar of mirrored tiles. Standing next to this and raising one leg out (wait for it!) one could create the impression of being unsupported in mid-air, as practised by a popular comedian of the time, Harry Worth. All my visits to the shops would involve passing the station and, through the railings, I would usually see a tank engine at the head of a Darlington train or taking water before its next duty. Alternatively, a view down Milton Street towards the carriage sidings would often be rewarded by the sight of a locomotive on empty-stock duties in the sidings or on a freight train in the distance, taking the avoiding lines. There was always a feeling of expectation here which made life very satisfying. Sometimes my brother and I would walk up the back street which was made up of smooth, rather small, cobbles. In fact, there was a network of back streets and

on one of them, at the back of Milton Street, stood a slaughterhouse. We often tried to peep through the slightest of gaps but, while we occasionally heard the sound of animals, never actually saw anything. One early memory I have of the back street concerns the gas lamps. In the summer, during the holidays when the nights remained light, it was sometimes difficult to get to sleep and on one occasion, hearing some movement near the back gate, I got up to look out of the window and saw a gaslighter using a pole or taper to light up the lamp. I would imagine that this practice ceased at some time during the nineteen-fifties when the street lamps were converted to electricity.

As younger children we were lucky to have the company of our cousins, Malcolm and Clive, who at that time were living with their parents at my grandmother's house, having returned from a spell in Malta. They were roughly the same age as us so we were natural playmates and, through them, made friends and played with other children in the street which, then, was free of cars. We ventured down to the beach and, of course, up to the railway but generally remained close to the house. Until the age of about twelve we were always accompanied on longer walks, which usually included a stroll on the

Plate 58. Newport-based, ex-NER 'J26' 0-6-0 No.65730, is about to skirt around South Bank station with a local freight.

Photo, J.F.Sedgwick.

sands and then a variety of options such as a return along the cliffs; through the woods that led to the caravan site and the carriage sidings; or towards the area known as Cat Nab and the Italian Gardens. The cliff walk between Saltburn and Marske always provided enjoyment because, not only could one look out to sea and note the ships making their way either towards or away from the Tees, but, across the fields in the other direction, the railway and its carriage sidings could be seen with smoke rising from the engine shed beyond. Behind the depot the Whitby line branched away, taking a detour of about two miles inland in order to cross the narrow valley at a viaduct over Skelton Beck, whereas the Whitby road dropped down to the beach by a series of hair-pin bends before rising steeply up the other side. In the days before improved power-weight ratios, buses and cars alike would often make heavy weather of these hills. The road met the beach at Cat Nab, the oldest part of Saltburn, comprising a few fishermen's cottages and a tavern known as the *Ship Inn*. Small boats registered in Whitby or Middlesbrough, bearing the letters WY or MH, would rest on the nearby shingle, not far from where Skelton Beck entered the sea. Beside the beck stood the miniature railway along which ran *Prince Charles,* a petrol-driven engine in the shape of one of Gresley's 'A4' Pacifics, with its rake of open coaches. An adjacent footpath kept company with the railway until it diverged, rising steeply into the woods. Here it

became part of a network of woodland paths under the towering structure of the Halfpenny Bridge that spanned the valley at a considerable height. While always appearing to be flimsy and mainly used by pedestrians it was, in fact, designed for vehicles as well.

Close to a junction of paths in this vicinity was what could be described, at first sight, as a folly but actually served a useful purpose. The Saltburn Improvement Company, the developers who built the nucleus of the town, removed the portico of Barnard Castle station (then only a few years old) as long ago as 1863 and placed it in the Valley Gardens for use as a shelter. It would undoubtedly have acted as a feature to attract the eye when the paths were laid out at the same time as the more formal Italian Gardens, a little further on and situated above the woodland terminus of the miniature railway. The paths beyond the Gardens led up to the extension of the upper promenade but also continued through the wooded valley, eventually passing under the viaduct of eleven arches that carried the line to Whitby. It was unusual to venture this far, however, and many walks would be confined to the firm sands (where a limited amount of motor racing took place in the nineteen-twenties) with a return via the woods, the cliff steps or even the cliff railway opposite the pier.

In time my cousins left Saltburn to live on a farm and my brother and I found our own amusements. Probably due to my persuasion we would spend more time by the

Plate 59. The terminus at Saltburn. Ex-NER 'A8' Pacific No.69894, having arrived at Saltburn, has advanced towards the Zetland Hotel and is now reversing round its train and the station. It will take water from the hose to the right of the train shed before returning to its duties. The gap between the properties above the locomotive's cab marks the entrance to Emerald Street where the author stayed whilst on holiday in Saltburn.

Photo, Neville Stead.

54

railway. A regular haunt was the cinder track by the caravan site from where we could keep an eye on the trains running into and out of Saltburn, the goods trains to and from Skinningrove steel works, and any movements from the engine shed and sidings. The track ran at a lower level than that of the railway although there was a point at which the levels were the same. However, at this point there were invariably two or three rows of coaches stored in the sidings to block the views. The carriages were a mixture of Gresley wooden-bodied vehicles and later examples from the Thompson era with their characteristic white oval toilet windows. Most of the coaches were red and cream or maroon although I seem to recall that one or two of the Gresley coaches were still in varnished teak brown. Articulated coaches were also in evidence, not only in the sidings but also on the Darlington trains. Views of the shed were obstructed by the lines of coaches but where the cinder track and railway were appropriately aligned it was possible to catch a glimpse of the usual class 'A5' or 'A8' tank engines by peering below the underbodies of the coaches which, of course, came into their own in the summer months when used for excursions. It was only at these times that the gates in the iron railings along Milton Street were opened, allowing day-trippers and holidaymakers to converge

Plate 60. Looking the other way from the previous picture towards the Zetland Hotel. The run-round loop can be seen to the left.

Photo, Neville Stead .

Plate 61 (below). On the journey home from Saltburn the first change of trains would usually take place at Darlington where an 'A3' Pacific or' V2' 2-6-2 would be the likely motive power for the route as far as Leeds. At the north end of Darlington an ex-LNER 'V2' No.60806 arrives with the 3.57pm Newcastle-Birmingham on 26th May 1956.

Photo, Ron Gee.

on the grassy excursion platform while we pressed our faces against the railings to take in all the activity. I never knew for sure where these trains were destined for but later learnt that there was regular excursion traffic to Blackpool and also to Morecambe from Saltburn. At the front end of these trains, and sometimes frustratingly hidden behind the signal box beyond the excursion platforms, would be a Thompson class 'B1' 4-6-0 or perhaps a 'K1' 2-6-0 or Gresley class 'V2' 2-6-2. Two of the 'B1s' I recall were *Gnu* and *Addax*, and, indeed, as many as forty of this class bore the names of deer so, at one time, I had quite a good knowledge of deer names (occasionally useful for crosswords) but if anyone had asked me to describe any of these animals then I would only have been able to point them in the direction of a class 'B1' 4-6-0! A train that was sometimes seen in the excursion platform bore the name 'The Teesside Nomad' which I assumed, as it was a named train, would probably be a service to London but I read later that it, too, was excursion stock. There were in fact through coaches for London at this time but the train left too early in the morning and returned too late at night for me to note the motive power in charge. Occasionally, a Gresley 'V1' or 'V3' 2-6-2 tank engine would be seen at the station and even a Worsdell 'J71' or 'J72' 0-6-0 tank engine would put in an appearance from time to time. The freight trains that gave Saltburn a wide berth were regularly in the hands of the 'J26' 0-6-0s and 'Q6' 0-8-0s of the NER, or the more modern 'WD' 2-8-0s. The freight trains could also be seen in the distance from the upper promenade, a plume of smoke or steam giving away their position as they made their way towards Hunt Cliff.

After a weekend or a week of underlining new numbers in my copy of *The abc of British Railway Locomotives* it would be time for the journey home which was less predictable than the outward trip. For a start, it would sometimes be on a Sunday but more usually on a weekday during our holidays. On the odd occasion we changed trains at Eaglescliffe but the normal practice was to return to Darlington, which suited me fine as it was one of my favourite locations. Its grand station had the right ambience for watching steam locomotives. Many are the names that I recall solidly stamped in cast iron on a nameplate or curved over a wheel splasher; names such as *Great Northern*, *Alcazar* and *Sir Charles Newton* on southbound expresses or *Cock 'o' the North*, *Earl Marischal*, *The White Knight* and *Knight of the Thistle* on trains for the north. On one occasion our train from Saltburn was held outside Darlington to allow for the southbound passage of a non-stop express. It duly passed by with one of Gresley's streamlined 'A4' Pacifics at the head so, on arrival, I sought out a young trainspotter and asked him for the name and number. He replied that it was *Mallard*. I had never seen the world's fastest steam locomotive and, although I underlined it in my locospotter's book, I did so unconvincingly as I never quite believed him. The next time I saw *Mallard* it was an exhibit in the National Railway Museum at York. It was at Darlington that my expectation of travelling on a named train for the first time was dashed. We had hoped to return as far as Leeds on 'The Queen of Scots' in one of its luxurious chocolate-and-cream Pullman cars, each bearing its own name, and hauled by a spotless Brunswick-green Gresley 'A3' Pacific, *Gainsborough*.

Unfortunately, the train was fully booked and I could only look with envy at the passengers sitting at their tables, each with a lamp and shade. The latter part of our journey home was often made in the dark and was generally more tiring so that by the time the train had drawn into platform three at Manchester Exchange my

Plate 63. A London express hauled by ex-LNER 'A4' Pacific No.60005 *Sir Charles Newton* pauses at Darlington as we wait for our train back to the north-west in the mid-fifties. *Photo, Eric Packer.*

interest in engines and their numbers had all but evaporated. Incidentally, our arrival platform was connected to platform eleven at Manchester Victoria and, together at 2194 feet long, they made up the longest platform in the country at the time, with the ability to accommodate three trains, all of which could gain access or egress without affecting the others.

On the odd occasion our journey to the north-east would take us via York, travelling on a train that originated at Liverpool Exchange and using the former Lancashire and Yorkshire route through Rochdale, Todmorden, Wakefield and Normanton. Motive power was usually a Stanier 'Jubilee' and our train, behind examples such as *Seahorse* and *Camperdown*, would start from Victoria station instead of the more usual Exchange station. York was one of the most exciting railway centres in the country. The sweeping curve of its large roof and the shafts of light that beamed down through the framework added to the impression of power and grace embodied in the locomotives as they brought their trains around the curve. Then there was the activity on the platforms as greetings and farewells took place beside the trains. Visitors, including the

many from abroad, would ask station staff for directions or alternatively puzzle over timetables, and at the far ends of the main platforms, remote in their own worlds, stood the hordes of trainspotters. It was from York where I first travelled on a named train, 'The Northumbrian', which ran from King's Cross to Newcastle. Standing on platform nine, north of the internal footbridge, it was possible to look across the curve of the platform to watch the stately progress of the train as it entered the station. It was only possible to see the top of the engine, steam issuing from its valves, as it rounded the curve, passed under the footbridge and came into view - a Thompson 'A2' Pacific, one of the most powerful express locomotives in the country at the time. As it passed by me I looked up to see the name *Airborne* on the side of its smoke deflector plate before it drew to a halt a little further on. The journey from York to Darlington was often exciting as the track was level and straight, allowing locomotives the chance to indulge in some high-speed running. Now was the chance, possibly, to tick off something new in the *I Spy* book such as the sign indicating the half-way point between London and Edinburgh, and an advertising hoarding consisting of two men supporting a horizontal ladder, presumably advertising some form of decorative service or product. I'm sure I did not dream this but I expect it is just possible that two men were actually walking off with the ladder and were just posing as we passed by! I also used to strain my eyes to catch a glimpse of The White Horse carved into the Hambleton Hills, a few miles to the east of Thirsk where, like Northallerton a little further on, concentration was needed to spot any stationary train or shunting operations.

This then was the pattern of travel between Manchester and Saltburn, mainly during Easter, Summer and Christmas holidays from 1951 to 1958 when my father bought his first car. By the end of 1957, however, another change had already taken place. The steam trains between Darlington and Saltburn were replaced by the new breed of diesel multiple units that had first been introduced to Britain's railways two years earlier.

Plate 64. An impressive combination of motive power ready to depart Leeds City station with the 9.55am Newcastle-Liverpool. Ex-LMSR 'Royal Scot' No.46123 *Royal Irish Fusilier* and ex-LMSR 'Patriot' No.45521 *Rhyl* are at the head of this train on 15th November 1960, though single-engine working was the general rule.   *Photo, Gavin Morrison.*

Had we spent Christmas that year at Saltburn, as we usually did, then we would have probably experienced the advantages of the new trains for ourselves but, instead, our holiday destination was the lovely Yorkshire village of Bishop Burton, near Beverley, where my uncle was in charge of poultry at a local farm. I think we only visited the farm three or four times but on each occasion our journey was different, the most notable feature being that we departed from no less than three separate Manchester stations to reach our destination. At Victoria we caught the express from Liverpool Exchange, hauled by a Stanier 'Jubilee', that took the Lancashire and Yorkshire route to York, although once we changed trains at Wakefield Kirkgate transferred to a local for Goole hauled by a Fowler 2-6-4 tank, and then a Thompson 'B1'- hauled train to Hull. From Exchange station we used the Liverpool-Hull service, again in the hands of a 'Jubilee' which, on this occasion, was *Aboukir*. At Leeds City a 'B1' took over for the remaining part of the journey to Hull.

From Manchester Central station there was another service to Hull which originated at Liverpool Central. The first part of this journey took us through suburbs to the south and east of Manchester before arriving at

Guide Bridge, on the electrified main line to Sheffield via Woodhead. Here motive power transferred to one of the seven Class 'EM2' Co-Co locomotives, designed for the line and using 1500 volts direct current from overhead wires. Although I had experienced electric trains on the Liverpool Overhead Railway, the Altrincham line and the Bury service (where the ancient-looking stock must have dated back to the early years of the century) it was still a novelty to sample haulage by a main-line electric locomotive. There were, after all, no more than a handful on regular passenger duties before the advent of the West Coast electrification less than three years later. This part of the journey was brief, however, and like all the other main Trans-Pennine routes it was the tunnel (at Woodhead) that was the main engineering feature. From Sheffield Victoria an engine-change would have seen another of the Thompson 'B1s' take over to cover the remaining miles to Hull Paragon, or Paraffin station as I used to call it as a child! The last part of our journey to Beverley, whether from Hull or York via Market Weighton, was invariably behind a Gresley 'D49' 4-4-0, popularly known as the 'Hunt' class. Names such as the *The Bedale* and *The Craven* are recalled but also

Plate 65. The end of another holiday as ex-LMSR class '5' 4-6-0 No.44857 pilots ex-LMSR 'Royal Scot' No.46119 *Lancashire Fusilier* through Manchester Victoria towards Manchester Exchange working the 9.55am Newcastle-Liverpool Lime Street on 8th September 1960. *Photo, Peter Fitton.*

Plate 66. Usual motive power at the head of the 11am Liverpool-Hull express as ex-LMSR 'Jubilee' 4-6-0 No.45708 *Resolution* (based at Farnley Junction) leaves Manchester Exchange behind, gathering speed through Victoria station on 8th September 1960. It is receiving rear-end assistance from sister engine No.45661 *Vernon.* *Photo, Peter Fitton.*

Lincolnshire as some of the class bore the names of counties. From Beverley station, with its North Eastern overall roof, we would catch a blue-and-white double-decker bus with its rounded roof, designed to negotiate the arched gates of the town. Once off the bus, near the village pond in Bishop Burton, there would be a walk up the long farm drive before a few days' fun and relaxation in very pleasant surroundings.

Around the farm there were fields and large tracts of broad-leaved woodland, providing an ideal playground for us to play with our cousins. In the fields we would play cricket in summer using stout sticks and a tennis ball or just disappear into the dense dark woods and seek adventure. The barns and their bales of hay were also favourite attractions but care had to be exercised to avoid the watchful eyes of the farmer. It was here where I learned to ride cousin Malcolm's half-size bicycle but only after suffering a few bumps and bruises. It was here, too, where one of the farm girls, Meg, showed us an injured barn owl sitting tamely on her wrist, its ghostly white face making quite an impression on me. Returning home after Christmas via Hull and Leeds I remember looking out of the window into the darkness, across the low-lying fields covered in snow around Selby, unaware that this would be the last time I would regularly travel by steam train.

Plate 67. Sometimes the journey to the north-east would be via York from where I travelled on a named train for the first time in the summer of 1957. The train was 'The Northumbrian' and the locomotive was ex-LNER A2/3 Pacific No.60511 Airborne, shortly after this shot of the same locomotive seen starting out from York on 6th July 1957 with the 8.05am Birmingham-Newcastle, having taken over from a Stanier class 5. *Photo, Michael Mensing.*

Plate 68. An alternative way of reaching East Yorkshire from Manchester was to travel from London Road (now Piccadilly) station to Hull via Sheffield. Standard motive power for the run to Sheffield were the 'EM2' Co-Co electric locomotives such as No.27006 *Pandora,* seen at Sheffield Victoria on 12th September 1959. *Photo, Peter Fitton.*

Plate 69. From Hull Paragon, ex-LNER 'D49s' handled the trains to Bridlington and Scarborough, and to York via Beverley. Here No.62766 *The Grafton* is awaiting departure at the head of an express train in 1951.

Photo, Rex Conway Steam Collection.

Plate 70. In the 1950s the 'D49s' operated from York on Hull and Harrogate services. Here an ex-LNER 'D49' No.62746 *The Middleton* leaves York on the 4.27pm to Harrogate.

Photo, Ron Gee.

Plate 71. Another 'D49' 4-4-0 No.62720 *Cambridgeshire* draws into Market Weighton station at the head of a Hull-York train in May 1952.

Photo, B.G.Tweed, Neville Stead Collection.

Plate 72. An ex-LNER 'B1' 4-6-0 No.61039 *Steinbok* leaves Beverley with a northbound holiday special. The station still retains its overall roof.

Photo, Neville Stead Collection.

Plate 73. Leeds City station as ex-LNER 'B1' 4-6-0 No.61038 *Blacktail* arrives from the east. This combination of locomotive and stock would have been similar to that on my last regular journey by steam before the family acquired a car.

Photo, Neville Stead Collection.

6. HAVE CAR WILL TRAVEL

We gathered in the playground before the school bell summoned us all. There was still a layer of frost on the tarmac as we discussed the disaster in tones that were at the same time excited and subdued. A few boys had brought newspapers with them on that day, 7 February 1958, and as we strained our necks to look over the shoulders of others, there, on the front pages, were the headlines "Manchester United plane crashes - 21 dead". The names of the dead players were recited time and again- Roger Byrne (captain), Tommy Taylor, Mark Jones, Eddie Colman, Billy Whelan, David Pegg and Geoff Bent. I had heard of Tommy Taylor because the boys who kicked a ball around the playground mentioned his name (everyone likes a striker) but I have to admit that, until then, our local team, just four miles up the road into Town, had meant little to me, whereas many other eight and nine-year-old boys in my class were supporters. The team was on the crest of a wave having won the Championship for a second year running, reached the Cup Final the year before and performed well in the emerging European Cup competition. Moreover, this had been achieved with a squad of young players. Yes, this day marked my first awareness of football. It had never really been mentioned before and there was no great interest in the family although my father had been taken many times by his father to see Aston Villa play between the Wars and my uncle Boris actually had trials in the nineteen-forties with Tottenham Hotspur as a goalkeeper. However, he was discouraged by his parents from making it a career and that was the end of the matter.

By coincidence my father had to make his first trip abroad with ICI in the same month. It was his first flight, a 'Douglas Dakota' DC3 to Oslo via London, and recent events had not been the ideal preparation. To make matters worse, the flight was delayed because of mechanical trouble which meant that the passengers had to leave the plane and later reboard as on that fateful day in Munich. However, all went well and there followed a succession of trips to Scandinavia and mainland Europe during the next two years on 'Dakotas', 'Argonauts', 'Elizabethan Ambassadors' and the popular 'Vickers Viscounts'. At the same time he received visitors from abroad keen to learn about the new technical developments at the Blackley Works and, as a consequence of this, my parents began to entertain visitors from different countries such as Denmark, Sweden and Italy which, whether or not we appreciated it at the time, must have helped in some small way to broaden our minds.

At about Easter 1958 my father bought his first car, a four-year-old, black (like most cars until the early nineteen-sixties) Rover 90, registration number ONE 951, which enabled us to explore much of the north of England and Wales on day trips, many of which would have been impractical by train. I don't recall shedding any tears for the era that had now passed as the novelty of car travel, coupled with its comfort and convenience, provided new pleasures and opened up new expectations. The journey to Saltburn remained the

Plate 74. Regularly seen at Saltburn during the 1950s were the ex-LNER 'L1' 2-6-4 tank engines and in this view No.67754 is ready to depart from Darlington with a Saltburn train. A 'J94' can be seen shunting in the background beyond the 'L1'.
Photo, The Stephenson Locomotive Society.

Plate 75. From the winter timetable of 1957 diesel multiple units replaced steam on the Darlington services and here, at platform 1, a Metro-Cammell unit forms the next such service at an otherwise deserted terminus. On the far left is the excursion platform while, to the right of the picture, a single line runs alongside platform 4. *Photo, Neville Stead.*

same contrast of blackened mill towns and attractive market towns beyond the Pennines, of moorland scenery and rich farmland, but it took much less time. In 1958 the first motorway was built (the Preston by-pass) but it would be many years before we would reap the benefit of fast travel. It took an hour to pass through Manchester and reach the other side of Oldham. Although there were several points where road and rail met in Greater Manchester the only places we ever noticed steam engines were on the viaduct outside Manchester Central station and in the Miles Platting area of Oldham Road where the Manchester to Leeds line crossed over at the junction there. It was on one return journey that we first encountered vast crowds of people in Manchester taking part in the Whit Walks that were still popular at that time.

Beyond Oldham the scenery changed as we reached the edge of the Pennines. Crossing the moors into Yorkshire was always interesting and sometimes exciting as the road skirted around reservoirs and clung to the edge of hillsides with very steep drops that were positively fearsome in fog. On more than one occasion, returning from Saltburn on a foggy evening, I recall my mother getting out of the car and guiding us forward to avoid creeping too close to the edge of the road. In this wild setting stood the isolated *Nont Sarah* inn which, no doubt, provided many a traveller with a welcome break in the days before motorised transport. From Huddersfield (where trolley buses remained a regular sight on our journey for many years) to Bradford via Brighouse, we passed through drab urban surroundings with little in the way of open space but beyond Yeadon Airport, serving Leeds and Bradford, the scenery changed and the Pennine gritstone gave way to a more mellow limestone, part of a geological band of rock that stretches from the north-east to the south-west, producing similar building stone in areas such as the Cotswolds. Hill farming now gave way to fields of crops but my attention was focused on the Leeds-Northallerton main line as it came off the Arthington

Plate 76. An ex-LNER V2 2-6-2 No.60910 rushes through Danby Wiske, between Darlington and Northallerton, shortly before the station closed after the summer of 1958.

Photo, Eric Packer.

Viaduct and ran alongside, intermittently, both south and north of Harrogate. Alas, I rarely saw any trains but it sent my pulse racing when, on one occasion, a clean-looking Peppercorn 'A1' Pacific No.60131 *Osprey* overtook us with a Pullman train. Soon we were in Harrogate with its wide open parkland known as 'The Strays', situated close to the town centre and adding much to the environment for its inhabitants. A few miles further on we passed through Ripon, another attractive town with market square and prominent cathedral. Its station lay at the far end of the town, close to the bridge that carried the railway over the river Ure. On one late return journey from Saltburn we arrived at Ripon just before 9pm, in time to see the official hornblower or wakeman (in his costume and tricorn hat) blow his horn, perpetuating a nightly tradition that can be traced back several hundred years. Apparently, at one time, it indicated that the wakeman had begun his night watch over the town.

Continuing north-eastwards we would cross the A1 trunk road, still known then as the Great North Road, and, before Thirsk, reach the high spot of the journey as far as I was concerned for that was where we crossed the East Coast Main Line at Thirsk station, which provided an eminently suitable toilet stop! Naturally, every possible excuse was used to prolong the stay (eg.

the need to stretch one's legs or get some fresh air) and often we would see at least one passing train. From here it was a short distance past the racecourse into the town. The goods station was situated close to the centre of Thirsk and on just one occasion I saw a BR class '2' 2-6-0 (probably one of Northallerton's allocation) shunting wagons. Now, though, we were about to begin the final leg of the journey along the A19 and A172, both winding roads at the time with bad records for accidents. As well as the splendid views of the Hambledon Hills and the Cleveland Hills our route took us through the attractive towns of Stokesley, Great Ayton and Guisborough where thinly-used branch lines were crossed. In the days of steam I only once saw a train near Stokesley but now the line to Whitby is all that exists, crossed north of Great Ayton under the distinctive volcano-like hill known as Roseberry Topping.

Although a little over 1000 feet it looks taller for rising steeply out of the farmland to the west. For some time I thought the hill was called Rosemary Topping but then there is something about the area that tends to corrupt one's thinking such as the signs to Sexhow and Mount Grace Priory. My uncle was never sure whether this latter sign was a direction or an instruction!

Once past the minute Upleatham church, one of the contenders for the smallest church in Britain, we were now almost within sight of the coast. The approach to Saltburn by car was visually more attractive than that by train. The road climbed up to the Saltburn Golf Course and on the brow of the hill a panoramic view of the North Sea opened up. A line of cargo ships and tankers could usually be seen making their way into and out of the docks along the Tees, serving the heavy industrial plants visible on the left, while on the right stood the impressive Hunt Cliff. Saltburn lay straight ahead, the eye drawn to the spire of its parish church where my mother and father were married, where I was christened and where, many years later, my grandmother's funeral service would take place. The journey had taken three-and-a-half hours, two hours less than by public transport and, in time, with road widening and straightening, by-passes and ultimately the construction of motorways, the journey time would reduce to little more than two hours!

Steam was still active at Saltburn station even though the Darlington service was now in the hands of diesel multiple units and the shed had closed at the beginning of 1958. The occasional 'A8' 4-6-2 tank engine worked

66

Plate 77. Memories of London Road station in Manchester as rebuilt ex-LMSR 'Royal Scot' 4-6-0 No.46137 *The Prince of Wales's Volunteers (South Lancashire)* leaves Manchester with the 12 noon train for London St. Pancras on 22nd March 1960, during the period prior to electrification of the route to Crewe when London Road was renamed Piccadilly.

Photo, Ron Gee.

into the terminus and the 'L1' 2-6-4 tanks, especially Nos.67754, 63 and 64, were often seen on a variety of duties including the handling of empty coaching stock, mainly in the summer. The car enabled us to visit other locations, occasionally, mainly along the East Coast Main Line. I recall two visits in particular which serve to demonstrate the changes that took place between 1958 and 1963. The first trip was to Danby Wiske, the station north of Northallerton. In 1958 this manned wayside station, like many others between York and Darlington, barely had a service. By this time only one train a day called each way and yet the platforms were tidy, garlanded with hanging baskets and tubs, and the small waiting room was still in use. There was also a short, single-track, gated siding into a bay at the southern end of the southbound platform which certainly gave the impression of being in use, presumably for the occasional loading of agricultural produce and farm animals. In any event it was a very pretty scene, set in the heart of Yorkshire farmland, especially on that warm summer's day. The main line was very straight here and

one could see two or three miles down the track through a succession of bridges. The eye was strained for the first sight of a train which initially would be a distant grey shadow gradually becoming darker until its form became clearer. Then the sound of the train would be transmitted to the rails and within seconds, amid growing excitement, it would flash by. On that day Gresley 'A4' Pacific No.60012 *Commonwealth of Australia* hauled the northbound 'Elizabethan', its driver and fireman having left their seats in the first coach of this non-stop train just a few minutes earlier to pass through the locomotive's corridor tender and relieve the crew who had been in charge for the first stage of the journey to Edinburgh. That summer was to be the last for Danby Wiske as passenger services were withdrawn soon afterwards and by the time we visited Cowton station, the next stop north in 1963, the farmland surroundings were similar but the station had been substantially dismantled. The 'Flying Scotsman' was hauled by a two-tone green 'Deltic' and Gresley Pacifics could be seen at the head of freight trains.

67

During the late nineteen-fifties my grandfather, who still lived in Birmingham, occasionally travelled up to Sale to spend a few days with us. His visits were always very welcome as he was patient, kind and generous and, in a low-key manner, instructive, often imparting little bits of knowledge. He also appreciated our interest in trains and took us to railway locations such as Hartford on the West Coast Main Line where we saw 'Coronation' class No.46242 *City of Glasgow* and 'Princess' class No.46207 *Princess Arthur of Connaught* (to a child this was a weird name), curiously in black livery at the head of the 'Merseyside Express'. This was at a time when, despite living only a few miles from this main line, we had seen very little of the LMS Pacifics. On another occasion he took us to Stockport and Cheadle Hulme travelling via London Road, Manchester. Our electric train from Sale terminated here and we transferred to a Buxton train behind a Fowler 2-6-4 tank engine. On a neighbouring platform stood a gleaming 'Britannia' Pacific, No.70033 *Charles Dickens*, at the head of a London express while the Eastern Region side of the terminus was represented on that day by Robinson 4-6-2 tank No.69806. At Cheadle Hulme 'Coronation' class No.46252 *City of Leicester* raced through with a train for Manchester while 'Royal Scot' class No.46162 *Queen's Westminster Rifleman* rounded the curve in the Macclesfield direction. At Stockport a northbound 'Royal Scot' 4-6-0 No.46169

The Boy Scout was followed by 'Patriot' No.45519 *Lady Godiva*, one of the unrebuilt variety, while, back at London Road, we took another look at *City of Leicester* on the turntable (in the vicinity of the present-day power box at Piccadilly station) prior to its working the southbound 'Comet' express to Euston. The rewarding afternoon of trainspotting came to a close after witnessing the late arrival of the 'Pines Express' behind No.46115 *Scots Guardsman*, another 'Royal Scot'. On occasions such as these there was little to rival the local steam scene.

1959 was a warm and dry year, so much so that when my father took us to Ladybower Reservoir in Derbyshire the water had disappeared revealing sun-baked mud and various buildings, including the old Derwent Valley bridge, that had been flooded when the reservoir was built. In fact, 1959 was the perfect year to see Scotland. It seemed as if there had not been a cloud in the sky for fifteen days as we enjoyed our first holiday away from relatives. Over two thousand miles were covered during that time when we stayed at hotels and guest houses starting with the Pinewood Hotel in Callander for two nights. It was a great feeling to step out of the hotel on that first morning and sample the clean air mixed in with the sweet scent of pine needles in the hotel garden, and to be allowed to walk up the road to the station before breakfast. I don't think we saw a train but it didn't matter; it was the atmosphere that

Plate 78. Another ex-LMSR 'Royal Scot' No.46158 *The Loyal Regiment* leaves Stockport Edgeley with the 2.25pm Manchester (London Road)-Birmingham train on Sunday 14th October 1956.
Photo, Ron Gee.

Plate 79. One of the MSJ&AR electric multiple units leaves London Road for Altrincham on 9th September 1958, shortly before the line between London Road and Oxford Road was closed completely to allow reconstruction works to take place at London Road. Thenceforward, the electric service to Altrincham ran from the bay platforms of Oxford Road station.

In pre-Grouping days the MSJ&AR was jointly owned by the L&NW and GC; and from 1923 by the LMS & LNER.

The Weir Committee on main-line electrification was set up by the government in 1929 and as a result the electrification of the MSJ&AR was the first scheme to be completed, in 1931, by recommendation of the Committee. Under the scheme, the MSJ&AR, from London Road to Altrincham, some 8½ miles, was electrified at 1500 volts d.c., the recommended system favoured at the time. At Altrincham, the MSJ&AR made an end-on connection with the CLC route via Northwich. A part of the MSJ&AR not electrified was that near Ordsall Lane, a short spur, which connects with the Liverpool & Manchester route and often used by WCML diversions routed by way of Eccles Junction via Tyldesley, rejoining the WCML at Wigan, Springs Branch, Manchester Lines Junction.

Photo, Ron Gee.

counted and the feeling that a train may arrive. Later, we did see one or two Stanier class '5s' on trains to and from Oban as indeed we did at our next stop at Pitlochry, where on one evening we relaxed by the Highland line and watched the southbound 'Royal Highlander' pass by behind a brace of class '5s'.

Much of the holiday itinerary kept us away from trains, however, as we made our way in stages to the north-west where it stayed light for so long. One night we set off at about 10pm from our little guest house beside Little Loch Broom to stroll along the road in an atmosphere of calm and stillness, which made the sudden flight of a disturbed red grouse all the more alarming. The sound of its rapid wingbeat could be

heard for some considerable time afterwards as it looked for safe cover in the heather by the shores of the loch. I awoke briefly at 3.30am the following morning and noticed that it was already light. Our most northerly overnight stop was at Ullapool where many of the houses at the time were wooden. From here we made a circular trip to Lochinvar along roads that were little more than dirt tracks and virtually deserted. There were times when half-an-hour would pass without the sight of another vehicle and when the car received a puncture it brought home how awkward it could be in the event of a breakdown. The west of Scotland was, in fact, well patrolled by smart AA men on motor bikes with sidecars and a regular feature at the time was the exchanging of salutes with all drivers who were members of the AA, as evidenced by those splendid yellow-and-silver metal badges that were pinned to the fronts of cars.

Returning south along the coast we were briefly involved in a chance encounter the odds against which must be very high indeed. While enjoying the warm sunshine on an otherwise deserted beach at Gruinard Bay we noticed a family walking along the sands in our direction. When they were close enough to be identified it was realised that the family lived on our road in Sale and the daughter was in my brother's class at school! So much for getting away from it all but soon we would return to civilization as we made overnight stops at Fort William and Oban. At both locations we saw steam engines but not close enough to identify, which was a

lost opportunity bearing in mind that at these outposts were Gresley 'K2s' and 'K4s' and Caledonian 0-4-4 tank engines that were about to succumb to dieselisation.

Our itinerary now took us to Edinburgh, crossing the Forth by a ferry which gave us a marvellous view of the huge, powerful and aesthetically-pleasing structure of the Forth Bridge, being crossed at the time by a Stanier class '5' with a passenger train. Two nights were spent in Edinburgh and the high spot of this memorable holiday for me was the trip from Waverley station, via the Forth Bridge, to Inverkeithing by steam train. I have no record of the motive power on that day - it may have been a Gresley 2-6-2 tank engine, a Thompson 'B1' 4-6-0 or perhaps something more glamorous but I don't think it mattered at the time. I certainly loved the atmosphere of railways and of steam locomotives in particular and I was taking down engine numbers and transferring them to my Ian Allan *ABC* book of locomotive numbers but I don't think I was a committed trainspotter. Of course, at that time it did not occur to me that steam engines were a dying breed despite the changes taking place at Saltburn. After all, they were still being built!

The warm summer meant happy times playing outside in the garden or in the school playground where, amongst other activities, I remember having graduated to the game of 'kiss-chase', the rules of which I cannot exactly recall except that it involved kissing and ...er..chasing! The boy or girl who thought up this game may have achieved his or her portion of 'fame for fifteen minutes', at least in the playground, as did one younger boy at our school who, for a very brief period, was able to attract an inquisitive crowd of children around him as he gave a faultless rendition of Cliff Richard's *Living Doll*. It was now the last term of the penultimate year at primary school and the two top classes were taken on the annual school trip to a destination that changed each year. In 1959 I was more than happy to visit London for the first time. Naturally we visited the usual tourist spots but I was able to add Euston station (complete with Doric arch) to my list of happy memories that day. As we filed out of the train to form a haphazard queue on the platform I was well satisfied as I admired the subdued power of our train engine 'Royal Scot' class 4-6-0 No.46152 *The King's Dragoon Guardsman* simmering at the buffer stops. For some reason our return journey took us into Mayfield station instead of the adjacent London Road.

Plate 80. Stanier 2-6-4 tank engine No.42606 is about to enter Oxford Road station with the 4.05pm London Road-Warrington service on 9th September 1958.

Photo, Ron Gee.

Plate 81. By the end of 1957 the ex-GCR types had all but disappeared from the Chester services, which were now mainly in the hands of ex-LMSR 2-6-4 tank engines such as this Fowler design, No.42303, seen leaving Altrincham & Bowdon station with a Chester train on 3rd November 1957.

Photo, D.Chatfield.

Apparently, Mayfield was used as an overflow for the main terminus but when London Road was rebuilt as Piccadilly station Mayfield closed to passengers, in August 1960, and was retained for parcels only.

Part of our summer holidays was spent at a new location, a farm on the edge of Wighill near Tadcaster. My cousins had moved from Bishop Burton to the large farm where my uncle had a wider range of responsibilities but still looked after the hens, some of which were free-range and others which were raised in small cages on the 'battery' principle. From the edge of

the village a gated drive led through a small area of parkland and then through a series of gates to a T-junction where a right turn down a short track ended at the substantial farm of Mr. Ackroyd. The main house was situated on the edge of a courtyard off which stood various barns, pens, sheds and a milking house. My uncle's family lived in a prefabricated bungalow close to the yard while nearby were fields, woods, dens and 'spooky' places. In fact, there was a seemingly endless expanse of gently rolling countryside and farm buildings at our disposal, which we made full use of

Plate 82. While work was taking place in connection with electrification of the route from Manchester to Crewe via Stockport, many trains were diverted via Sandbach, Northwich and Altrincham. BR 'Britannia' class 4-6-2 No.70004 *William Shakespeare* is seen approaching Hale station on 16th July 1960 with the diverted 'Pines Express.'

Photo, D.Chatfield.

Plate 83. The 10.35am Chester Northgate-Manchester Central service with ex-LMSR Stanier 2-6-4 tank engine No.42428 calls at Knutsford station on 14th May 1960.
Photo, D.Chatfield.

subject to the occasional stern warning from Mr. Ackroyd and with good reason, too, for a farm was and still is, potentially, a very dangerous place. I managed to cut myself on a rusty circular saw, was badly winded when falling more than ten feet from bales of hay stored in a barn, and once found myself at the controls of a tractor having been shown how to operate it by my cousins. Death or serious injury lurked just around the corner but we survived our adventures more or less intact. On one occasion we converted a few hundred palings that had been stored neatly, near to the bungalow, into a three-roomed shack. Construction techniques were very basic and involved firstly stacking the palings in criss-cross sequence and then placing them side-by-side to form a roof after leaving a gap, of course, to gain entry and egress. We were very proud of our 'second home' where we even had some of our meals but it all came to an end when one day the patient farmer told us to dimantle the 'house' and re-stack the palings.

We kept well out of the way when the large combine harvester visited the farm in August but we were allowed to follow the baling operation and stack the bales of hay. The modern machinery on Mr. Ackroyd's farm contrasted sharply with that of the neighbouring farmer who appeared to be about eighty. He was a man of a bygone age and of unusual appearance especially when he sat upon his horse-drawn binder in a long black coat and hat, conjuring up the appearance of some hardened Wild West character who was quite beyond any attempt to civilize. Beyond his fields lay substantial broad-leaved woodlands where we would seek adventures and use as an unseen route to various places such as the mysterious, solitary house at the far edge of the woods. It was occupied by a poor family, clearly living a precarious existence, as evidenced by the bare walls in each room and the spartan furniture.

The teenage boy, Ross, who my cousins knew, showed us how to operate an air rifle which he used, apparently, to shoot crows, rabbits and pigeons. Like the ancient farmer there was a wild, untamed streak in this boy and I thought that he may have been responsible for the death of a sparrow hawk that I discovered at the foot of a large oak tree near the farm. It was the first hawk I'd knowingly identified but its unmistakable light striped chest bore no signs of impact by pellet. It was only some

72

Plate 84. A familiar sight in the north-east. Ex-LNER 'B1' 4-6-0 No.61018 *Gnu* restarts its train at the south end of York. I learned a lot about the names of deer from this class!
Photo, The Stephenson Locomotive Society.

years later, after reading Rachel Carson's book *Silent Spring,* that I realised it had almost certainly died of poisoning by a pesticide residue such as DDT. It was at about this time when the effect of such chemicals was having an alarming effect on wild life.

There was another mysterious house nearby in what was known as Wighill Park and, because it was a ruin, it inevitably drew us to its crumbling form. We knew it as 'The Grange', a creamy-white edifice that had once been owned by a Yorkshire and England cricketer of long ago, Lord Hawke. I believe that there was a 'keep out' notice but, as the building was situated away from

other houses, it received our attention when there were no adults in the vicinity. It was a potential deathtrap as we sat inside the towering, crumbling and fragile walls dropping stones down a deep well which, though covered by a large slab, was nevertheless moveable by children. So we explored and flirted with the potential dangers within the farm and its immediate surroundings but emerged unscathed, though more sober, looking back through the eyes of an adult and parent. The subject of flirtation has reminded me that it was on this farm where, at the tender age of eleven, going on twelve, I looked at a woman for the first time as more

Plate 85. A visit to York would invariably provide much of interest to a railway enthusiast apart from the spectacle of the main-line expresses. One of York's allocation of ex-NER 'J72' 0-6-0 tank engines No.68735 negotiates the crossing at the north end of the station on 9th May 1953.
Photo, J.D.Darby.

73

Plate 86. The doyen of its class, BR designed 4-6-2 No.70000 *Britannia,* has plenty of steam to spare on arrival at York. This engine carries the modified smoke deflectors, fitted after a serious accident on the Western Region involving sister engine No.70026 *Polar Star.* At the inquiry, the original style of deflector with protruding handgrip *(as in plate 82)* was said to have contributed to the accident, in that it hindered the driver's vision. Not all locomotives of the class received modification, particularly those allocated to the London Midland Region. *Photo, B.Nichols.*

Plate 87. Another popular railway centre was Crewe. Many would argue that the Stanier-designed 'Coronation' class 4-6-2 locomotives were the most powerful ever to run on Britain's railways, especially if the yardstick for measuring that is 'drawbar power'. On 25th May 1961, No.46235 *City of Birmingham* awaits departure with a southbound express.

Photo, David Stratton.

than just a pretty face. Her name was Tura, a buxom farm girl who, with rosy complexion and tight jeans could, to borrow a quotation, 'cause lycanthropy in a boy scout'! But, as the song goes, 'I was too young to know'.

On usually one day of our holidays at Wighill my mother and aunt would spend the day shopping in York, catching the bus from Tadcaster and leaving us at York station for a few hours to watch trains. The highlights on these occasions were the northbound and southbound 'Elizabethan' and 'Flying Scotsman' expresses which would pass slowly but majestically through the station between platforms eight and nine with, more often than not, a Gresley 'A4' Pacific in charge. From the north end the Scarborough trains would arrive and depart often behind class 'B16' 4-6-0s while, at the south end, there was a good chance of seeing a Stanier class '5' or 'Jubilee' on a train for Sheffield or further destination. One train that I looked forward to seeing was the Colchester-Newcastle express which changed engines at York and would bring an East Anglian-based 'Britannia' to the city. *John Bunyan* and *Britannia* were two of the class I recall seeing as they came off their train to be replaced by an 'A1', 'A3' or 'V2' on the occasions that I saw the train. In time, we ventured out of the station and made our way up Leeman Road to the sheds where we would note some of the many locomotives on view in the yards but never summoned up the courage to look inside the depot. While in York we once paid a visit to the old railway museum where I climbed into the cab of a steam locomotive, ex-GNR 4-4-2 *Henry Oakley*, for the first time.

If York was the Mecca for steam along the East Coast Main Line then Crewe was certainly its equivalent in the west. My first visit to the station was very brief as my parents were parting company with some elderly relatives there, but in the few minutes spent on the platform I was delighted to see 'Coronation' class No.46232 *Duchess of Montrose* pass through with the southbound 'Caledonian' express, especially as I had recently acquired a Hornby Dublo train set including a model of the same engine. Subsequent visits by car were usually to a point about three miles south of Crewe, where we would park on a quiet lane running alongside the eastern side of the line. From here there was an excellent view but, by the time of our second or third trip, the first gantries had been erected in readiness for electrification. Over the next three years I was able to underline many new names in my locospotter's book including examples from all the former LMS express

types as well as 'Britannias' and the unique class '8P' No.71000 *Duke of Gloucester*. I was also interested to note the pioneer diesels 10000 and 10001 in tandem and the experimental gas turbine locomotive GT3 but, during the same period, there was a significant increase in the number of diesel locomotives and multiple units that even I could not fail to notice.

It was, therefore, an enjoyable interlude to travel entirely by steam on the second of my school trips to North Wales in the summer of 1960. On a pleasant sunny day the children climbed aboard the special train hauled by a Stanier class '5' 4-6-0 at Timperley station on the MSJ&A line north of Altrincham. Our initial destination was Rhyl where we changed trains and boarded 'The Welsh Chieftain', consisting of six coaches and an observation car (once part of the 'Devon Belle' and, since preservation, in use on the Paignton and Torbay Steam Railway). The BR class '4' 4-6-0 at the front end was No.75054 which took us on a circular tour of North Wales, following a pattern of similar trains over previous years bearing names such as the 'North Wales Land Cruise'. As we left Rhyl I noted one of the few numbers that day, No.52119, an example of the old Lancashire and Yorkshire Railway 0-6-0s, some of which, for some reason, found themselves ending their lives in this part of the world.

On that day I took my first photographs. My brother and I had just acquired our first camera, a Kodak 44A, which took a roll of twelve pictures, and the very first picture was of an LNWR 0-8-0 No.49314 at Flint, taken while our train was moving! Further moving shots were taken of the Menai Bridge and of Harlech Castle, both of which looked as if they had been embellished with 'go faster' stripes when we saw the results! The pictures taken inside the train were, not surprisingly, under-exposed while the distant shot of a group of classmates on Barmouth beach failed to identify any of them, even with a magnifying glass! The only photograph that passed the double criteria of being clear as to subject matter and being in focus was of part of the observation car. Luckily it was of the sloping end leaving the viewer in no doubt as to the nature of the vehicle.

It was an enjoyable trip though, passing through Caernarvon and along the now-closed section of the line to Afon Wen, taking in the views of several castles, the spectacular crossing of the Mawddach estuary on a lengthy wooden trestle bridge and heading north through Dolgelley (at about this time the station's name was changed to Dolgellau), Bala Junction and the Cynwyd of my younger childhood holidays. In just five short years it already felt like a distant memory as I glimpsed briefly at the station for positively the last time from a train. From Corwen we returned to Rhyl via the old LNWR line through Ruthin and Denbigh which, by then, was goods only and due to close shortly, while the former GWR route from Barmouth would also cease operations in a few years.

All too soon the last day of school was upon us, the pages of the autograph books filled up with signatures and messages, final goodbyes were exchanged and I walked out of the gates of Woodheys Primary School for the last time, not for one moment pausing to reflect on the last seven years of highs and lows since that first eventful day - the sports days, the Christmas parties where I learnt to do a little Scottish dancing, the stage performance as a clown in an exotic purple satin outfit and pointed hat that my mother made, the day we stood by the side of the playground watching a tractor with attachments cutting the grass, only to witness a girl lose her balance and injure her hand under the wheels of the tractor, or the day when I sat in the canteen staring with cruel innocence at the boy opposite who had that day returned to school having lost his younger brother in a road accident.

Plate 88. Ex-LYR Aspinall-designed 0-6-0 No.52119, seen at Rhyl on 5th July 1960, at about the same time as I saw the locomotive whilst on a school trip around North Wales.

Photo, Jim Peden

Plate 89. Later the same day the school children pass through Cynwyd on 'The Welsh Chieftain', hauled by BR class '4' 4-6-0 No.75054. The train (a summer-only land cruise service) ran from Rhyl to Caernarvon, Afon Wen and Barmouth (where the train was berthed while passengers spent an hour or two at the resort), before returning via Dolgelley, Corwen and Denbigh to Rhyl. Large sections of this route were closed in the 1960s.

Photo, Eric Packer.

7. SOME SERIOUS TRAINSPOTTING

I'm pretty sure that it was Christmas 1959 when I received my first football annual. It must have been because there was a feature on Billy Wright who had recently retired having become the first player to gain one hundred caps for England. He also captained Wolverhampton Wanderers, arguably the most successful side of the nineteen-fifties. The article referred to an injury he sustained at the outset of his career which nearly forced him to abandon the game, but he overcame this and went on to lead his club and country, where he remained at the heart of the defence for 105 matches. Retiring at the age of 36 he had become one of the 'greats' in the English game. It seemed natural to me, therefore, to support Wolves even though my local team was a more illustrious side. But they were a West Midlands team and I hailed from that part of the world and the fact that they had won league titles in successive years and were on course for a third tipped the balance in their favour.

The expression 'kiss of death' briefly comes to mind when I think of the subsequent history of Wolves since I gave them my support! Having said that, it all started well enough and 1960 may well have been their most successful year as they won the FA Cup and, indeed, missed the first League and Cup double of the twentieth century by just one point when, in the last game of the season, Burnley beat Manchester City 2-1 to clinch the title. The Cup Final of that year was the first that I can remember watching, when Wolves beat Blackburn Rovers 3-0. It brought to an end a glorious chapter in the history of the team, who were to lose heavily to Barcelona in both legs of the subsequent European Cup Winners' Cup competition and also in the league to Tottenham Hotspur, who achieved what Wolves so narrowly failed to do by completing a famous 'double' the following year. I was taken to Old Trafford on several occasions as my interest in football developed and for three successive seasons saw them beat a Manchester United side with Munich survivors such as Harry Gregg, Bill Foulkes, Dennis Violett, Albert Scanlon and, of course, Bobby Charlton.

I was now at North Cestrian Grammar School in Altrincham and made friends with a boy who lived close to the main bus route, so we travelled to and from school together and, in time, I would stop at his house on the way home to listen to his records. His parents' house was situated opposite a parade of shops and he told me that he had seen the Manchester United goalkeeper, Harry Gregg, call regularly at the newsagents across the road for his paper. Sure enough, on my next visit, the burly figure of this Northern Ireland international appeared and it subsequently became part of our routine to watch out for him. Before long we recognized another United player, Bill Foulkes, who also lived locally. By now I was not only watching football but playing in competitive matches for my 'house' at school where I scored a few goals and, presumably, on the strength of this, was selected to play for my school. I only played a handful of games, insufficient to gain a badge at the end of the year but enough to appear on the school photograph of the team. My problem was that I shied away from tackling and, consequently, my weak star waned and I would never play for the school again, at any sport for that matter.

Plate 90. For several months from the summer of 1960 a number of the Metrovick Co-Bo diesels, based at Derby, were stored at Trafford Park shed, owing to a disagreement over maintenance between BR and the locomotive contractors. D5710 is seen on shed at Trafford Park at the time.

Photo, Author.

Plate 91. The first locomotive in steam that I 'cabbed', while on a visit to Trafford Park shed, was BR class '4' 2-6-0 No.76088, seen leaving Ashley with the 5.07pm Manchester Central-Chester Northgate on 30th May 1960.
Photo, Raymond Hughes.

North Cestrian was quite different from the purpose-built primary school I had just left in that it occupied the rooms of a former substantial villa, set in extensive grounds comprising two bowling greens (created for a previous commercial user), a tarmac playground and a large lawn at the front which was used for the boys' recreation, subject to ground conditions being suitable. There were tennis courts, various paths and plenty of greenery for the wildlife, including squirrels and even a grass snake that one boy discovered and, in a show of bravado, draped round his neck. I thought briefly at the time 'what if it isn't a grass snake' and, coincidentally, just a few years later, I read about a local policeman who found what he thought to be just such a snake in the centre of Altrincham and took it to the RSPCA only to be told that it was in fact a green mamba! One unusual daily routine at school occurred each lunchtime when all the pupils had to troop a distance of nearly a mile to our dining rooms at Seamons Moss Mission Hall. It was good exercise but left little time for recreation and it would be many years after I had left the school before a new dining hall was built in the grounds.

There were aspects of the school I particularly enjoyed including the strong sense of identity (the 'Wheatsheaf' was our emblem, worn on our blazers) and its commitment to good manners (we were advised to touch our caps when passing a lady in the street!). The school motto was 'Delapsus Resurgam' or 'When I fall I shall rise' and I recall doing plenty of falling and rising, certainly in terms of class marks! Discipline was by no means excessive but, in any event, did not seem to be required as there was a noticeable element of self-discipline. Detention was the main punishment but a slap across the face was not unknown and on just one occasion I received a slap for talking in class. A novel punishment was meted out by our English master in the first year. He would chalk in purple on the blackboard and any boy caught talking in class was brought to the front and had his nose gently rubbed in it, much to the amusement of the others. These were all acceptable forms of discipline to us but I was once at the receiving end of a bizarre incident when I was caught talking again. At the front of the science laboratory and, without warning, a handful of glass tubes was flung down on to the worktop in front of me where they shattered, mercifully (for everyone concerned) causing no injury. The science master walked out and the lesson came to a prompt and premature end and, while he would later become our headmaster and steer the school to new heights, he would also suffer personal tragedy when his son committed suicide at home.

Once, a boy was paraded in front of the whole school in assembly as a bad example to everyone. He had been caught swearing at the lady in the 'tuck' shop and it appears that a four-letter word was used. Possibly the boy's previous record had been taken into account as he had been brought to the headmaster once before when, during a lesson, he blew some chewing gum out of a bazooka in the vain hope that it would stick to the ceiling only to see it pursue too low a trajectory and land on the geometry master's bald head!

Travelling to school on the bus I had three

opportunities to see steam trains. At West Timperley and Broadheath on the former CLC and LNWR lines respectively, between Stockport and Warrington, and at Altrincham where, from the top deck of the bus (the 47 or 48 of Manchester Corporation's fleet of red-and-cream buses), a bird's eye view of the station could be obtained. Apart from the electric and diesel services to and from Manchester there was always a chance of seeing one of the regular limestone trains that ran between the quarries in Derbyshire and the ICI works near Northwich. By this time I had acquired an Ian Allan *Combined Volume* of steam,

Plate 92. An ex-LMSR class '8F' takes an eastbound coal empties over the Bridgewater Canal at Broadheath Junction on 9th May 1959.

Photo, Tom Noble, D.Chatfield Collection.

diesel and electric locomotive numbers and, being accustomed to travelling by myself or with friends to and from school, I was now allowed a little independence and, in 1960, made my first trip to Trafford Park sheds. Up until this time most of my trainspotting had been due to being in the right place on holidays or on day trips but now, for the first time, it was number-taking by design! It was becoming serious.

Each time I left the bus on Chester Road and walked up Ravenswood Road I felt the same sense of excitement, wondering whether any express locomotives or, perhaps, something unusual would be on-shed but, on that first occasion I had no idea what to expect. Diagonally across from the far end of

Ravenswood Road was a footbridge leading away from the houses and out into the open above the tracks of the former CLC main line between Manchester Central and Liverpool Central. Here with my brother or with a school friend we would linger awhile to see a 'semi-fast' between the two cities before stepping down to the other side, crossing the neck of the sidings, and taking the cinder track to the large shed with the towering structure of Manchester United's football ground above us to the right. On that first visit we could not bring ourselves to open the shed door for fear of being met by a railwayman and ushered out, so we walked around the back and found ourselves in an area where engines were stored in the open and where others were coaled. Here we stumbled upon Fowler 2-6-2 tanks Nos.40009 and 40018, an LNER 'J10' (of MS&LR origin) and an LMS class '2' 4-4-0 (a very promising start). We then ventured

Plate 93. The ex-LMSR Ivatt class '2' 2-6-2 tank engines were seen on a variety of local duties including the Manchester Central-Chester Northgate trains and the Oxford Road-Warrington services. On 4th August 1962 No.41213 propels its train away from Broadheath station with the 12.25pm service from Oxford Road.

Photo, Raymond Hughes.

Plate 94. Another of the LMSR, Ivatt-designed 2-6-2 tanks is seen at Oxford Road station prior to departure from the bay platform with a train for Warrington about 1962. The locomotive, No.41211, is push-pull fitted and will push this train to its destination. The signalbox in the background stands adjacent to the 'through' lines.

A number of these locomotives, Nos.41210-4/6/7, had arrived new at Plodder Lane shed in November 1948, after No.41215 had been on trial in August of that year. The push-pull nature of these little tank engines was considered ideal for working the local services over former L&NW routes from Manchester Exchange, Bolton Great Moor Street, Tyldesley and Kenyon Junction; having a quick turn of foot they were well liked by their crews. In 1953 they were replaced en bloc by the BR 84xxx version of the same design, the only difference being that the BR engines had the benefit of a speedo. Plodder Lane was the first shed to close in the Manchester area in 1954.   *Photo, Raymond Hughes.*

to the front of the shed, screened from officialdom by lines of locomotives, some awaiting their next turn of duty and others requiring attention and to which were attached signs with the words 'Not to be moved'. The top-link locomotives on shed were two 'Britannias' Nos.70015 *Apollo* and 70017 *Arrow* but also present were LMS 2-6-2 and 2-6-4 tank engines, Stanier class '5' 4-6-0s and class '8F' 2-8-0s, and Fowler class '3s', '4s' and '5s'. Naturally, the Fowler, Stanier and Fairburn designs formed the bulk of the allocation on each visit but there was usually something new or interesting to note such as the migration of many of the Metrovick Co-Bo diesels that had been built in 1958 and were allocated to Derby. Some of this class were stored at the depot during a disagreement between BR and the locomotive contractors concerning maintenance. Occasionally, an LNER 'B1' 4-6-0 would appear on shed having possibly worked into Manchester on a train from Sheffield, and Stanier 'Jubilees' were also often seen.

The 'Britannias' did not stay long but on subsequent visits I was more than delighted to see, in their place, the 'Royal Scots' including No.46115 *Scots Guardsman* and No.46143 *The South Staffordshire Regiment* (one of the class that had been timed at 100mph, and only recently, hauling 'The Palatine', the top service between Manchester Central and London). Inside the shed I 'cabbed' my first locomotive, excluding those in preservation. It was a BR class '4' 2-6-0 No.76088 but it was a very special moment when I climbed aboard 'Royal Scot' class No.46140 *The King's Royal Rifle Corps,* in steam but without its crew and hidden from the foreman's office! After a few visits I gained more confidence and, for some reason, the staff and shed foreman did not trouble me though I was always careful to look where I was going and, more importantly, to show that I was exercising care when in view of railway staff. As a young teenager I had no knowledge of the history of the shed, so was unaware that, though owned by the Cheshire Lines Committee originally, the locomotives were provided by the Great Central Railway and later by the LNER. This accounted for the appearance on our trains to Chester in the nineteen-fifties of LNER types such as the 'D10s', 'D11s' and 'C13s' but by 1960 these had disappeared. The Midland Railway and later the LMS also serviced their locomotives here, so up to the time of my first visits there had been a wide variety of classes but, still, I always enjoyed looking around the shed and, on leaving, once again I liked to hang around on the footbridge waiting for the passage of a Manchester-Liverpool train behind a Stanier or Fairburn 2-6-4 tank or sometimes a Stanier class '5' 4-6-0. Occasionally the wait was rewarded by a freight train in the hands of an LNER 'O1' or 'O4' 2-8-0 and it was the unexpected locomotives such as these that typified the pleasures of trainspotting.

In the spring of 1961 my father replaced his car with a newer Rover 105 and in the Whitsun break the family undertook a second touring holiday, this time to Devon and Cornwall. As in Scotland we were blessed with good weather and, after visiting Cheddar Gorge and Wells cathedral, we reached the north Somerset coast and our first overnight stop at a guest house, just yards from Blue Anchor station. It was a very pleasurable experience to run down to the station before breakfast and watch a Taunton train arrive behind a large GWR 2-6-2 tank engine and, once it had left, to walk a little further to the beach . Once again, and as at Saltburn, the combination of sea and steam was compelling. Happily, as Blue Anchor is on the present West Somerset Railway, these images can still be enjoyed. We travelled near to the coast to Ilfracombe and settled in at our next hotel near the beach at Woolacombe. In this hotel I was made aware, for the second time in my life, of the attractions of a woman, this time a voluptuous blonde who worked behind the reception desk but, fortunately, there was something more important to think about and that was the close proximity of Southern steam. I, still, had never seen a Southern Railway steam locomotive unless I included *Gladstone,* a museum exhibit at York.

I did not have to wait long because on the evening of our overnight stop we drove up to Morthoe station, at the summit of the steeply-graded line between Barnstaple and Ilfracombe. It was a bright evening with a gentle breeze blowing from the sea, enough to deaden

Plate 95. Also seen at Manchester Oxford Road station's bay platform is a spotless d.c.electric train, in green livery, for Altrincham on 12th July 1961, whilst in the adjoining platform an a.c electric set waits to depart. *Photo, David Stratton.*

Plate 96. As the crow flew, West Timperley was the closest station to home and lay a few hundred yards to the east of the section of track visible from my home. An Ivatt class '4' No.43033 is seen departing with a Stockport-Warrington local train. This locomotive was a regular sighting in the area and at Trafford Park shed for a while.

Photo, Raymond Hughes.

Plate 97. As a meeting place of three lines Skelton Junction was a natural focal point for trainspotters. Arriving at the junction with a freight from the Northwich direction is ex-'WD' 2-8-0 No.90367. Behind the train the CLC line rises towards West Timperley and Glazebrook.

Photo, Raymond Hughes.

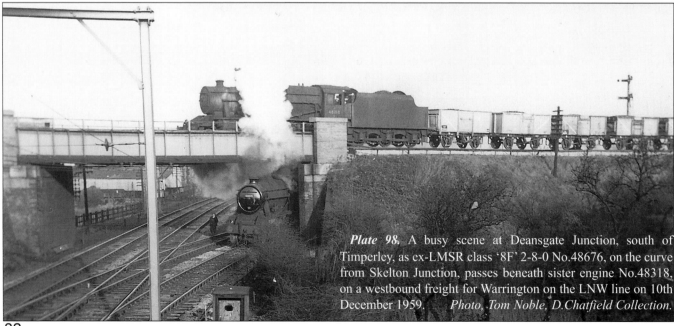

Plate 98. A busy scene at Deansgate Junction, south of Timperley, as ex-LMSR class '8F' 2-8-0 No.48676, on the curve from Skelton Junction, passes beneath sister engine No.48318, on a westbound freight for Warrington on the LNW line on 10th December 1959. *Photo, Tom Noble, D.Chatfield Collection.*

Plate 99. Until the early-sixties it was possible to see one of the ex-Midland class '3F' 0-6-0s in the small goods yards at stations such as Stretford and Altrincham. On 29th July 1955, Longsight's No.43717 is seen at Altrincham & Bowdon goods yard at the back of the station. It would have worked a pick-up goods from Manchester, shunting at yards on the MSJ&AR en route.

Photo, D.Chatfield.

Plate 100. Long after the diesel multiple units had taken over the passenger services on the Manchester Central-Chester Northgate route the 8.18am commuter service to Manchester Central (and the 4.40pm return service) remained a steam working. On 12th July 1962 the train arrives at Hale station worked by an ex-LMSR Hughes 2-6-0 'Crab' No.42792, deputising for the more normal 2-6-4 tank engine. This picture is particularly interesting as, judging from the appearance of the commuters, it seems to capture the period when fashions were changing from the fifties to the sixties.

Photo, David Stratton.

Plate 101. At Hale station ex-LMSR class '8F' No.48511 raises the echoes as it gets to grips with a limestone train bound for Northwich
Photo,

Raymond Hughes.

Plate 102. From the early-1960s most local passenger trains were either DMUs or EMUs and the two types are seen together at Altrincham. On the left is one of the BR Derby Works units delivered in the late-1950s and, on the right, a MSJ&AR unit No.M28589 of the 1930s. This was presumably a Sunday as it was unusual for DMUs to be seen at the platforms used by the electric units.
Photo, Raymond Hughes.

Plate 103. Ex-Southern Railway 'West Country' 4-6-2 No.34003 *Plymouth* departs Barnstaple station with a train for Exeter.

Photo, Neville Stead.

the sound of the locomotive working hard up the punishing gradients, varying between 1 in 80 and 1 in 40 for five miles. The wisp of smoke drifting across the moorland gave the train away but it was a few minutes before it came into view, three green coaches behind a Maunsell class 'N' 2-6-0. It rounded the curve on the approach to the station and, as the brakes were applied, I noted down its number, 31875, the first to be underlined in the Southern Region section of the *Combined Volume*. There was a brief pause, but little activity, before the train restarted for Ilfracombe and all was quiet again, apart from the breeze. However, it did not seem too long before another train approached from Barnstaple. When it came into view it was clearly a longer train and at the head was the unmistakable outline of one of Bulleid's unrebuilt 'West Country' class 4-6-2s. I carefully noted its number and name as 34030 *Watersmeet* eased its train to a standstill, and studied its unusually smooth lines as one or two people clambered out with suitcases (perhaps this service had arrived from London). Soon it resumed its journey to the coast and we returned to the hotel. My first view of Southern steam confirmed my impression that they were the least pleasing, aesthetically, of locomotives but, nevertheless, that brief stop at Morthoe remained a special memory.

The next few days were spent exploring the coastline of Devon and Cornwall, calling at Clovelly, Tintagel, Newquay and a working lighthouse at some forgotten location, before arriving at St. Ives. We stopped overnight at the nearby village of Lelant, served by a station on the branch line, and I saw small GWR 2-6-2 tank engines in charge of the local service to St. Ives, but the following morning I noticed that, from the bedroom window of the guest house, there was an unimpeded view of the main line to Penzance. There was plenty of activity, too, although most of the trains appeared to be hauled by the Western Region diesel hydraulics, including the two different 'Warship' classes. Later that day, on leaving Penzance, I caught a fleeting glimpse of the engine shed there and noted a number of locomotives in steam, so the diesel revolution had not yet completely displaced the old order.

We continued our journey around Cornwall and back into Devon making overnight stops at fishing villages and farmhouses, including one near the village of Loddiswell, where a pre-breakfast stroll took us up to a railway bridge over the quiet lane and, fortuitously, gave us a good view of another of the small GWR 2-6-2 tank engines with a branch line train on its way to the

Plate 104. The 'Kings' had already been displaced from main-line services to Plymouth by the North British and Maybach 'Warship' classes of diesel hydraulic locomotives in 1961. D600 *Active*, first of the North British type, is seen at Plymouth North Road on 14th August 1959 with an express for Manchester.

It ended its days at Barry scrapyard in South Wales but, unlike the many steam locomotives there, it did not survive the cutter's torch.

Photo, David Stratton.

terminus at Kingsbridge. Similarly at Paignton, another early morning walk, to work up an appetite for a hearty English breakfast, brought us to a level crossing just as 'Castle' class *Gladiator* was passing with a train, possibly for the capital. On the way to Paignton we had crossed the river Dart by a ferry from Dartmouth, which was promoted at the time as the only BR station without a railway line, from which tickets could be purchased! One of the most popular locations for railway photographers must surely be the coastal line at Dawlish and, luckily, a cafe here just yards from the railway was chosen as our coffee stop. From the comfort of our table we were able to watch a procession of trains passing along the seafront including GWR types and an unidentified 'Britannia' as well as the increasingly common diesel locomotives. In fact, that day turned out to be a memorable one as there was a further chance to indulge in trainspotting at Exeter St. Davids in the afternoon while Mum and Dad shopped in the city centre. Exeter is one of the few locations where the top link locomotives of two regions meet and, like Chester, where trains from London approach from different directions! Unfortunately, no 'King' or 'Merchant Navy' types were seen but many Western and Southern Region classes were noted including two examples of the handful of the Southern's 'Z' class 0-8-0 tank engines that were banking trains up the steeply-graded curve towards Exeter Central.

Although our holiday in the south-west was now over there was still the summer break in Saltburn to enjoy,

but the Thompson 'L1' 2-6-4 tanks that could still be seen around the station and the sidings with empty coaching stock were living on borrowed time and, after that summer, they were not seen again in Saltburn. My cousins had, earlier in the year, moved from Wighill to nearby Clifford, a village whose houses were built mainly of the warm golden limestone prevalent on the east side of Yorkshire. My uncle had taken a caretaking position with a wealthy solicitor and property owner, a Mr. Appleby, whose home at Springfield House was situated in substantial grounds on Old Mill Lane. It was his job to tend the gardens and to manage the large areas allocated to vegetables and fruit and, with his employment, came the tenure of Springfield Cottage, adjoining the main house. As far as we were concerned the house and gardens provided a safe haven for adventures and sporting activities as well as providing a home for some of the local wild life and it was here where I saw a lizard and a newt for the first time. From the entrance leading to the cottage, a gravel path passed between the buildings on one side and two lawns and large ornamental ponds that had become overgrown with weeds, on the other. At a junction of paths to the rear of the house one way led round to the main driveway, and was unofficially out of bounds, while the other path proceeded between two more lawns and an old summer house, sitting on top of a small mound. The path eventually led to the greenhouses and, through a gate set in a high wall, to the vegetable gardens. It was all very nice to look at and hard work to maintain but

Plate 105. From the comfort of a seat in the cafe, on the left of this picture, I watched a procession of trains at Dawlish on the South Devon coast. Ex-GWR 'Modified Hall' 4-6-0 No.6982 *Melmerby Hall* is seen with a passenger train heading for Newton Abbot in 1963.   *Photo, Rex Conway Steam Collection.*

'hide-and-seek' was never more enjoyable with its wealth of suitable hiding places in trees, hedges, sheds and greenhouses. The lawns were large enough to play cricket and far enough away from buildings to use a cricket ball instead of the more usual tennis ball and many competitive times were had when the 'sides' each consisted of two boys and a father. As if this was not enough there was also a swing, an iron swing, which had been used by Mr. Appleby's daughter, Louise, but was now the source of some exhilirating contests between the four boys. We would take turns in swinging to a height that, we judged, would help give us the best trajectory and the longest landing distance after jumping off ! This was a truly compelling past-time as there was always the chance of edging ahead of the previous best distance but it was surprising, looking back, that none of us suffered any damage. Away from the cottage it was a short distance to a nearby stream, alongside which ran a path leading to fields and woods, at the base of Windmill Hill, from where there was a commanding view over the countryside to the north. The hedgerows here provided a rewarding bounty for blackberry pickers and for nearly three decades it became a regular venue at the end of each summer.

Plate 106. One of the two members of the ex-Southern Railway 'Z' class 0-8-0 tank engines seen at Exeter St. Davids during the holiday in June 1961. Employed on banking duties up to Exeter Central, No. 30956 was photographed nearly a year later at Exeter Central station   *Photo, Peter Fitton.*

Plate 107. A final glimpse of steam in the south-west as ex-GWR 'Castle' class 4-6-0 No.5079 *Lysander* arrives at Exeter St Davids with an express. An ex-Southern Railway 'N' class 2-6-0 No.31831 stands at the opposite platform.

Photo, D.K.Jones Collection.

While on holiday at Clifford in August 1961 my father decided to take the four boys to Essendine and Little Bytham on the East Coast Main Line. It was a long drive but during our stay we saw plenty of trains at speed. From our position at the goods dock, by the dismantled station at Little Bytham, there was a good view to the overbridge carrying the former Midland line to King's Lynn, close to where it took over from the Midland and Great Northern Joint Railway. There was no sign of life on that line and it may well have been closed by this time but, below, on the racetrack, there was plenty of life as we noted several Gresley 'A3' 4-6-2s, some of which were now sporting German-type half-size smoke deflectors while others, such as *Flying Scotsman* on a southbound express, were seen in unaltered state. Only one Gresley 'A4' was seen, *Wild Swan*, with a train for the north, while Peppercorn 'A1' No.60123 *H. A. Ivatt* was in charge of the 'Queen of Scots' Pullman train and a 'V2' at the head of the 'Tees Thames' for Middlesbrough and Saltburn. Diesel locomotives, especially the English Electric Type '4s' (later class '40s'), were very much in evidence, including D209 on the southbound 'Tees Tyne Pullman' and my first view of one of the new Deltics, D9007

Pinza on crew-training duties. Little did I appreciate at the time that these powerful new diesels would soon help bring about the downfall of so many of the graceful-looking Pacifics that had handled the top express trains along this route for a quarter of a century.

At home, my parents were still entertaining foreign visitors to ICI but the guests were now arriving from further afield such as eastern Europe and the Middle East. One such visitor, a Mr. Dolay, came to our house on more than one occasion. He owned a plastics company in Turkey but was also a senior figure in Turkish politics and when Turkey went through a period of instability in the nineteen-sixties he was arrested and imprisoned for three years. The prime minister was not so lucky; he was executed. My father was also travelling further, spending six weeks in South Africa in 1960 and a similar period towards the end of 1961 in India, and it was on one bright Saturday morning in that November when he sprang a surprise on Nigel and me - our first flight. The arrangement was that we would fly to Liverpool and return by train to Manchester. It is likely that the cost of a flight between these two cities was about the cheapest to be had anywhere at twenty-five shillings (£1-25) for an adult fare and half price for us.

88

Boarding a plane in those days at Manchester Airport (or Ringway as it was then) was much simpler as the plane would usually be parked outside the terminal building instead of alongside one of the gates, off the long corridors extending outwards from the central block. The terminal, before receiving its large chandeliers of 'drooping spaghetti', was a more homely place as we boarded a British European Airways Vickers Viscount of the 'Discovery' series bearing the name *Sir William Dampier*. The plane was bound for Dublin on a regular service that called at Liverpool and the Isle of Man and, on that Saturday morning, took off with a light complement of passengers. Needless to say, the journey lasted only a few minutes during which we obtained clear views of the radio telescope at Jodrell Bank, the Manchester Ship Canal and the West Coast Main Line and it was a particular thrill to do some of the viewing from the pilot's cabin, to which we were invited to spend a few minutes. As we began to lose height near the Mersey estuary we were ushered back to our seats and, in no time at all, the plane touched down at Speke airport and a memorable flight came to an end. From the airport we took a bus into Liverpool city centre and, for the first time, entered the large cavernous space of Lime Street station for the return service to Manchester, travelling on a new up-market diesel multiple unit service, the 'Trans-Pennine', which had recently replaced the Stanier 'Jubilees' on the express service to Hull. The Newcastle service had also been dieselised by this time so the sight of a clean-looking 'Royal Scot' class 4-6-0 No.46108 *Seaforth Highlander* at the terminus was particularly welcome.

During 1961 my interest in 'pop' music developed as more sources of listening and viewing became available. There was no 'pop' channel then and the weekend provided the bulk of the programmes devoted to this type of music. On Saturday morning we listened to *Children's Favourites,* introduced at that time by 'Uncle Mac', and then often stayed tune to *Saturday Club*, hosted by Brian Matthew, and featuring a blend of recorded and live music from some of the top artists of the day. *Children's Favourites,* was not a true 'pop' programme, its content including a wide range of material from the latest 'pop' releases to hymns, classical music extracts and novelty songs. I have no doubt that it helped to widen the musical horizons of children in a light-hearted way and that its passing was mourned by many at the time. On Sundays, the long-standing *Pick of the Pops,* introduced by Alan Freeman, was a 'must' in order to track the movement in the charts of our favourite records. On television, the pioneer 'pop' programmes had been replaced by *Juke Box Jury*, featuring a panel of four celebrities who would sit in judgment of the latest record releases, and *Thank Your Lucky Stars*, showcasing current 'hit' songs performed in the studio by the artists concerned. New releases were also reviewed on this programme by a panel drawn from the public who would give a score out of five and a regular on this panel was Janice from Birmingham, whose "oi'll give it foive" became a catchphrase of the day. Apart from the radio and television there was also my friend's record player to listen to after school and, at Rodger Varley's house, we would listen to his collection of singles by Cliff Richard, The Shadows and various American artists such as Del Shannon, Duane Eddy and Bobby Vee.

Plate 108. In August 1961 I visited Little Bytham to watch East Coast Main Line steam. On that day ex-LNER 'A3' Pacific No.60112 *St. Simon* was seen on both northbound and southbound turns. The following summer it is seen hurrying an up relief, composed of an assortment of stock, at Marholm King, north of Peterborough, on 16th June 1962.

Photo, Peter Fitton

Plate 109. During the visit to Little Bytham only one of the Gresley 'A4' Pacifics, No.60021 *Wild Swan*, was seen and somehow we managed to miss the passage of the famous non-stop 'Elizabethan' express but, at about the same time, on 7th August 1961, ex-LNER 'A4' No.60014 *Silver Link* is seen at the head of the London Kings Cross-Edinburgh Waverley express, further north at Doncaster, just a few weeks before the service ran for the last time. *Photo, Peter Fitton.*

Quite often, on a Saturday morning we were allowed to go with Rodger to the *Odeon* cinema in Sale where the matinee would consist of Batman and Robin films, cartoons and a session during which records were played while children were allowed to walk on stage and mime. It was a good idea to give youngsters the chance to play at performing on stage and Del Shannon's *Runaway* never sounded better than in that auditorium.

Late in 1961 I bought my first record. My father had recently purchased a record player on spindly legs, very much a product of its time, and a compilation album of Rossini and Verdi overtures provided the ideal music to test this fairly basic piece of 'musical' furniture. No woofers or tweeters on that machine, just an on/off switch, volume control and the legs! It was rousing stuff but it was a special moment when I was able to spend my own money, six shillings and ninepence, on that first single, *The Savage* by The Shadows. It was not one of their better top ten hits but I suppose I was just keen to acquire something by Britain's top group of the day. 'Pop' music was tolerated at home in limited amounts but when my grandfather visited us for the last time at the end of the year he said, in an encouraging way, that he quite liked *Peace Pipe*, the 'B' side. I looked forward to playing more records for him in the future but the

opportunity never arose as, early in February 1962, we received a phone call to say that Papa (as we had always called him) had died. By the end of that decade all but one of his six brothers and sisters had died, too.

Plate 110. An English Electric type '4' 1Co-Co1 locomotive is seen south of Crewe with an express train for London Euston in 1960. *Photo, Eric Packer.*

8. PUTTING THE BOOKS AWAY

If I had to choose one year when 'pop' music meant more to me than at any other time it would have to be 1962. It was nothing to do with following any particular act but perhaps linked to the intensity of my interest in the songs and the charts. I had just bought my first single and the year started with three of the biggest records of the time vying for the no. 1 spot, namely Cliff Richard's *The Young Ones*, Presley's *Can't Help Falling In Love* and Chubby Checker's *Let's Twist Again*. This was at the height of the 'twisting' craze and, indeed, at a time when many dances such as the 'Locomotion' enjoyed brief popularity. Much of the output was still American but there were many memorable songs, simple and melodic, that have already stood the test of time. Looking back at the nineteen-sixties I would have to admit that 1962 was not typical of the decade of liberalism, socialism, of protest marches and of the 'new wave' of British 'pop' music; instead it was the end of an era.

The era of steam was also, clearly, drawing to a close and my preoccupation with 'pop' music eased the growing feeling of melancholy I felt each time I read the pages of the *Trains Illustrated* which, by now, had changed its name, ominously, to *Modern Railways*. There was now widespread withdrawal of many older classes of locomotives and dieselisation of most of the principal express trains but the scrapping of the first 'King' in the first half of 1962 still came as a shock (especially as I had not knowingly seen any examples of this illustrious class). Further shocks were to follow when the first examples of my favourite 'Royal Scot' class were also withdrawn including the eponymously named pioneer, and yet, at the age of thirteen going on fourteen I did not have the means to travel far and see the types of locomotives that were reducing and, indeed, disappearing in large numbers. Of course, I continued to make periodic trips to Trafford Park shed where a 'Scot' or 'Jubilee' could still be seen alongside the more commonplace LMS classes but now Sulzer Type '4' diesels ('Peaks') were in evidence at the shed as they had, for some time in fact, taken over the main London services from Manchester Central.

York station was revisited that summer while on holiday at Clifford but now virtually all the regular express trains were diesel-hauled and the Brush Type '4s' (later class 47s) in their two-tone green livery were seen for the first time. Saltburn, too, was still a regular holiday destination and there were still tank engines handling empty stock but these were, rather incongruously, Stanier 2-6-4 tanks that were so commonplace around Manchester. Sulzer

Plate 111. Seen several times at Trafford Park shed and caught on camera on 1st October 1961 is ex-LMSR Stanier 2-6-4 tank engine No.42580.

Photo, C.A.Appleton, Jim Peden Collection.

Plate 112. A later visit to Trafford Park shed reveals ex-LMSR 'Royal Scot' class 4-6-0 No.46115 *Scots Guardsman* awaiting its next turn of duty from Manchester Central station while, to the right, is BR class '4' 4-6-0 No.75042.
Photo, Nigel Packer.

Type '2' diesels (later class '24' & '26') handled parcels trains but the excursions were providing some impressive motive power and it was an unforgettable moment catching sight of a Gresley Pacific at the terminus for the first time. As usual, on hearing a whistle, I hurried up Emerald Street, turned right along Milton Street in time to see coaches being propelled into the excursion platform beyond the iron railings. Eventually the tender and finally the locomotive revealed itself and the excitement I felt was something that I could only expect another trainspotter to understand. Gresley 'A3' No.60074 *Harvester* had been one of the regulars on the Liverpool-Newcastle services of my younger childhood and here it was gracing the grassy platform that saw only occasional use. I stood admiring the engine until close to departure time when I ran up to the caravan site along, what was then a cinder track, to a viewing point. There I waited until *Harvester* passed by, negotiating points and beginning to get into its stride, and I remained there until the last coach had rounded the curve towards Marske. I saw another 'A3' Pacific in Saltburn during the same period on what may have been an excursion, though it used the main platform. This was an example of the class with the half-size smoke deflectors and merited the purchase of platform tickets to obtain a closer look. While taking a photograph of 'A3' No.60047 *Donovan* I noticed a boy peering out of the cab and, unable to resist the opportunity, asked the driver if I could climb aboard. The request was granted and, in no time, I was enjoying the warmth of the cab, the smell of oil, fire and coal and the view from the fireman's seat. Leaning out of the side window across the layout at the terminus I briefly imagined myself as an engine driver; I looked at the

gauges, the levers and peered through the front window at the long boiler and then looked back along the rake of Thompson and Gresley coaches that stretched back to the far side of the train shed. The few minutes spent on the footplate had been moments to savour and this was fitting as I don't recall seeing another steam-hauled passenger train at the terminus (at least, not in BR days).

One of the few places where I knew steam could still be seen in abundance was the line that was visible from the cherry tree. The only problem now was that I was beginning to feel a little self-conscious about sitting in the tree and as I had been given a bicycle for my thirteenth birthday it was only natural that I should explore the open countryside between our house and the railway.

The route was via a series of tracks that led away from a housing estate, which had expanded during the previous ten years, alongside fields, over the 'pink' bridge (as it was called), through a farmyard and along a cinder track that led directly to a gated crossing by the railway. Incidentally, the bridge was not really pink. No, it was the brook that was pink, and not just watery, but creamy! We never found out how it came to be that colour but knew not to fall in! Next to the crossing gates was a cast-iron warning sign erected by the Cheshire Lines Committee and it says something for the times we lived in then that such an old sign should survive so long without being removed. There was a moral imperative then that governed most people's actions and which, sadly, like the steam trains, has faded into the past. By the time of these lineside visits the bulk of the freight trains were in the hands of one of the more numerous classes such as the Stanier class '5s' or class '8Fs', Fowler class '4s' or '5s', 'WD' 2-8-0s and BR class '9s'. On the local passenger service between

Stockport Tiviot Dale and Warrington or Liverpool Central, motive power was usually a Stanier or Fairburn 2-6-4 tank while, in summer, there was still a healthy procession of trains including excursions hauled by 'Jubilees', the occasional rebuilt 'Scot' or 'Patriot', 'Britannias' and LNER 'B1s'. It was while cycling along a narrow track and watching a 'Jubilee' on an excursion that I lost control of my bicycle and ran into a barbed wire fence and suffered deep cuts to my leg. Not being one to suffer pain lightly or to appreciate the sight of blood my facial contortions would have made a presentable death-scene on stage. As it was, my brother was now on the bike (some people can be really mercenary) and I limped behind calling at the first house for help. By happy coincidence the occupant just happened to be a doctor, who referred to the advantage of having blood that clotted easily in such situations. He then telephoned my parents. The rest of that afternoon was spent in Altrincham General Hospital where I received ten stitches to my leg.

It was a while before I cycled that way again but, during the summer, there were other pleasures such as my first and only caravan holiday to date. The caravan belonged to friends of friends and was berthed in a field overlooking Cardigan Bay at Llanbedrog, near Pwllheli. The weather was warm and sunny and, indeed, it was one of the few occasions when I splashed around in the sea off a coast in Britain in bathing trunks. We visited the usual tourist attractions such as Caernarvon Castle, Barmouth and Bettws-y-Coed but, for me, it was the train trips that stole the show. The first was a run on the scenic Vale of Rheidol Railway to Devil's Bridge. The locomotives, *Prince of Wales* and *Owain Glyndwr* were BR stock at that time and painted GWR green while the terminus at Aberystwyth was the original before being repositioned a little further out. 'Manor' class 4-6-0s still seemed to be in charge of many of the passenger trains at the adjacent BR station and we saw the 'Cambrian Coast Express' arrive behind No.7801 *Anthony Manor*. The pleasures of that day, including my first narrow-gauge journey, were eclipsed, however, by the treats in store on the second trip, a blend of BR steam travel (the first for over a year) and a run along the spectacular Festiniog Railway. Our journey began at Pwllheli behind BR class '4' 4-6-0 No.75021 on what may have been a train for Ruabon. The BR standard classes appeared to have had replaced some of the Great Western types on the local trains and, as if to confirm this, a BR class '3' 2-6-2 tank engine No.82031

occupied the adjoining platform with a train for Machynlleth. We alighted at Minffordd, where there was a good connection with the higher level narrow-gauge station, and caught a train to Tan-y-bwlch behind the diminutive *Prince*, built in 1865 and therefore probably the oldest locomotive still in regular service at the time. The renowned driver from King's Cross, Bill Hoole, had recently retired to this area and was a volunteer driver on the line. Who knows, he may have been handling our engine on that day but, suffice to say, the speed of the train did not warrant any reference to a stopwatch! The Festiniog Railway was still in its infancy as a preservation group at that time and Tan-y-bwlch was as far as the train went. In fact, the railway was in the process of surmounting the problem caused by the abandonment of its original course due to the construction of a reservoir. The solution was to build a deviation route incorporating a loop at Dduallt whereby the line curved round to gain height in order to cross over itself and skirt around the reservoir. Thus the railway preservationists showed what they were capable of achieving and helped to give the movement respectability. Our return journey to Pwllheli, incidentally, was a great bonus for me as the motive power was Great Western, a 2-6-0, No.6386, in green livery, on what turned out to be my last journey behind a GWR engine in BR days.

Hardly had we returned from our holiday when another trip was planned of a valedictory nature. It was either through the columns of *Modern Railways* or in a newspaper article that we learnt that the 'Kings' were to run for the last time on the Paddington-Wolverhampton service, the last of their traditional routes to hold out to the diesels. My father had spent much of his life in Birmingham and he had a strong affinity with the Great Western and to Snow Hill station, so it was probably at his instigation that we made the journey down to Birmingham to see the 'Kings' on 8th September 1962, their last day in service. On that Saturday I walked out onto the platform of a rather jaded-looking, but fascinating Snow Hill station, my eyes immediately drawn to the tunnels at the south end from which appeared, as if by magic, a succession of engines shrouded in smoke and steam. Then we wandered around the station so that I could familiarize myself with the unfamiliar surroundings and quickly discovered what we had come to see. Simmering in the northern bay platform, alongside diesel multiple units bound for Dudley, stood No.6002 *King William 1V*,

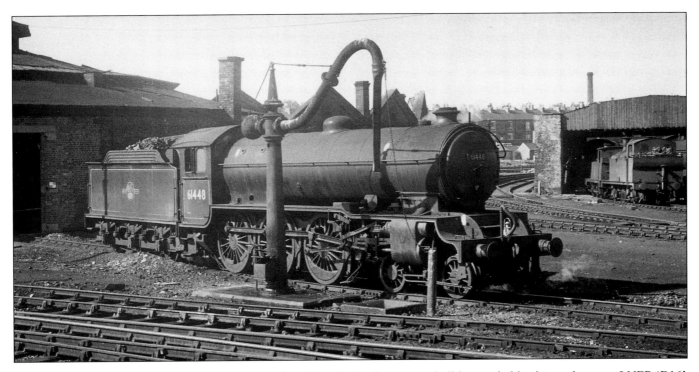

Plate 113. For a few years an annual visit was made to York during the summer holidays and this picture shows ex-LNER 'B16' 4-6-0 No.61448, seen on one of the last visits in the summer of 1963. One of the Thompson rebuilds of the original design by Raven, 61448 stands outside the old Midland roundhouse on 18th September 1961. *Photo, Peter Fitton.*

spotlessly clean and simply oozing power. In some of the photographs I had seen of 'Kings' in magazines I had found it quite difficult to tell them apart from 'Castles' but now that I had the chance to study the locomotive at close quarters it seemed so much bigger. It was a little disappointing that we saw just three 'Kings' that day but we saw plenty of Great Western types including 'Castles','Counties', 'Granges', 'Halls', Collett 2-8-0s and 2-6-0s, large 'Prairie' tanks and, of course, the ubiquitous pannier tanks. We also had our first view of the 'Western' diesel hydraulics, impressive in their different experimental liveries of sand, green and maroon. In between all this my brother and I even managed to find time to have our names embossed on a strip of metal punched out by a machine on the platform. Shortly after watching the arrival and departure of a London express behind No.6007 *King William III* we caught a DMU to Tyseley, giving us the chance to experience the tunnels south of Snow Hill. At Tyseley we saw the northbound 'Cambrian Coast Express' behind No.5026 *Criccieth Castle* and also one of the large Churchward 2-8-0s on a freight train but, back at Snow Hill, the arrival of No.4074 *Caldicot Castle* was greeted with wild delight by one trainspotter who needed that engine to complete his sightings of all

that class. Before we left, No.6022 *King Edward III* arrived on a northbound express and, with other excited youngsters, I grasped at the chance to climb into the cab for a minute or two before it majestically resumed its journey north for the last time. This was just one of a series of 'last days' that would gather momentum until that grim day in August 1968.

It had been a good summer for watching steam trains, apart from the incident with the bicycle; in fact, it had been a good year all-round. In spring we acquired a dog, but only on a caretaking basis as it was destined to perform very useful work as a guide dog. Everything was arranged by the Guide Dog Association who, after consultations, would transfer a puppy (typically about eight-weeks-old) for the first year of its life to a family willing to feed and exercise it. At the end of this period the dog would undergo rigorous training at a Guide Dog Centre before being teamed up with a blind person. Holly was a labrador puppy with a gentle and happy-go-lucky temperament who gave the family a lot of pleasure but the inevitable downside was having to part company with her at the end of the first year. She was not the first pet; there had been my mother's dog, Micky, in Birmingham with whom I had spent the first three years of my childhood and a black-and-white cat called Winston, shortly after moving to Sale, but he liked his independence too much. Holly, though, was different, or perhaps we were of an age when we could appreciate her more. This eulogizing does not mean to say that she had a blameless character; she did cause the odd problem. At the beginning Holly was given a large, round wicker basket and, perhaps we should have expected trouble when, one morning, she was discovered having shredded several carrots that were stored in the kitchen. It was put down to a moment of madness and she seemed to show some remorse after some stern words but, within a short time, she struck again. One morning my father went down to the kitchen and discovered that the sides of the basket had been demolished with no piece of wicker longer than two inches! To a certain extent this orgy of destruction (it must have been an all-night job) helped to wean her off this habit, though she later broke up an old badminton racket (presumably for old time's sake). It was probably her gradual maturity more than anything else that turned her into a reformed character but there was one aspect about her that did not change - her love of water. If the water was trickling from a waste pipe into a drain she would paw at it furiously or if we were anywhere near a river or by the sea she would make a bee line for the water and it was uncanny how she would always wait until we were within range before shaking herself dry! Her crowning moment came at Clifford where, on a summer's afternoon in the garden of Springfield House, a hose pipe had been left running, creating a mudbath near the fruit bushes. The water had not been running long but sufficiently for Holly to discover it and roll around in it until only the whites of her eyes were visible! Hosed down she regained her respectability and continued to give us many happy times until the following spring when a representative from the Guide Dog Association called to take her back for training. It was a terribly sad moment and there were tears all round but, at least she was going on to fulfil her true role, teaming up with a blind man and performing many years of useful service.

Christmas that year was spent, as usual, at Saltburn.

Plate 114. Scheduled to depart at 10.55am, this York-based ex-LNER 'V2' 2-6-2 No.60810 is seen at platform 9 in York station with a Saturdays-only Manchester-Scarborough train on 10th August 1963.   *Photo, Peter Fitton.*

In winter the process of washing and going to bed at my grandmother's house was an ordeal as the heating was always inadequate in the bathroom and the water was either lukewarm or cold. Then, once inside the bed, it would take too long before we could feel the benefit of the weighty blankets and, during that winter of the 'Big Freeze', these discomforts were felt even more keenly. Our cousins were there as well for Christmas so it was a full house, supplemented by visits during the day from local relatives, including my great-uncle Herbert, who usually called on Sundays from Middlesbrough. I remember that one of my Christmas presents that year was a solid-looking telescope which, by good fortune, was quickly put to profitable use. One evening I entered the bedroom and noticed a light shining through the flimsy curtains. Looking through the window I could see that the light was coming from a room of a house across the other side of the back alley and a young woman appeared to be sitting at a dressing-table. I hurried to get this wonderful new present and soon I

was back at the window spying on a teenage girl combing her hair and preening herself. Then she proceeded to undress. This was exciting. This was fun. I called to Malcolm, Clive and Nigel. That was stupid! The telescope passed from one to another like a hot potato from one pair of quivering hands to another until the girl, dressed only in her panties, walked from the dressing-table and, all of a sudden, the light went out. I felt, instinctively, that she knew there were lads across the alley and I wondered whether she returned to the window under cover of darkness to see the faint outline of four lads at the opposite window, tongues hanging out and fully extended telescope. Needless to say, we returned to the scene during the next few days but to no avail. Had she twigged ? Had she left? Had she been, like us, just a visitor?

Less than two months later and very much in the grip of the most prolonged cold spell in my lifetime, Nigel and I paid a visit to Trafford Park shed. We set off after an early lunch and, having completed the routine task of

Plate 115. More activity at York in the shape of ex-LNER 'A3' 4-6-2 No.60066 *Merry Hampton* with the 10.10am Hull-Edinburgh, scheduled to depart York at 12.25pm on 10th August 1963. Though it bears the Kings Cross shed code, 34A, the depot had, in fact, closed by the time this photograph was taken.

Photo, Peter Fitton.

Plate 116. Another view at York station on 10th August 1963 with ex-LNER 'A1' Pacific No.60128 *Bongrace,* about to depart with the 2pm to Newcastle from one of the north-end bay platforms.

Photo, Peter Fitton.

Plate 117. An English Electric type '4' 1Co-Co1 No.D237 is seen ready to depart York with an express for the south on 27th April 1963.

Photo, David Stratton.

Plate 118. In the final years of steam at Saltburn the last freight locomotives to be seen in the area were ex-NER 'Q6' 0-8-0s and ex-'WD' 2-8-0s such as No.90435 of Thornaby shed, seen at Crag Hall. *Photo, Neville Stead.*

jotting all the numbers down, I decided, in a moment of mad impetuosity, to try for Hartford station on the West Coast Main Line. How I could so hopelessly miscalculate time-scales is still beyond me but, before long, we were sitting in a diesel multiple unit bound for Chester. As we entered the Cheshire countryside the snow on the ground appeared to be appreciably thicker and it was growing dark. By Knutsford snow was falling and, now, even I had to admit that the misjudged expedition should be called off. We aborted the journey at Plumley which, in open country, the platforms covered in a foot of snow, and large flakes silently falling through the weak glare of the station lights, could rarely have looked more enchanting. As we waited for the delayed train back to Manchester thoughts of how my mother would react were now uppermost in my mind. It was long after tea-time when Nigel and I trudged back home through the snow and, by coincidence, met Mum with Holly, in the process of searching for us. I suspect that her sense of relief at finding us safe and well overcame the natural instinct to give us a good ticking off.

Plate 119. The author is seen looking out of the cab of visiting ex-LNER 'A3' Pacific No.60047 *Donovan* as it awaits departure from platform 1 of Saltburn station with a returning excursion in 1962. More coaching stock can be seen occupying the adjacent platform. *Photo. Nigel Packer.*

98

Plate 120. Towards the end of the summer holidays of 1962 the family spent a week in a caravan near the village of Llanbedrog. From there it was a short drive to Pwllheli, and one afternoon we took the train from this seaside terminal to Minffordd, where there was a connection with the Festiniog Railway. The return journey behind a GWR 'Mogul' proved to be my last trip by Great Western steam but, while waiting to depart on the outward trip, the train on the adjoining platform was captured on film. The train is believed to be a local for Machynlleth behind BR class '3' 2-6-2 No.82031, in the green livery favoured by the Western Region for many of its locomotives.

Photo, Eric Packer.

Not surprisingly it was some time before we were allowed out again unaccompanied but, instead, we were treated to a day trip to Shrewsbury, following a tried and tested format whereby Mum spent the afternoon at the shops while we watched the trains at Shrewsbury station. There was still plenty of steam here although Western Region diesels of 'Warship', 'Hymek', and 'Western' classes were also in evidence, bringing in trains from the south that would be taken northwards by steam locomotives such as 'Royal Scot' class No.46167 *The Hertfordshire Regiment*. One solitary 'Castle' class 4-6-0 No.5091 *Cleeve Abbey* stood in a bay platform with a Wolverhampton local while 'Counties', 'Halls', 'Granges', Collett 2-8-0s, large 'Prairie' tanks and 'Pannier' tanks performed a variety of duties. Surprisingly, we did not see one of the 'Manor' class 4-6-0s that one associates with Shrewsbury but neither did we see the 'Cambrian Coast Express', one of the regular 'Manor' workings.

The pages of the monthly magazines were showing, all too clearly, the massive inroads made into the ranks of all locomotives, new and old, express or freight, and I was now very keen to grab a last chance to see those classes that I had never seen before. This meant that I needed to visit Scotland and the south of England, in particular. The only safe way to accomplish this was to take part in organized trips so, along with another boy from my school, David Nevell, I joined the South

Lancashire Locomotive Club run by Mr. Walklet. Our first trip was by overnight coach to Scotland in late June 1963, calling first at Motherwell shed at the unearthly hour of 4am. Most of the number-taking here was carried out in the dark but there were a lot of engines and, already, I had achieved my goal of spotting examples of types I had not seen before, including the Caledonian 0-6-0 tanks and 'WD' 2-10-0s. At St. Rollox, Kipps and Eastfield there were some of the remaining North British types such as the 'J36', 'J83', 'J88', 'N15' and 'Y9s' while at Corkerhill further pre-Grouping locomotives including Caledonian 0-4-4 tanks and Midland Railway 4-4-0s were seen in a state that left no doubt as to their future. Parkhead shed was particularly depressing as we noted three of the withdrawn Polmadie 'Royal Scots' (the other two were at Corkerhill), all the Scottish-based 'Clans' (another class I had not seen before), and 'Coronation' class No.46227 *Duchess of Devonshire*, one of the first of its type to be withdrawn. There was still plenty of life, however, at Polmadie shed including Caledonian and North British classes still in steam, but our trip was only just in time as, for instance, all the former Caledonian types had been withdrawn from service by the end of the year. The locomotives in steam here included two 'Coronations', No.46223 *Princess Alice* and No.46230 *Duchess of Buccleuch*, 'Royal Scot' No.46132 *The King's Regiment, Liverpool* and preserved former

Plate 121. No sooner had school restarted when a visit was made to Birmingham to see the last day of the 'King' class on the Paddington-Wolverhampton services. At Birmingham Snow Hill ex-GWR 'King' class 4-6-0 No.6007 *King William III* arrives from the north with a Paddington express, eagerly watched by a group of enthusiasts on 8th September 1962. On the right, in a siding, stands ex-GWR 'Grange' class 4-6-0 No.6855 *Saighton Grange,* possibly on pilot duties.

Photo, Eric Packer.

Plate 122. After the 'Big Freeze' during the winter of 1962-3, a family day out to Shrewsbury provided the ideal opportunity for some trainspotting at the station, a popular meeting point of Great Western and LMS steam. At the south end of the station an ex-GWR 'County' class 4-6-0, No.1002 *County of Berks,* draws up to BR class '4' 2-6-4 tank engine No.80097 in the bay platform.

Photo, Eric Packer.

Highland Railway 4-6-0 No.103, shining like a beacon in its yellow livery among the rows of more grubby inmates of 66A. As a bonus, 'Coronation' class No.46245 *City of London*, in clean maroon livery, passed by the shed on a service train from Glasgow Central.

On the way south again we called in at Beattock shed where, apart from various types of LMS tank engines employed on banking duties, a sole Pickersgill 4-4-0 No.54507 awaited its final journey to the scrapyard having been withdrawn nearly two years earlier. Indeed,

it was a feature of this trip that many of the locomotives seen that day had already been withdrawn the previous year and, in one or two cases, in 1961. As we returned from the depot to the station we were rewarded by the spectacle of another maroon 'Coronation' No.46255 *City of Hereford* at the head of a special train, racing through at high speed and clearly not expecting a banker as it began the climb to Beattock summit in style. To see two of these most impressive and powerful locomotives in clean condition and in fine form on the Caledonian main line was a fitting climax to our visit of Scottish sheds,

Plate 123. A last 'spotting' trip to Crewe in 1963 was rewarded with views of a 'Coronation' and a 'Royal Scot'. Here we see ex-LMSR 'Coronation' Pacific No.46246 *City of Manchester* after arrival with a train from the north.   *B.Nichols.*

but there were still two more calls to be made, albeit over the border at Carlisle. At Kingmoor shed many engines were in steam including 'Coronations', 'Scots', 'Britannias', 'Clans' and even a Gresley 'A4', No.60023 *Golden Eagle* (one of three seen that day). Withdrawn 'Princess' class No.46201 *Princess Elizabeth*, in green livery, survived the cutter's torch to play its part in the preservation movement, in contrast to No.46200 *The Princess Royal*, its sister engine, still looking magnificent to the end in maroon at Carlisle Upperby. It had been a very rewarding day with the prime objective of seeing some of the pre-Grouping classes achieved but with some unexpected bonuses, including the Stanier Pacifics in service, the Gresley 'A4s' and a quartet of old historic locomotives inside Dawsholm shed. *Glen Douglas, Gordon Highlander* and Caledonian Railway 123 would be seen again but, for some inexplicable reason, *Ben Alder* was later scrapped after being sidelined for preservation for so many years.

To emphasise how important this trip had been, in terms of timing, a visit later in the year to London depots revealed that two of the main sheds, Camden and

Plate 124. Finsbury Park depot was visited during a 'locospotters' trip around London sheds in late-1963 and here, the distinctive, ghostly-white livery of the experimental Brush Co-Co Type 4, *Lion*, stands out like a beacon among fellow shed-mates including English Electric 1 Co-Co 1 Type '4' No.D272. *Lion* enjoyed a brief life on both Western and Eastern Regions between 1962 and 1965.   *Photo, Author.*

King's Cross, had already closed their doors to steam, Cricklewood and Devons Bow had become dieselised and Stratford, once boasting the largest allocation of steam locomotives in the country, now played host to two 'J15s', an 'N7' and a 'B12' (three of the quartet being secured for preservation). There was still plenty of steam at Kentish Town, Willesden and Old Oak Common, however, even if the lines of locomotives awaiting disposal (including one 'King', No.6028 *King George VI*) at the latter depot were alarmingly long. One diesel aroused my interest at Finsbury Park. It was the mysterious-looking Type '4' prototype *Lion*, painted white and similar in body shape to the class '47', undergoing trials on the Eastern Region at the time. Ironically, it was scrapped before many of the steam engines it was designed to replace. Early in 1964 a trip around Manchester sheds lulled us into a false sense of optimism as there were still large numbers of locomotives in steam, but many of these were of the more numerous classes that would survive until the end. Only at Horwich Works were there one or two gems such as the former Lancashire and Yorkshire 0-6-0

saddle tank No.11305 and former works shunter *Wren*, but in the breaker's yard lay the remains of two LYR 0-4-0 saddle tanks alongside a Stanier 2-6-0, about to suffer the same fate. Meanwhile, outside the works, stood three Stanier class '8F' 2-8-0s, recently reprieved from the scrapline and overhauled for re-use at a time when Horwich Works was about to abandon its long tradition of repairing locomotives.

In the summer of 1963 my brother and I made two unaccompanied railway trips. The first was to Doncaster, setting off from Manchester Central behind a Fairburn 2-6-4 tank engine through the southern and eastern suburbs of the city to Guide Bridge, where an 'EM2' electric locomotive took the train onwards to Sheffield Victoria via the Woodhead Tunnel. Gresley 'K3s' were noted in a scrapyard west of Sheffield while numerous Robinson 'O4s' had their numbers noted as the diesel multiple unit, to which we had transferred, rounded the curve at Mexborough. Doncaster itself was a little disappointing as there were few LNER Pacifics to be seen and only one 'streak', No.60026 *Miles Beevor*. The second trip, in July, was to be our last

Plate 125. During the summer of 1963 a trip was made to Doncaster via the Woodhead line (behind one of the 'EM2' Co-Co electrics as far as Sheffield), but only one of Gresley's celebrated 'A4' Pacifics, No.60026 *Miles Beevor,* was seen that day. A month or so earlier another 'A4' Pacific, No.60006 S*ir Ralph Wedgwood,* passes through Doncaster station on 15th June, the last day of steam from King's Cross, with the Anglo-Scottish Car Carrier, a train often seen when visiting the East Coast Main Line.
Photo, Peter Fitton.

Plate 126. In July 1963 my brother and I took the train to Preston to catch a glimpse of two of the unrebuilt 'Patriots,' No. 45543 *Home Guard* and the unnamed No.45550, that were stored at the former engine shed. The depot had been largely destroyed by fire in 1960 but was used to store locomotives pending disposal for scrap. All of the unrebuilt examples of this class were withdrawn from service by this time so it was very much a last chance to see these engines before they disappeared for ever. We did manage to view the locomotives and, as a bonus, travelled up to Preston behind one of the rebuilt 'Patriots,' No.45531 *Sir Frederick Harrison,* on a Blackpool train. In this picture 'Patriot' 4-6-0 No.45550 faces the camera with 45543 *Home Guard* behind. To the left is a Stanier class '3' 2-6-2 tank engine.

Photo, Peter Fitton.

journey behind a steam locomotive in BR service. We had previously made trips to Manchester Victoria to watch the procession of passenger and freight trains, many of which were still steam-hauled. On this occasion, however, I wanted to visit Preston where, at the closed, fire-damaged depot there were still examples of unrebuilt 'Patriots' in store. It was appropriate therefore that the locomotive at the head of the Blackpool train, that we boarded at platform 12, should be a rebuilt example of the same class, No.45531 *Sir Frederick Harrison* (a director of the London and North Western Railway). It looked very impressive in its polished green livery, in marked contrast with the two unrebuilt examples, Nos.45543 *Home Guard* and 45550 (un-named) that awaited scrapping along with some ex-LNWR 0-8-0s. We were refused permission to take photographs by BR employees but, given the condition of the building, this was hardly surprising. Our train was

one of the few that was steam-hauled during our stop at Preston but 'Royal Scot' class 4-6-0 No.46118 *Royal Welch Fusilier* passed through with a parcels train and BR class '7' 4-6-2 No.70000 *Britannia* put in an appearance on a freight train. The return journey was via Wigan North Western on a DMU, from which we caught a glimpse of the diminutive LYR 0-4-0 saddle tank, No.51232, in the New Bailey goods yard in Salford, where it had been the last steam shunter until its recent withdrawal. At the time there was a picture of this locomotive in *The Daily Telegraph*, showing a schoolboy standing on the buffer beam and peering into its funnel, prior to its being towed away to Horwich Works for scrap and where I saw its remains some months later.

The newspapers of the time were more concerned, of course, with the implications of the Beeching Report, which proposed that passengers and freight should be

103

carried at high speed between the larger towns and cities, leaving road transport to serve the smaller centres of population. Branch lines and stations had already closed in large numbers, however, and British Railways was well on the way to transforming its locomotive stock and turning its attention to passenger and freight vehicles. Soon, those under-used carriages, stored in sidings such as those at Saltburn, that satisfied the demand at holiday times, would disappear. The once familiar sight on summer Saturdays of a procession of excursion trains would consequently come to an end. The writing was on the wall for close-coupled goods trains that produced such a familiar clanging sound and for the countless wagons stored in marshalling yards and in sidings. The railway industry was in a depressed state, under-going massive upheaval, and morale among employees was, not surprisingly, low. One only had to look at the condition of the steam locomotives and, indeed, the railway stations to see that the industry had low self-esteem and it was hardly good for public relations.

At times like this it was good to turn one's thoughts to music, which captured the headlines in a big way during 1963. The seeds of this massive British 'pop' boom were sown in 1962. I remember that after tea on most evenings we would watch one of Granada Television's regional programmes *People and Places* and, in October that year, The Beatles made their debut on the programme at about the same time as their first release *Love Me Do*. They made further appearances on the programme and its successor, *Scene At 6.30*, and gained their first national exposure on *Thank Your Lucky Stars* the following January, when they also made their debut on *Saturday Club*. This exposure helped the group achieve its first big success with *Please Please Me* and, from then on, their fame and fortune just snowballed. By the end of 1963 they had made their famous appearance on *The Royal Variety Performance* and the term 'Beatlemania' had been coined by the Press. Other Liverpool groups prospered at the same time such as The Searchers, Gerry and the Pacemakers, The Merseybeats and Billy J. Kramer and the Dakotas, before other groups made their mark from Manchester and London. In fact, the new wave of British 'pop' music was dominated by groups and the old format of singer, with or without backing group, had suddenly become less fashionable. Of course, all the talk at school was now on the subject of the new groups and the fashions,

Plate 127. The run behind 'Patriot' No.45531 *Sir Frederick Harrison* in July 1963 proved to be my last trip behind a steam locomotive before the end of steam in 1968. Here is the locomotive at Carnforth over a year later, on 30th August 1964, with a Sunday milk train from Carlisle to Crewe.
Photo, Peter Fitton.

104

in particular the hair styles, that were changing to reflect the new images. But it wasn't just the music that was changing, it was the mood in the country. Old standards were now being supplanted by new attitudes, for better or worse. Censorship was becoming less restrictive and, through the new satirical TV programmes such as *That Was The Week That Was*, there was a growing cynical view of figures in authority. Episodes such as the Christine Keeler affair, which brought about the downfall of senior Tory minister, John Profumo, only helped to fan the flames of this cynicism.

Yes, change was all around and, in the summer of 1963, we left Overton Crescent, home for the previous twelve years, and moved to Moss Lane, a tree-lined road in Sale with larger detached houses set back in substantial gardens. Now I could sing at the top of my voice, knowing that the neighbours wouldn't hear, and play my new reel-to-reel tape recorder, taping the latest sounds on Radio Luxembourg. It was Nigel who had been listening to this radio station when the programme was interrupted by a news announcement that President Kennedy had been shot. He ran downstairs to tell us the news and my father immediately switched on the television, which had already broken into its scheduled programmes to cover the shooting and its confused aftermath. Then came the further announcement that the president had died and, over the next few days, there were repeated flashbacks on TV of the motorcade, the shooting, and the anguish of Jacqueline Kennedy. It was difficult to comprehend this appalling crime involving, arguably the most powerful man in the world, but history shows us repeatedly that, with power can come great risks. Perhaps it was the televising of the shooting and its unexpectedness that was so deeply shocking but, by the end of that remarkable decade, we had almost become inured to otherwise horrific acts such as the slaying of Martin Luther King and then Robert Kennedy.

It is normal in times of distress or great sadness to seek sources of comfort. Music was certainly one such source but steam locomotives, now very much in decline, were less so. From our new home I could still hear trains but I could not see them. In truth, I now felt remote from the CLC line that I could once survey from the comfort of home and this feeling became stronger when, passing by the old house some months later, I noticed that the new owner had cut down the beloved cherry tree and some of the hedges to create an open-

Plate 128. Returning from Preston we also managed to catch a glimpse of the L&YR 'Pug' 0-4-0 that had been the yard shunter at Irwell Goods Yard, Salford, now one of the large car parks for Manchester city centre. In this view, L&YR 'Pug' saddle tank No.51230 is side-by-side with a larger L&YR 0-6-0 saddle tank No.51496 on 8th October 1957. The lines out of Victoria and Exchange stations are on the viaduct above. Examples of both these small locomotives have been preserved at the Keighley & Worth Valley Railway.

Photo, Jim Peden.

Plate 129. The sheer volume of traffic at Manchester Victoria made it a popular venue for enthusiasts at weekends and during holidays. On 8th September 1960, an ex-LMSR Fairburn 2-6-4 tank engine No.42696, fresh from a visit to Derby Works, awaits its next duty at the eastern end of the station.

Photo, Peter Fitton.

Plate 130. Approaching Manchester Victoria from Miles Platting on the same day, and seen beneath a fine array of signals, is ex-LMSR Fowler 0-6-0 No.44601, with a train of stone hoppers. Under construction at the time is Manchester Victoria East signal box. Obscured by the locomotive are the lines to Red Bank Carriage Sidings and Collyhurst which were lifted in the late 1990s.

Photo, Peter Fitton.

Plate 131. Seen entering platform 14 at Manchester Victoria with the 7.25a.m. from Blackpool North on 21st April 1965 is ex-LMSR class '5' 4-6-0 No.45076. *Photo, Peter Fitton.*

plan garden that, sadly, bore little resemblance to that which had been part of my world as a child. The railway sounds I could now hear were clearest at night, when the lights were out and the bedroom window open, but there were various sounds ranging from the constant background hum of the traffic on the A56 trunk road, half-a-mile away, to the more transient sounds of a plane or train. The hooting of owls was also frequently heard and, on one occasion, very clearly when the large bulky form of a tawny owl alighted on top of the open bedroom window. It may well have been the same owl that was referred to in our local newspaper, shortly afterwards, in a report about a girl living nearby who woke up in the night to see a tawny owl sitting on a cupboard across the room ! There were two sounds I listened out for at this time. The first was the drone of a piston-engine plane as it made its way across the night sky. Almost certainly a Douglas 'DC4' or 'DC6' providing a mail service, its drone appeared to be audible for a long time, especially on a clear night. The other sound was that of a train at speed, of coaches rather than wagons. I later found out that this was the Liverpool-York mail train, still steam-hauled, making progress along the LNWR line between Warrington and Stockport.

One night in January 1964, while lying in bed before drifting off to sleep, I became aware of a rumble like thunder except for a slight difference; perhaps the rumble stopped more abruptly than thunder. I felt convinced that a crash had occurred, possibly involving a plane or train but, beyond that I could not tell. All went quiet again and, after reflecting on the ominous sound, I fell asleep but, the following morning I was curious to listen out for any news item or read a newspaper report of any mishap. Scanning the paper I noticed a small item at the bottom of the front page, reserved for the latest news, referring to a train crash at Altrincham. As there was a line passing from north to south through the town and two lines crossing from east to west I could not be sure of the precise location, but as soon as a later radio report mentioned Sinderland Road I set off on my bicycle along the farm paths and across the 'pink' bridge to the crossing over the CLC line. From here the wreckage, the cranes and all the activity could be seen a further four hundred yards away at the LNWR line, west of Broadheath station. A large crowd had gathered around a bridge over the line where the Liverpool-York mail train had caught up the preceding freight, forcing the mail coaches to telescope upwards like two hands pressed together in prayer. Beyond the bridge lay 'Jubilee' No.45695 *Minotaur*, on its side, battered and bruised and clearly having run its last journey. The driver of the 'mail' was seriously injured and transferred to Stockport Infirmary but, fortunately, there were no

107

Plate 132. Also on 21st April 1965, ex-LMSR Stanier-designed 'Jubilee' class 4-6-0 No.45563 *Australia* arrives at Manchester Victoria's platform 16 with the 7.00a.m. from Barrow.

Photo, Peter Fitton.

Plate 133. The sound of the Liverpool-York mail train was regularly heard from the bedroom as I drifted off to sleep. One night, in January 1964, there was a sound like thunder and the following morning the crash was reported. The scene captured on camera the following day shows the remains of ex-LMSR 'Jubilee' 4-6-0 No.45695 *Minotaur* after its final revenue-earning trip.

Photo, Raymond Hughes.

other casualties. The guard on the freight train leapt from his van before impact and escaped serious injury but it is easy to imagine the shock he must have felt as he saw the 'Jubilee' and its train closing in on him. There were other steam locomotives on the scene that morning including 'Britannia' No.70052 *Firth of Tay*, in charge of the breakdown train, Stanier 2-6-0 No.42970 and BR class '5' 4-6-0 No.73067, standing like sentinels over the mailbags that had been gathered together to a collection point. The wreckage was substantially cleared by the following day while *Minotaur* was placed in a siding nearby, where it remained for some time afterwards before being purchased for scrap.

Early in 1964 I travelled for the last time with the South Lancashire Locomotive Club, visiting sheds of the Southern Region between London and Brighton. It was an important trip for me because, apart from my brief glimpses of the Southern three years earlier in the south-west, this was the one-and-only day I spent trainspotting exclusively on that region. It went a long way to boosting the list of Southern Region engine numbers to a respectable level and, by the end of the day, I was able

to boast numbers from 'Merchant Navy' (for the first time), 'West Country', 'Battle of Britain', 'N', 'U', 'S15', 'W', 'Q' and 'Q1', 'H', 'USA' tanks and 'M7' classes. Many engines were still in steam but, at Nine Elms, the first two examples of the 'Merchant Navy' class had been withdrawn and, of the sheds on our itinerary, Norwood Junction and Horsham were both empty. The Southern could at least lay claim to having the last all-steam main line (between Waterloo and Exeter) but this only added to the feeling of depression. I stopped reading the railway journals when the list of withdrawals included engines barely five years old (how could this possibly make economic sense?) and even my enthusiasm for railway trips was beginning to wane. During the year I saw steam for the last time in Saltburn, an LMS tank on a parcels train and a 'WD' 2-8-0 with a train of mineral wagons on the avoiding line to Skinningrove Iron and Steel Works. Nigel and I had taken a train to Darlington the previous year when the highlight was Gresley 'A4' No.60017 *Silver Fox* on an express train, and in 1964 to Newcastle, where Peppercorn 'A1' No.60150 *Willbrook* and 'V3s' on empty stock were the main attractions.

Plate 134. The changing scene at Manchester Central station as Sulzer 1 Co-Co 1 Type '4' 'Peak' No.D26 waits at the head of a London train on 25th May 1961.The substantial building behind the locomotive is the former Great Northern Railway Goods Warehouse
Photo, David Stratton.

Plate 135. An ex-GNR 'K3' 2-6-0 No.61853 pauses at Knutsford with an evening mail train on 6th June 1962. These locomotives were also seen on a morning parcels service in the Altrincham bay platform that used to attract a wide variety of motive power including a 'V2' on one occasion. *Photo, D.Chatfield.*

Plate 136. A last look at the passenger service from Stockport Tiviot Dale which lasted until November 1964. Early the previous year ex-LMSR Stanier 2-6-4 tank No.42598 moves empty stock from the station having arrived with a train from Liverpool Central on 23rd March 1963. This site is now occupied by the M60 motorway. *Photo, Peter Fitton.*

Plate 137. Under the graceful arch of Manchester Central station with two DMU trains on 3rd May 1969, the last day of services before closure.

Photo, David Stratton.

From home I visited the CLC line, near West Timperley, for the last time. There was still regular steam but the passenger service between Stockport and Warrington was withdrawn that year and the stations closed. One interesting steam working which I often saw from the upper deck of the bus to school was a parcels train in the bay platform at Altrincham station. The interest was mainly due to the variety of motive power employed. Over the years I had seen small Ivatt 2-6-0s, Stanier and Fairburn 2-6-4 tank engines, BR standard classes and LNER 'K3s', 'B1s' and even a 'V2' on one occasion.

During a family holiday to Scotland in 1964 the only steam engine seen was an LNER 'B1' No. 61030 *Nyala* on a northbound freight, passing our picnic spot alongside the Waverley route. Sulzer Type '2' diesels (class '24' and '26') were in charge of most trains seen at places such as Callander (a station that was, by now, in decline) and Pitlochry. In fact, the holiday as a whole lacked the magic of our visit five years earlier. Perhaps I had lost that carefree innocent spirit or maybe it was the weather. What I recall most from that holiday was

my first glimpse of a golden eagle, soaring above Glen Torridon in large sweeps, watched enthusiastically through binoculars by several bird watchers. We had already seen an osprey at Loch Garten a few days earlier so it may have been that, on this lonely road, the seeds of a new interest were sown. Even at home a curious ornithological discovery was made. Shortly after moving to Moss Lane we began to notice, for the first time, a small pigeon in the garden that we later discovered was a collared dove. The curious aspect of this sighting was that, even though we had moved less than a mile from our previous home, we had never seen this bird before.

It was purely by chance that we learnt, through a book on local wildlife, that the bird was very much on the increase in the country, spreading from its traditional area of southern England, and seen in a localized area of Sale. How accurate this observation was I don't know but its subsequent spread throughout the country shows that the bird has been one of the success stories in this country against the general trend.

Returning to the trains I made my final trip in search of steam in the summer of 1964. It was with David Nevell to Derby, Leicester and Nottingham and, although the journey was behind a diesel locomotive, a Sulzer Type '4' ('Peak'), the quality of the scenery alone made the trip worthwhile as we threaded our way through the Derbyshire Dales, along a route that is now closed between Buxton and Matlock. At Derby there were 'Jubilees', Stanier class '5s', tank engines and BR standard classes but the abiding moment for me came at Leicester Central where we stood on the platform as 'Royal Scot' No.46125 *3rd Carabinier* was turned on the turntable in the adjacent yard and then watered. By then it was only weeks away from withdrawal and this would be the last time I would see one of this famous class in service. As I began my fifth year at school with GCE 'O' Levels just nine months away I made a positive attempt to curtail my trainspotting activities and put away the Combined Volume into storage, to be referred to on occasion, but otherwise bringing my days of number-taking to an end. Or did it ?

9. THE END ?

Trains and steam engines now took a back seat but my love of 'pop' music was still strong and there was more choice than ever on radio and television. I kept up with the changes in the 'pop' charts by listening to *Pick of the Pops* on Sunday afternoon while Friday nights were reserved for a new programme, *Ready Steady Go*, introduced with the words 'The weekend starts here!' Part of its appeal was the club-like atmosphere and the blend of new and current acts with famous names from the past. The Beatles and The Rolling Stones made appearances on both this show and on a new BBC programme, *Top of the Pops*, that is still broadcast today. 1964 saw the first major challenge to the mainstream 'pop' programmes, at least on the radio,

when a new 'pirate radio station', Radio Caroline, started broadcasting music offshore from a boat, utilizing a loophole in the existing law preventing commercial radio broadcasting on land. It would be three years before the loophole was plugged and by that time the BBC's own 'pop' channel, Radio 1, had arrived. In the meantime I attended my first 'pop' concerts in Manchester and witnessed some of the excitement that had been reported in the newspapers. The shows were often good value for money with, sometimes, as many as ten acts on the bill and usually headlined by an American star. One memorable concert I attended in Manchester featured the Everly Brothers and Little Richard who, before he had finished his performance,

Plate 140. Manchester Central station sees the departure of a Buxton commuter train behind ex-LMSR 'Jubilee' 4-6-0 No.45705 *Seahorse* on 29th June 1965.   *Photo, Tom Heavyside.*

had removed his shirt and taken his dynamic rock 'n' roll act from the stage and briefly into the auditorium. On stage that night was a little-known band performing their first single release, 'Come On', but within a few months The Rolling Stones would provide the main challenge to the supremacy of The Beatles. In October 1964 I finally got the chance to see The Beatles at the ABC in Ardwick, Manchester, at the height of Beatlemania and, suffice to say, I found it difficult to hear the music over the constant screaming, but the atmosphere was electric and more intimate when compared to some of the modern concert venues.

At the age of sixteen I was becoming more interested in the world around me although the definition of 'world' was a narrow one consisting of music, football, trains (but less so now) and, oh yes, girls. To be honest, they were positively leaping up the popularity stakes although, being a home-loving lad, my contact with the opposite sex was fairly limited. I was in a 'boys only' school so that didn't help either, even though there were girls next door at the Loreto Convent, divided from us by a high wall. We could hear their squealing and giggling at break time but that was it until after school when, walking to the town centre to catch the bus home, there would be a lot of furtive glances at a variety of girls from the Convent, Culceth Hall and Altrincham Grammar School for Girls. There was the occasional party that I was invited to and, if the parents were away, Postman's Knock was likely to be the central theme, with all the kissing that was so eagerly awaited. But proper girlfriends had not yet come my way and, in any event, there was the small matter of impending 'O' Levels that needed addressing. The school operated a competitive system of marking involving the posting up of weekly positions of pupils in each classroom, based on work in the class and at home. Until the fifth year I only came first once and was generally 'Mr. Average' but in that autumn term there was a dramatic improvement and, similarly, in the following spring the marks were good and in only one week during the year was I not in the top ten. I was confident about my chances in all subjects apart from English Literature, where my teacher had written in the report, "Poor performance followed by an amazing improvement - alas too late!"

It looked as if I was hitting peak form at just the right time and then, in May, I fell in love. Friends of my parents visited us for the first time in several years and their daughter, Andrea, had matured into an attractive fifteen-year-old. We seemed to hit it off at once and, as her sixteenth birthday was due in May, this provided me with an ideal opportunity to write to her. There then followed a surge of correspondence on the subjects of true love, music, films, fashions and how Tom Jones peered into a tent at an outdoor show and winked at her! There were visits on the coach or with my parents (she lived in Sutton Coldfield) and for much of that summer the romance consumed all my emotional energy. And it showed, for when my examination results came out I had failed in Geography (my best subject), French (my second best subject), Geology (my favourite subject) and Physics (a loss leader!) and while, by the time of my retakes, I had passed in eight subjects the omens did not look good for the sixth form. Still, studying could not have been further from my mind during the holidays and it was only in the days preceding the publishing of the results when I started to have nagging doubts about how I would fare.

Earlier in the year my father had advised me that I was to be sent on holiday to Poland with other school-children as part of a tour organized by the Educational Interchange Council. The proposed visit had been given some press coverage and had clearly captured my father's imagination. I put up some resistance to the idea, in common with anything else that was likely to be for my benefit, but once the three-week holiday had begun I was quite surprised at how quickly I left my thoughts of home behind. I travelled on the Southern Region for the first time, albeit by electric train from London Victoria to Dover, and then at Ostend we all boarded a continental express which, from memory, was bound for Moscow. I recall seeing very little steam as we ate up the miles through Belgium, resting for a few minutes at the larger stations such as Brussels and Liege. During the night the train pressed on through West Germany: Cologne at nine, Dortmund at midnight and Hannover by three in the morning. Finally, it came to rest at the border town of Marienborn where there was a passport check. By 6am we were behind the 'Iron Curtain' and at the East German border town of Helmstedt. Here there was a ninety-minute wait while aggressive armed guards, in military uniform and jack boots, distributed Communist propaganda leaflets and checked the passports very carefully. One of the guards, realising that he had become the subject of a photograph taken, unwisely, by a member of the party, had the film destroyed. Everyone felt uneasy here and the presence of watch towers along the route ahead did nothing to allay these feelings. In

Berlin, too, there was another long stop as we watched military guards, with light machine guns, patrolling the platforms. They were even visible on the small ledges below the roof of the station. The train was now two hours behind schedule but it made up time as it sped through wooded countryside towards the Polish border, where further passport checks were encountered. My memory of the Polish countryside on this journey was of endless fields farmed, apparently, without the benefit of much machinery, but with horse-drawn carts and many peasants, with head scarves, carrying out back-breaking work. By the time we had reached Poznan it was the afternoon and tiredness was, once again, overtaking us but the last leg was made eventful by, not one but two derailments, one affecting a locomotive and the other damaging a Moscow-Berlin express. The words of Lady Bracknell in *The Importance of Being Ernest* briefly came to mind as we skirted slowly round the mishaps. After twenty-eight hours of confinement since Ostend we arrived at Warsaw, where there was a great reception as we were presented with bouquets of flowers from our Polish counterparts (the children with whom we were exchanging visits, together with their parents), waiting on the platform. The first week was spent at a reception centre from where we visited places of interest in and around Warsaw, much of which had to be reconstructed after the War. From there the party moved on to Krakow, the old capital of Poland, and from where we visited the remarkable salt mines of Wieliczka, boasting an underground chapel as well as

many impressive sculptures hewn out of rock salt. It was inside this mine where my relationship with Liz flourished. I'd spent the previous two days with Barbara but, while in another compartment with a group of other children, enjoying a friendly banter, Liz asked me if she could feel my chest (not that there was much to feel) and I agreed on condition that I could feel hers first! From that moment we got on like a house on fire but, unfortunately, the cabin I shared with three others was situated next to the tour leaders and one evening, in the middle of a steamy session, our neighbours must have become suspicious as there was soon a knock at the door. After a brief pause to make ourselves presentable I opened the door to be greeted by a stern look and a strict lecture which sobered us up for some time afterwards. But what was to be expected of fifty young adults between the ages of sixteen and twenty-four, brought together away from home, some for the first time ?

If romance was in the air then the atmosphere was certainly conducive as we travelled south to the beautiful mountain resort of Zakopane, situated in the Tatra Mountains near to the Czechoslovakian frontier. From Krakow it is less than one hundred miles to this resort but the overnight journey seemed to last for hours. It was a classic journey that I imagined reading about in a fairy tale, and one essential ingredient was the steam engine at the head of the train. Alas, I can remember little of the engine itself except that, when I inspected it the following morning at the terminus, it was clearly a fairly old locomotive with a separate tender. I took a photograph but, sadly, due to a fault, it was never processed. In any event it was the sound it made and the pictures

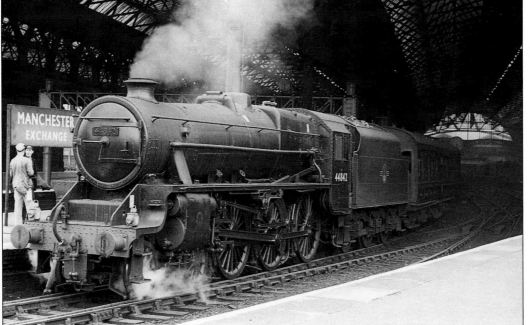

Plate 141. The teminus section of Manchester Exchange station. Standing at platform 2 is ex-LMSR class 5 4-6-0 No.44842 with the 4.30pm to Llandudno on 23rd June 1965. *Photo, Peter Fitton.*

115

that were created in my mind that captured my imagination. The bunk beds that we slept on were tolerably comfortable but sometimes I had difficulty in sleeping so, on that night, it was a pleasure to listen to the old engine toiling up the steep gradients as we climbed into the hills. The sounds of the exhaust beat found echoes everywhere in the still of the night and, as I have already mentioned, it felt like a fairy tale journey in which we were making our way up to the roof top of the world, safe from the pitch black outside that concealed many dangers (perhaps there were wolves and lynx out there). To the sound of that repetitive exhaust beat I must have drifted off to sleep only to wake up the following morning and find that, to some extent, we had left the real world! Not only was the engine of another age but the whole town, with its wooden houses and horse-drawn transport, presented a beautiful picture of a way of life detached from the world with which I was familiar. While in Zakopane we listened to Polish folk music and walked in the mountains, some of which were as high as 7000 feet (sorry, over 2000 metres!) before heading north again for an altogether more sobering appointment. The town of Oswiecim lies on the edge of the industrial region of Silesia and on the outskirts of the town stands the former German concentration camp of Auschwitz, where some four million Jews were put to death by the Nazis. After gazing in silence at the masses of human hair and belongings of the victims, and reflecting upon the horrors of the gas chambers and the ovens, wreaths were laid for the Britons who died there, just twenty years earlier and more. Carrying the appalling images away with us we headed back to Warsaw. At some point along the way (it may have been Katowice) the train was shunted into sidings for a while and, conveniently, right alongside, stood a Tk148 tank engine with an access platform in between. Using this convenient bridging point, a group of us gained access into the cab with the permission of the friendly Polish crew. It was an unexpected bonus that briefly whetted my appetite for steam at home. The last few days were spent in the jaded concrete homes of our hosts before leaving Warsaw with mixed feelings of regret and relief, amidst a large crowd of Polish friends. It had been a memorable experience.

The summer holiday seemed to pass in a blur. I returned home to resume correspondence with Andrea, to receive my 'O' Level results, and to find that we had a new guide dog puppy, Quorna. At the same time, my Polish counterpart, Karina, arrived to spend three weeks with us. We met her at Manchester Central station and, during her stay, took her to the Lake District, Derbyshire, Wales, Yorkshire and, of course, Saltburn, where she got on well with my grandmother who, at last, had a chance to practice her rusty Polish. In September I became a sixth former and developed an air of confidence. After all, girls had entered my life, I'd experienced life behind the 'Iron Curtain' and now I was furthering my education. I had even taken up golf through the school and enjoyed it so much that, on one occasion, I played with a school friend in dense fog when, for a time, we discovered that we had been playing on parallel fairways ! All in all I was beginning to feel quite adult but had I caught up with the 'swinging sixties' ? Not a bit of it ! I still dressed up in a jacket, shirt and tie, I still bought rock 'n' roll compilations and Elvis Presley records, and held no views at all about war or racial problems, except when forced to confront issues through the Debating Society at school. For this reason alone it was a very useful society in which to be a participant.

During the mid-sixties there were new developments in television. The BBC had already added a second channel in 1964 and now the first experiments were taking place with colour. In 1967 the BBC also became involved with the first worldwide live satellite hook-up during which The Beatles recorded their latest single *All You Need Is Love*. Satire had nearly run its course with the more sophisticated *BBC-3* having replaced the earlier, more abrasive forms. However, it was on this late-Saturday evening programme that the film critic Kenneth Tynan uttered the forbidden 'F' word, yet another example of the old barriers falling. On the subject of this programme I'm reminded of a conversation at Andrea's house that was amusing at the time. Her parents had visitors on the Sunday and the talk eventually turned to television. "Did you watch *BBC-3* last night ?" The innocent reply was "No, we haven't got it yet!" In my humble opinion the best comedy was to be found, not on television, but on the radio. Sunday lunchtimes were never more enjoyable than when listening to the classic series *Round The Horne*, featuring the genial host, Kenneth Horne, who provided the perfect foil to the comic talents of various actors including the unique Kenneth Williams. They depended on first-class scripts that developed double entendres and innuendoes to art forms. Television, however, was in a class of its own when staging the big events and

116

they did not come much bigger than the World Cup in 1966. Football fans had already been treated to a weekly diet of football highlights courtesy of *Match of the Day*, introduced in 1964, but this was the real thing and, looking back, the only regret was that it was denied colour televising by about one year. When England won, heroes were made of the stars such as Banks, Moore, Charlton, Peters, Ball and Hurst. The nation was on a high until the autumn brought the unforgettable tragedy of Aberfan, when a pit village lost so many of its children, buried by a huge spoil heap.

At school it was decided to put the sixth formers in for 'A' Level Geography in one year. Having failed to secure an 'O' Level pass, even after retaking the exam, I was more than a little sceptical about my chances at this higher level. However, I was pleasantly surprised to discover that I had, indeed, achieved a pass grade and I could now afford to look ahead with some optimism. By now, one or two of my classmates were arriving at school in cars and I, too, was eager to drive. My parents arranged for me to have lessons and by October 1966 I had passed at the second attempt. Shortly afterwards I bought a 1953 Morris Minor Convertible and, with it, a measure of independence. For instance, I went to clubs in Manchester for the first time. The three that stand out in my mind were The Oasis, The Twisted Wheel and The Jigsaw and, of these, it was the last-named that I frequented with a view to seeing top bands performing in an intimate setting, similar to The Cavern Club in Liverpool. Manfred Mann, The Yardbirds (with Jeff Beck in the line-up) and Geno Washington played there during this period and that New Year's Eve, with cousin Malcolm, we participated in the party atmosphere which culminated, when the chimes struck twelve, in an orgy of kissing, the likes of which I had not experienced before and am unlikely to enjoy again. In time, The Jigsaw was closed down, apparently due to a problem associated with drugs - a sign of changing times. In the run-up to Christmas I took employment for the first time in my life, helping with the Christmas post in Altrincham. It was good fun, apart from having to get up so early, and we quickly learnt how to distribute letters and parcels as quickly as possible within our area so that we could make some free time in the pub for a drink and dominoes. I was even allowed, very briefly, to drive the van until I nearly wrote off an old Humber Hawk. It was certainly different from driving the little Morris and, after the near miss, I was quite relieved to limit my activities to delivering the post, including a plucked goose with an address tag and a small remnant of the parcel in which it had originally been wrapped!

Soon I was sitting important examinations again and thinking a little more about my future. I had an instinct to try estate agency but, after a chat with an accountant known to my father, I changed my mind. How could I refuse when told that if I hadn't earned £2,000 by the time I was thirty I would have missed the boat! It sounded good to me so I applied for appropriate degree courses but, when the 'A' Level results were published, I discovered that my three passes fell short of the required grades. I dare say that I would have been accepted on some courses but it was accountancy that I had opted for and becoming a part-time student while earning money seemed like a good alternative. I joined Binder Hamlyn, a top firm of accountants, with another classmate from school, earning the princely sum of £10 a week! Everything started very impressively with a flight down to London to meet staff at the London office and first-class return tickets on the train. Apart from my occasional trip on one of the ageing local electric trains this was about the first time that I'd travelled by train in England for two years and I was very impressed by the speed and comfort. The new electric service between London and Manchester had only recently been inaugurated and the 2 hours 40 minutes schedules were a very substantial improvement on previous timings. During the following three weeks we were to attend an induction course at Westminster and enjoy the benefit of further first-class travel for our weekly trips. We were based at a small hotel on Cromwell Road where, in the bar one night, we met a singer called Solomon King. He told us that he was trying to break into the music scene and that he would soon be releasing a record called *She Wears My Ring*. Within a few weeks the song became a big hit but, as quickly as he rose to fame, his star waned. Meanwhile, working in the office off St. Ann's Square, Manchester, was not quite as exciting as I had first imagined. I was based in the audit department and seemed to spend much of my first year out on audits at cotton warehouses in the centre of Manchester (most, if not all, have disappeared) or at mills in Rochdale and Oldham. One of my main duties was to add up columns of figures in books of account, in my head! Business attitudes, within a few years, would change but at that time there was still a strong air of formality and a strict pecking order with articled clerks at the bottom of the pile, collecting the sandwiches, carrying books and papers, and generally being sent on errands. There was

Plate 142. BR class '5' 4-6-0 No.73128 is seen on station pilot duties at Manchester Exchange station on 30th March 1968. The station had been opened by the L&NWR in June 1884 and closed in May 1969. Since then part of the station has been used as a car park. *Photo, Tom Heavyside.*

Best had grown up with the club and dazzled the Old Trafford crowds with his skills. A new generation of players were seen near home, Pat Crerand living round the corner from us and David Sadler, the centre back, living next door. Both players were in the side that won the European Cup in 1968 when United beat Benfica 4-1.

There was a show-business feel to Manchester United and, for that matter, to our office as well. Our cashier was President of the Herman's Hermits Fan Club and had written a song that appeared on one of their strong-selling albums in America, where they were particularly successful. One of our senior audit clerks, Richard Pearson, had also written a song for the group and made a few thousand pounds in the process. Richard was apparently a talented pianist and was once a member of a 'pop' group called The Four Pennies, leaving to study accountancy before their no.1 hit, *Juliet*. I had also started to write songs, since the previous summer, in fact, while waiting for my 'A' Level results, but they sounded too much like the music I was fond of (and that was unfashionable) and I was limited to a handful of chords on the guitar. I had a long way to go.

I had been at Binder Hamlyn barely two months when, while browsing at magazines in Smiths, I flicked through the pages of the *Railway Magazine* and noticed, to my astonishment, that under the section of locomotive news there was only one locomotive left on the Eastern Region. At first I thought I had misread the passage but then, checking other magazines, realised the awful truth that in the three years since I had put away my *Combined Volume,* the ranks of the Eastern Region's locomotives had indeed been reduced to a solitary 'K1' 2-6-0 No.62005. Feeling a sudden sense of urgency I decided there and then to 'come out of retirement' and keep in touch with what was going on, especially as much of the remaining steam activity was confined to the north-west.

some fun to be had, however, and the Subbuteo competition within the office occupied many lunch breaks, especially as a league of teams had been formed. Football was obviously a popular topic of conversation and both the Manchester teams had their loyal band of supporters in the office. At that time both clubs were successful but Manchester United were the current league champions and in Europe once again. The team had changed since the days when we looked out for Harry Gregg at the paper shop. Denis Law, Pat Crerand and Alex Stepney had all been purchased and George

118

Once I discovered that the whole of the dwindling stock of steam locomotives was programmed for extinction the following August I decided to take my renewed interest a stage further and bought a cine camera on hire purchase. It turned out to be rather late in the day as few sequences were actually filmed. 'Britannia' class *Oliver Cromwell* is seen leaving Manchester Victoria with a special train while two Stanier class '5s' stand at the station awaiting banking duties, a Stanier class '8F' 2-8-0 passes Newton Heath engine shed with a freight on the Oldham line, and there are shots of Rose Grove depot, but that was basically it until the last day. There were some photographs as well but it was a meagre output considering my supposed enthusiasm. I had paid my last visit to Trafford Park, which had already closed, but there were just five withdrawn locomotives on shed, all Stanier class '5s', Nos.44665, 45150, 45285, 45315 and 45316. I took a couple of pictures but it was eerie and depressing, there was no sense of eager anticipation and, as I closed the shed door and returned to the footbridge for the last time, there was a feeling of sadness. I called in at Patricroft shed where there were many more locomotives including the Stanier class '5s' and '8Fs', and BR class '5s' and class '9s', but none of them in steam. At Bolton shed it was a similar situation enlivened only by the passage of the sole-surviving 'Britannia' Pacific *Oliver Cromwell*, once again on a

special train. At Newton Heath and Rose Grove sheds there was, at least, some sign of life as late as 3rd July and I suspect that this was the last time I saw steam on normal revenue-earning service. I called at Lostock Hall depot which, along with Rose Grove and Carnforth, was the last to close on 4th August 1968, when the last scheduled passenger trains also ran between Preston and Blackpool and Preston and Liverpool Exchange. Then, finally, on that last Sunday of 11th August when the 'fifteen guinea special' ran from Liverpool Lime Street to Carlisle and back, we followed the train, taking photographs of Stanier class '5' No.45110 passing Patricroft in the morning, and 'Britannia' No.70013 *Oliver Cromwell* near Ais Gill, on the Settle and Carlisle line. The 'Britannia' caught me a little by surprise and the shot was spoilt by the tall strands of rose-bay willow-herb waving in the wind. Later, at the north end of Mallerstang Common, we watched the returning special behind two class '5s' Nos.44781 and 44871, a wisp of steam issuing from the valves as the train passed by and on to a right-hand curve ahead. The last coach disappeared from view and then it was all over. But not quite. On our way back to Settle we caught sight of *Oliver Cromwell* again, running light at Horton in Ribblesdale. Unknown to most people at the time, it was making its way to Bressingham Gardens in Norfolk, where it has remained ever since.

Plate 143. The scene at Manchester Victoria station with a BR class '9F' 2-10-0 No.92113 alongside platform 12 with a Moston-Brindle Heath (Salford) freight. An ex-LMSR Ivatt class '2' 2-6-0 can be seen awaiting the next banking duties 'Wall Side'.

Photo, Tony Oldfield.

Plate 144. Station pilot, ex-LMSR class '5' 4-6-0 No.45240, takes water alongside platform 17 at Manchester Victoria on 30th March 1968.

Photo, Tom Heavyside.

Plate 145.(below) With little more than a year to go before the end of steam on British Railways, two ex-LMSR class '5' 4-6-0s give the impression that steam is very much in evidence at Manchester Victoria. No.44803 is at rest with a parcels service alongside platform 11 while No.45101 awaits its next banking duty on 29th July 1967.

Photo, Tom Heavyside.

Plate 146. Trafford Park shed less than a year from closure with two ex-LMSR class '8F' 2-8-0s Nos.48613 & 48332, seen on 28th June 1967. The shed closed its doors on 4th March 1968. *Photo, Tom Heavyside.*

Plate 147. The Heysham Boat Train arrives at Manchester Victoria's platform 16 behind ex-LMSR class '5' No.45107 in July 1965. On the right an ex-LMSR class '2' 2-6-0 No.46501 is about to replenish its tender at platform 17.

Photo, Tony Oldfield.

Plate 148. On 19th June 1968, at Bolton shed, ex-LMSR class '8F' 2-8-0 No.48773 and ex-LMSR class 5 4-6-0 No.44802 stand below the coaling plant prior to their next duties. *Photo, Peter Fitton.*

Plate 149. Inside Patricroft shed on 6th April 1968 where two more Stanier '8Fs', including No.48374, receive some dappled sunshine. Patricroft shed, situated alongside Stephenson's Liverpool-Manchester main line, was to close later in the year and much of the site disappeared under the M602 motorway, the rest of it being taken up by industrial units. *Photo, Tom Heavyside.*

Plate 150. At Newton Heath shed on 8th June 1968 ex-LMSR class '5' 4-6-0 No.45350 is turned with the help of two children. This Rose Grove engine was one of the last survivors of the steam age, holding out until the beginning of August, just days before the end of steam.

Photo, Tom Heavyside.

Life without steam would be difficult to get used to even though there had been plenty of time to prepare for the loss. Nothing would be the same again without the unique animated movements, sounds and smells of steam locomotives, but there were still a few places around the country where enthusiasts could relive the 'old days'. Already the smell of engine smoke and the sound of whistles had returned to Yorkshire, where the Keighley & Worth Valley Railway Society had re-opened the old Midland branch line to Oxenhope and, of course, the Bluebell Railway and some narrow-gauge lines in Wales had become well-established at running services with steam engines. A reliable car would be an essential prerequisite if I was to visit these far-flung preserved lines and, while the old Morris Minor was reliable, I was always worried about putting it into top gear because reverse was alongside it in the bottom right-hand corner. There was a lot of play in the old gear lever and I was never sure whether I was sliding the gear into fourth or throwing it into reverse, with possible disastrous consequences. It did not make for relaxed driving so I sold the car in the February for just £5 less than I paid for it, but it was not the test drive that sold the car. That was a disaster. First of all it was very slow. On a steep hill a milk float passed us; it was going the same way! Then, approaching a T-junction, we indicated to turn right. The indicator was a semaphore recessed into the side of the car and operated by a knob

Plate 151. Lostock Hall shed, south of Preston, on 4th August 1968, with a line-up of ex-LMSR, Stanier-designed locomotives including, from the left, class '5' 4-6-0s Nos.45305 and 44894 and '8F' No.48476, all used on special trains later that day.

Photo, Peter Fitton.

10. THE PRESERVATION ERA

My life had changed quickly, it seemed, in a short space of time. Here I was in a business suit and an income that allowed me some luxuries such as a car and, late in 1969, a holiday to Paris. My brother was at university and, although I was still content to travel with my parents to Saltburn and Clifford, it did not feel the same. Saltburn was beginning to look run-down, probably a mixture of neglect and vandalism, while its station looked as if it was living on borrowed time. Rusting rails bore testimony to the loss of the excursion traffic and there was an air of dereliction about the place. The only crumb of comfort was that the Victorian Society had listed the station as being suitable for retention but would it be able to withstand the pressure for redevelopment? Meanwhile the house and gardens at Clifford hadn't changed much but my cousin Malcolm had now moved out to his own house and Clive had joined the Hong Kong police force. I now had a young cousin, Jane, a late addition to the family, and she was now my only excuse for sitting on the metal swing, but there was no chance to jump off recklessly this time! In retrospect, what I needed was to make a complete break and live in London possibly and force myself to take on a new challenge, but life was comfortable at home and reasonably cheap.

I was still writing songs, adding a few more chords to my accompaniments, and trying something new by hiring a recording studio to record a demonstration tape. I paid three visits to Starphonic Studios in Fallowfield and, on the first two visits, managed to record ten songs each session. I then took the tapes to Eroica Studios (affectionately known as Erotica Studios) in Altrincham where they were converted to discs. The next step should have been to make contact with music publishers and recording companies but I did not have the confidence to take this extra step at the time so the discs languished at home. On Saturday nights at the local tennis and rugby clubs local bands would play and it was while dancing at one club that I came across a band called 'The Bitter End'. I summoned up the courage to introduce myself and discovered that they were quite happy to add a backing to my songs and record them in the studios. I was now able to add a more professional sound without having to pay and they gained a little experience of studio work. They brought their friends with them and, if it wasn't quite like The Beatles in their filmed recording of *All You Need Is Love*, then at least it was fun. The lead singer was not present at the session so I took over the vocals as I was feeling more assured in a studio environment. It was just a shame about my voice! Anyway, feeling more confident about this batch of songs, I paid my first visit to the recording companies in London and experienced the first of many fruitless journeys.

At the same time I was making parallel attempts to write a book. I had acquired H. C. Casserley's *Preserved Steam Locomotives* and felt that there was a market for a book on preserved railways as well. The first thing I had to do was to visit some of these railways and so I decided to try out the Dart Valley Railway, which had just been officially opened by none other than Doctor Beeching! It was the picture in the *Railway Magazine* of a small Prairie tank engine at Buckfastleigh that sold me the idea of visiting this reincarnated Great Western branch line. I could have travelled down by car but opted for the train instead which, with a class 47 at the head, took the line from Crewe, through Shrewsbury and the Severn Tunnel (a first for me) to Bristol and Newton Abbot, where I spent some minutes studying the minute proportions of the sole-surviving locomotive of the broad gauge era, the appropriately named *Tiny*. My guest house for the next six nights was conveniently situated within walking distance of Buckfastleigh station on the A38 trunk road and, during that time, I tried to absorb as much of the line as possible, watching the activity and taking trips down the branch. I relaxed on Buckfastleigh and Staverton stations, took strolls in the surrounding countryside, watching as the pannier tanks shuffled their trains through the sylvan setting of the Dart Valley, and sat in the auto trains as Nos.6412 and 6435 took turns on the services. At that time, the line to Ashburton was still intact and small Prairie tank No.4555 worked that section during the week with weedkiller trains, suggesting that the railway was upbeat about its chances of retaining that section. In the bar each night I found myself chatting to one of the construction workers engaged in the building of the new A38 dual carriageway. He was convinced that the railway would be severed and, as a railway enthusiast, I could hardly take any other stance than the opposite view. But, since when has a railway taken precedence over a road in recent times? Well, not on this occasion either, and the chance of seeing the branch-line trains in the delightful terminus at Ashburton was lost.

The week spent in Devon fired my enthusiasm and, in the coming months, I produced a manuscript on preserved railways and other relics and began the laborious process of sending copies to various publishers. The most encouraging reply was from Philip Unwin, who had by then retired from Allen and Unwin. In his letter he apologized for his typing errors and gave me some useful constructive criticism on how to make the finished product more commercially-orientated. Although this was very much appreciated I was also involved, half-heartedly, in studying for my accountancy examinations and writing songs so, surprising as it may seem, I did not find it easy to focus on the revisions that were considered necessary to the manuscript. The truth of the matter is that time drifted by until it was too late and I read in a magazine that the M.P. Gerald Nabarro (who was perfectly capable of finding time in his busy life) had written a book on preserved steam railways. It dealt with the subject matter in a different style but I took the view that there was no room for two books on this subject and put the whole project on hold. Since then, other works have taken over from Nabarro's contribution while my manuscript continues to gather dust.

During the course of preparing the manuscript I naturally visited other railways including the first preserved standard gauge line, the Bluebell Railway. I hired a Morris 1300 from London and found it to be a most enjoyable car to drive along the country roads of Sussex and Surrey. Horsted Keynes is not the easiest of stations to find, even now, but on my first visit I was truly thankful that the car did plenty of miles to the

Plate 156. A new era of steam, on lines run by preservationists, actually began way back in 1951 with the opening of the Talyllyn Railway, a narrow-gauge line. At the end of that decade the first standard-gauge line, the Bluebell Railway, began operations in Sussex but the preservation movement got into its stride from 1968 when the first of a new wave of schemes commenced its operation of train services at the Keighley & Worth Valley Railway in June 1968. Ex-LMSR Ivatt 2-6-2 tank engine No.41241 hauled the opening-day train and this same engine is seen approaching Keighley on 10th April 1971. *Photo, Tom Heavyside.*

Plate 157. The Dart Valley Railway opened for business the year after the Worth Valley line and there had been hopes that the whole of the original branch to Ashburton would be re-opened. Unfortunately, this proved not to be the case as the A38 road scheme breached the line beyond Buckfastleigh. However, we can still enjoy the sight and sound of steam in the Dart Valley as illustrated above by this shot of ex-GWR 0-4-2 tank engine No.1420, working the 11.30am to Totnes Riverside soon after leaving Buckfastleigh on 15th October 1971.   *Photo, Tom Heavyside.*

gallon! Anyway, when I eventually drove into the station approach all was quiet and, as at Buckfastleigh, there was a feeling of travelling back in time. There was not a soul about as I walked to the ticket office and no one on the platforms. There wasn't a sound apart from the echoes of my footsteps as I made my way down the subway to the island platform. Admittedly, the train was not due for another fifteen minutes and, in time, I was joined by a dozen or more fellow travellers but those first few minutes were golden and full of nostalgia. Here I was, deep in the heart of the English countryside and all I could here was the ticking of the clock on platform 2. Eventually, the aura of calm was broken by an approaching train, just three coaches behind a class 'P' 0-6-0 No.27 (formerly 31027). The engine ran round its train, a few of us looked on as the fireman attended to the business of coupling No.27 to the first coach, and soon we were on our way to Sheffield Park. At around

about the same period I paid my first visit to the Severn Valley Railway, running from the picturesque town of Bridgnorth to Hampton Loade. There was some excellent coaching stock and several locomotives of mainly LMS origin although my return trip was behind GWR 0-6-0 No.3205. I looked around at the attractive station, the busy shed and yard, admired the views from the train and felt, instinctively, that this line was going places.

Back in the modern world I was already well aware that I had no great talent for accountancy and, if I was to get by, then it would be by hard graft alone. This did not sound very appealing especially as I was having to study by correspondence course in the evenings. However, I was still an articled clerk and the workplace was hardly ever dull. Apart from the busy office where there was a lot of good humour, I worked in a variety of buildings including mills, factories, hotels, shops and offices. As audits took place just once or twice a year we usually had to make do with whatever space the client could make available for us. Sometimes there would be the luxury of a boardroom table but, on one occasion, I recall having to work on local MP and engineering boss, Tom Normanton's cocktail cabinet! There were many varied destinations such as Colwyn Bay in 1969, when I travelled by train from Manchester Exchange station for the last time, shortly before it was closed. Then there were the ten weeks in Sheffield when on several occasions I caught the train from Piccadilly behind Bo-Bo class 'EM1s' (the more usual 'EM2s' had by then gone into storage pending shipment to the Netherlands for service there). Motive power included the veteran No.26000 *Tommy* (built for the LNER) on more than one occasion. The timing of these journeys was fortunate as the Woodhead route would shortly lose its regular passenger service and another large city station, Sheffield Victoria, would close. Of all the destinations for audits, it was the mills in north Manchester that I remember best of all. They were teeming with women, naughty women who, when we approached on the mill floor, would eye us up and then, after we had passed by,

giggle or burst into raucous laughter. There was plenty of flirting and, whenever dating a girl, all attempts at secrecy were usually, ruthlessly exposed. Then there was the music over the Tannoy systems. It was, more often than not, Radio 1 (in its early days) and, in particular, the Jimmy Young Show that I remember. It wasn't easy having to concentrate on books of account while listening to the latest recipe!

It was in the offices of Binder Hamlyn where I met a charming young man, James Gibson, who was at Cambridge University at the time but working during his holidays. He had lost his parents early on and had been brought up by an uncle who lived in a large house on the edge of the Cheshire village of Sandiway. We got on well and it was he who introduced me to the National Society for Cancer Relief, the Manchester branch of which held its committee meetings in the Town Hall. I attended a couple of meetings but felt that I was not able to contribute much so, after speaking to the Regional Organizer, decided to set up a committee for Sale and Altrincham. So began a two-year stint as chairman of the local branch during which junior branches were set up at the local grammar schools and fundraising events

Plate 158. On my first visit to the Bluebell Railway in 1969, ex-SECR 'P' class 0-6-0 Tank engine No.27 was in steam. On 11th July 1971 it was the turn of sister engine No.323 *Bluebell*, seen here leaving Horsted Keynes with a train for Sheffield Park.

Photo, Tom Heavyside.

Plate 159. One of the most successful (and longest) of preserved railways, the Severn Valley Railway opened in 1970 and on 17th August 1974 Ivatt class '2' 2-6-0 No.46443 leaves Hampton Loade with the 4.15pm Bewdley-Bridgnorth train.

Photo, Tom Heavyside.

were organized. The charity shop was most profitable but the football match between a boys' team and a girls' side (Legs X1) which Manchester United star, Pat Crerand, agreed to referee, was very enjoyable. The most memorable occasion though was the visit of the popular comedian and entertainer, Arthur Askey, who agreed to take time off from pantomime rehearsals in Manchester to attend a coffee morning at Sale Town Hall. It was an education to watch the way that he put everyone at their ease with his relaxed manner, smiling face and his wit.

By 1970 I was ready to replace my car. Although I had been pleased with the reliability of the Morris I needed something with more power. There had been one or two incidents that perhaps persuaded me it was time to move on such as the accelerator cable that snapped, on the outside lane of the busy Chester Road, at rush hour! Or when the car collapsed, on the outside lane of City Road, at rush hour! Apparently, there was a problem with the kingpin that caused the front wheel to collapse. I know that the window must have been open because I saw a woman pointing at the car and shouting to another woman "It's on fire!" I opened the car door immediately and prepared to eject but it soon became apparent that, as the car ground to a halt, the flames she had seen had been sparks. Still, it helped to concentrate the mind! A Wolseley 1500 was to be my next car. It was beige

(good for disguising rust), had that extra power I needed and, at £60, was money well spent in my view. While I enjoyed driving I can't pretend that commuting to work gave me any pleasure and there were spells when I used the ageing electric trains between Sale and Manchester.

One evening, in early December 1970, I was watching television, a film, when the phone rang. My father answered and, even though it was difficult to hear the conversation, I could tell by his tones that something was wrong. It had been my uncle to say that Malcolm had been killed in a car crash. He, too, had been commuting in his Mini when he hit a patch of black ice, lost control and ran into an oncoming vehicle. Naturally, Christmas was a more subdued affair that year but the bright blue sky and sunshine on Boxing Day tempted the family out for a day trip into Derbyshire, where we got as far as Ladybower Reservoir before heading back via Buxton. Although there was plenty of sunshine there was also a cool north-easterly wind developing, so we were glad to get back into the car and leave Buxton along the moorland road to Macclesfield. It's a steep road out of the town and height is gained quickly on the way to the *Cat and Fiddle* pub, one of the highest in the country. As we approached a right-hand bend we noticed a car in a lay-by and a man waving us down. My father slowed down but, as we took the next left-hand bend, the car lost all adhesion and veered across the

131

Plate 160. While the preservation movement was experiencing boom times the national railway network was continuing to decline and the first generation of diesel and electric locomotives was beginning to dwindle in numbers. One of the casualties was the passenger service from Manchester Piccadilly to Sheffield Victoria station, hauled at that time by the 'EM1' class Bo-Bo electric locomotives (the 'EM2' types having found employment in the Netherlands). Passenger services ceased in January 1970 leaving only the freight services and occasional diverted traffic running to and from Sheffield. Nearly ten years after the end of passenger services, an 'EM1' (by then known as class '76'), No.76046 emerges from the Woodhead Tunnel with a Great Western Society special to Manchester on 21st April 1979. *Photo, Tom Heavyside.*

road, tumbling into a deep ravine, overturning twice and landing upside down in a small stream. My father switched off the ignition the moment we left the road but the car undoubtedly saved our lives. It was a Rover 2000, one of whose safety features included a stiffened cage-like passenger compartment, designed to withstand collapse in just the sort of situation in which we found ourselves. The benefit of wearing seat belts was also amply demonstrated and, apart from some minor cuts suffered by my mother when the windscreen shattered, we climbed out unscathed, much to the surprise of onlookers. The cause of the ice on the road, incidentally, was water running off a slope and across the road but cooled by the easterly wind blowing in the opposite direction.

It was with a definite sense of relief that a new calendar was hung up and, in a few short weeks, spring would beckon. Symbolically, 1971 was indeed the beginning

of spring for the main-line steam movement as the first steam-hauled special of a new era was organized. The locomotive in charge that day, 'King' class No.6000 *King George V*, was a pioneer in its own right, being the first of its class and having travelled to the United States early in its career. On this occasion the locomotive, based at Bulmers in Hereford, hauled a rake of green-and-cream Pullman coaches and I set off with trainspotting friend, David Nevell, catching up with the train at Oxford. There was no M40 in those days but somehow we also managed to reach Hatton station in time to see the 'King' run through in late-afternoon sunlight. However, I had no great inclination to follow the succession of steam-hauled trains that appeared in various parts of the country unless they happened to be on the doorstep. Instead, I preferred the preserved lines and centres in varying stages of development such as the North Yorkshire Railway, the Lakeside Railway and

Dinting Railway Centre, occupying a former GCR depot near Glossop. The East Lancashire Railway was still in its infancy and hoping to operate from Helmshore station, on the Accrington branch from Bury, before changing to its present location. While many locomotives enjoyed a new lease of life in steam, others such as *City of Birmingham* were kept as static exhibits in museums. This was one of a type known officially as the 'Coronation' class but the names of individual members included, primarily, 'Duchesses' and 'Cities'. On visiting the transport museum in Birmingham I threw one of the attendants into a state of confusion and panic when I asked him where the 'Duchess' was! It was some time before we understood one another, at which point he was able to breathe a sigh of relief and I'd almost forgotten what I had come to see. In my defence, the class was often referred to as a 'Duchess'- even if this was a 'City'!

Now that the issue of 'Duchesses' and 'Cities' has been clarified it is time to mention Barry Scrapyard, a name that probably suggests to the layman it is time to skip a paragraph or two but which, in fact, became a catalyst in the preservation of steam locomotives. I can't remember when I first discovered its existence, but it was probably through the pages of the *Railway Magazine*. I think that, initially, there was an assumption that the locomotives in the yard would be scrapped but, when it became clear that some had been saved, there was a growing realization that Barry could provide the motive power needed for new railway schemes. It soon became a 'Mecca' for enthusiasts and, in 1969, I made the first of three visits. I was not quite sure what to expect but was staggered at the sheer scale of the place where 215 locomotives stood in varying stages of decay. It was amazing to see the *Duke of Gloucester* which, I assumed, had been scrapped shortly after its withdrawal in 1962. Likewise, I was delighted to see two 'Kings' while catching my first-ever views of Somerset and Dorset 2-8-0s, GWR 42XX and 52XX 2-8-0 tanks, and 72XX 2-8-2 tanks. There were no less than thirty-seven different classes of steam locomotives represented on my first trip and, of these, nine classes could only be seen at Barry Scrapyard. It took a while before the purchase of these rusting hulks gathered momentum but, once it had, there was no stopping it and nearly all of those engines seen on that first visit

Plate 161. For all those enthusiasts who were keen to see steam on the main line again, a big leap forward came with the 'Return to Steam' special in 1971, hauled by ex-GWR 'King' class No.6000 *King George V*. The locomotive is seen at Church Stretton at a later date working 'The Palatine' special. Next to the engine is the 'Bulmer Cider' Pullman car, a reminder that *King George V* was based at the Bulmer Cider site in Hereford for many years.

Photo, Peter Fitton.

Plate 162. Soon after the end of steam in 1968 enthusiasts learnt of the existence of over two hundred steam locomotives that still awaited scrapping. Soon, the large scrapyard at Barry, South Wales, became a Mecca for preservationists and enthusiasts alike, providing a source of motive power for new and existing preservation schemes. BR class '4' 2-6-4 tank No.80097 heads a line of locomotives that were all saved including a large GWR 'Prairie' tank, an ex-Southern Railway 'West Country' Pacific No.34072 *257 Squadron* and a BR class '9' 2-10-0, on 22nd June 1972.

Photo, Peter Fitton.

Plate 163. In the early days of preservation one of the more unusual settings was the open farmland at Lochty in Fife where ex-LNER 'A4' Pacific No.60009 *Union of South Africa* was based.

Photo, Author.

were saved. These included main-line successes such as *City of Wells, Taw Valley, Canadian Pacific, Defiant, Leander, King Edward I* and, of course, *Duke of Gloucester.* It was a remarkable story and the name of its owner, Dai Woodham, will always be associated with that stage of the preservation movement. On my last 'pilgrimage' to Barry Island I hired a Volkswagen Beetle and, arriving in the dark on a Saturday night late in 1972, walked across to the hotel to the sound of Lieutenant Pigeon's *Mouldy Old Dough* that was blaring out of an open bedroom window. I entered the reception area, only to be bitten on the ankle by an Alsatian, which suddenly appeared from behind the desk. Apart

from a little graze and being somewhat taken aback I was none the worse for the experience and, after receiving apologies from the hotel manager, I took the matter no further except to wonder whether all guests got this treatment! Anyway, I spent much of the following morning at the scrapyard before heading north to call at the Dean Forest Railway at Parkend. While driving through the suburbs of Cardiff I stopped to post a letter and, making my way back to the car, heard a dog barking aggressively. I turned round to see another Alsatian running towards me so I quickly dived back into the car to find the dog's head appearing beside the front passenger window and barking furiously. I started the

Plate 164. Another preserved railway that opened in the 1970s was the Lakeside & Haverthwaite Railway, operating the relatively short distance of just over three miles between Haverthwaite and Lakeside, on the shores of lake Windermere. It is the only line where, at the time of writing, ex-LMSR 2-6-4 tank engines can be seen on passenger trains. Here we see ex-LMSR Fairburn 2-6-4 No.2073 leaving Newby Bridge with the 6.05pm Lakeside-Haverthwaite on 22nd July 1973.

Photo, Tom Heavyside.

car and drove off, pursued by the dog, and soon came to a halt at traffic lights where, once again, the Alsatian ran up to the car barking. It was only after resuming my journey when I was able to shake it off but, to this day, I have no idea what it was that angered the two dogs (though possibly it could have been the same one). Perhaps I was tainted by the curse of the yellow Volkswagen but, otherwise, I am unable to explain the incidents that 'dogged' this trip!

Dogs were to become part of my life again in 1971 when my mother picked up a 'stray' that she found wandering in the street. It was a good-looking ginger-and-white mongrel with velvet ears that looked as if they had been grafted on afterwards. It settled in quickly and everything was fine until one day when an old schoolfriend, Roger Thornton, and I took Kim out for a walk. We let him off the lead in a field, where it enjoyed a good run but, when it came to putting the lead back on again, Kim would have none of it. No manner of

coaxing would entice it back to the lead so we walked back home and it followed us. This arrangement worked satisfactorily until, in a moment of madness, it ran into the road and was hit by a passing car. It took a bad knock and howled but otherwise seemed to survive intact. However, within a fortnight, and without reason, it bit my father. In the weeks that followed it had bitten the whole family, who were now treating Kim with considerable caution. The end came when, in a mad frenzy, it bared its teeth and snarled viciously at all of us. It could only be kept at bay with chairs until, eventually, it became more subdued, at which point it was taken to the vet and put down. It had been a tense few weeks, almost like living as a hostage in one's own house with an escaped psychopath! Just as I was getting used to a relaxed atmosphere Mum picked up another stray. This time it was a bearded collie of perfect temperament who quickly became a much-loved member of the family and remained with us for ten years.

Plate 165. In 1971 the distinctive electric units of the MSJ&AR were replaced by the standard West Coast Main Line EMUs. One of the original d.c. sets, No.M28593, stands at the terminus end of Altrincham station on 29th April 1971 during the last week of service. Judging from the length of the young woman's mini-skirt one can only assume that they had reached their height of popularity - at least among young men.
Photo, David Stratton.

Towards the end of 1971 my parents received a letter from Karina, the Polish girl with whom I had exchanged holidays in 1965. Then, as a fifteen-year-old, she was pretty and lively but the photograph she enclosed with the letter showed her to be a much more attractive and mature girl and I, for one, was looking forward to meeting her. She expressed the wish to revisit England and, with Mum and Dad's agreement, she stayed with us for over two months. We got on very well together and, shortly after St. Valentine's Day, a passionate relationship developed that continued until she returned to Warsaw. In April we managed to spend a week away together and she didn't seem to mind the prospect of seven days in a former railwayman's cottage by the side of the West Coast Main Line, just south of Scout Green signalbox, as English Electric and Sulzer Type '4s' hurried down from Shap with Anglo-Scottish expresses. We spent much of the time absorbed in each other's company and talked about spending a winter holiday in the Polish mountain resort of Zakopane, which evoked happy memories of my last visit. So there was something to look forward to as she boarded the boat at Hull bound for Gdansk. Meanwhile I had left Binder Hamlyn, following the expiry of my articles and having failed to pass my finals, and looked for a firm that

would give me better experience at preparing final accounts and taking full control of an audit from beginning to end. I found a small firm in Stockport and immediately settled. The atmosphere was more relaxed and friendly and, at lunchtimes, we enjoyed regular darts matches until a cricket game was devised using paper that had been screwed up into a ball and kept in shape by sellotape, wrapped round it many times. The batsman would stand in front of a high-back chair (the wicket) while the bowler pitched the paper ball on the table and, with a bit of luck, the ball would be struck with a wages book (the bat)! If you hit the window you were out but certain parts of the walls attracted six 'runs'. However, the standard of fielding was good and made for some competitive games in which, sometimes, the partners participated.

It was here where I met Joyce, who was also working as an audit clerk. Our first audit together was at a garage just round the corner from Strawberry Recording Studios in Stockport. From our window we could see the musicians arriving each morning, including members of the band 10cc who were based there. We worked on other audits together and, in autumn, had our first date at the Free Trade Hall in Manchester to see Victor Borge in concert. From then on we saw each other often, although there were occasions when the relationship faltered. For instance, there was the time when we agreed to meet on Wilmslow station but, after waiting fifteen minutes for her to arrive, I decided to catch the train back to Stockport. Just as the train drew out of Wilmslow another train was slowing down in the opposite direction. I spotted her and, luckily, she saw me too. We could have spent the whole day passing each other like this had it not been for the fact that the next train from Wilmslow reached Stockport before I had a chance to set off again for Wilmslow. Her patience was tested again when we spent a winter's afternoon by the side of Ladybower Reservoir. We had left the car just off the road in a large forest through which we had to pass to gain access to the reservoir but, once at the water's edge we strolled and chatted, oblivious of the growing darkness. It was only when we entered the forest again that we realised just how dark it was and, being out in the country without lights and alone (all the sensible people had gone home), progress was slow. We had to resort to feeling our way through the trees in the silent darkness, broken only by the cracking of twigs and the cursing as we bumped into fallen branches. It may have been as little as half-an-hour back to the car but, believe me, it seemed like an eternity and I was more than relieved to switch the ignition on and light up our surroundings. My car was a second Wolseley 1500 but, if anything, it was worse than the first. It had an annoying leak which had a habit of filling up the passenger footwell with water, to the point where I was having to provide Joyce with Wellington boots. To make matters worse the water was tidal! When the car accelerated the water would rush to the rear footwell and, when the car braked, it would rush back under the front seat, up the foot stop below the glove compartment, forming a wave as it rolled back to the footwell. I briefly toyed with the idea of adding a few pebbles and shells but wisely concluded that it would not be appreciated.

As Christmas approached, my thoughts turned towards the holiday I was to spend in the Tatra Mountains with Karina the following January and then, just before New Year's Eve, a telegram arrived, informing me that her father had died and that the holiday had to be cancelled. It was a big blow for her as she had already lost her mother two years previously but, there was little I could do, so I decided to take a break anyway and looked for a holiday that was available at short notice. A few days later I was on my way to Palma in Majorca to compensate for losing out on the romantic interlude in Poland. The flight was not enjoyable, there being a considerable amount of turbulence, and when we landed, the pilot seemed to brake at the last minute bringing the plane to such a sudden stop that I felt as if we were moving sideways! But, seven days in Majorca enabled me to relax, even if it didn't feel that much warmer than in England. I returned feeling rejuvenated and wondering if there was much of a future with Karina.

The next two years were spent developing my relationship with Joyce, discussing our likes and dislikes, noting our differences and trying to assess whether we were compatible. We spent a lot of time in each other's company and visits to railways were minimal. Instead, there were day trips to Stratford to see *Romeo and*

Plate 166. An example of the new a.c electric stock stands at platform 1 at Altrincham on 5th May 1971 during the first week of service.

Photo, David Stratton.

Plate 167. A train of limestone hoppers from Tunstead Quarry, near Buxton, passes through Hale station on its way to the ICI works at Northwich behind typical motive power of the time, a BR Sulzer Type '2' (by this time redesignated a class '25'), in 1974.
Photo, David Stratton.

Juliet (Timothy Dalton played Romeo), to Edinburgh for the Tattoo and a holiday in Paris. We went to concerts and clubs such as the Golden Garter in Wythenshawe, south Manchester, where, on a memorable evening, we saw Morecambe and Wise at the height of their fame. The same cabaret club sticks in my mind for another reason. A popular northern comic of the time, Colin Crompton, was top of the bill and we were just about to enjoy the first course at our table. In the process of helping to guide a tomato juice from the hands of the waitress to my table mat, the glass found its own way down, spilling a considerable amount of juice onto my lap. But I didn't appreciate how much had been spilt because the lights were low and the cabaret had begun. Anyway, I thought that half a glass of tomato juice was par for the course (the first course). After the meal I reluctantly, as usual, made my way to the dance floor and there, under the glare of the spotlights, I followed the look of horror on Joyce's face down to my trousers, where there was more red around my zip than on my bank statement! There was no alternative but to return home for a change of clothes and so we made our way out, between the tables, Joyce leading, with me so close behind that it probably raised a few eyebrows. In train parlance we definitely looked like a double-header!

By 1974 I had moved on, joining Renold Chain as a

financial accountant. I was on over £2,500 now and I remembered the words of the accountant who advised me to enter the profession, "if you are not on £2,000 by the time you are thirty you've missed the boat". Well I had missed the boat in that I had not passed my examinations but, here I was, on well over £2,000 and some years away from my thirtieth birthday. Of course, in the intervening years there had been the small matter of inflation that caused house prices to rocket. At a time when it had never been better to purchase property I decided to rent a flat. Still, it provided Joyce and me with a measure of independence and spare cash to spend on a Triumph Vitesse 2 litre convertible, a considerable advance on the Wolseley 1500, even if it didn't have an indoor pool! Although the Vitesse was not a true sports car, its 6-cylinder engine gave it a smooth sporty performance at cheaper insurance rates. Its engine was very accessible and, very importantly, it was a most reliable car so it was only natural that, after fifteen months, I should sell it and buy the car that would give me more aggravation than any other, as well as become a drain on my resources! How much aggravation it would cause will be explained a little later.

In 1974 we had the first of regular visits from a distinguished relation, Sir William Glock who, some years earlier, had been Controller of Radio 3. In this role

138

he ensured that a much greater proportion of modern music reached the public ear as well as developing the format of the Promenade Concerts. His mother, Gertrude, was the sister of my father's mother and, while my father and William had remained in contact with each other, it had been some time since they had met. Now William had taken up a post, on a fortnightly basis, teaching music appreciation at the Royal Northern College of Music and, on the night before his classes, he would often have a meal with us and chat about music, his experiences at the BBC and in Germany (where he studied piano under Schnabel during the 1920s and early 1930s). Mum and Dad continued to entertain foreign visitors to ICI including, for the first time, Japanese business men. I remember a lot of bowing when greetings were exchanged but the Japanese bow was often so low that the head reached a point, level with the waist!

In the same year I started to keep a diary for the first time and, in the pages, recorded the occasional engine number. At first, I noted only the numbers of locomotives at the head of trains on which I happened to be travelling, such as the class '87' on a London train (the old 'D' and 'E' prefixes had disappeared under the new TOPS system of numbering). By 1975 I was also noting the numbers of certain classes I had seen, such as the Deltics on a visit to York to see steam. It was some 'special' that day when 'V2' Green Arrow arrived, to be replaced by the combined forces of 'B1' Mayflower and 'A3' Flying Scotsman. I later hurried round to York depot and filmed the departing special from the cab of Green Arrow. Unfortunately, there was no sound facility on my cine camera and some of the effect was lost. While in York a visit to the newly-opened National Railway Museum was a 'must'. It was altogether on a grander scale and more informative than before but the engines still did not move and, without movement, the onlooker missed out on the unique smell and the sound

Plate 168. Memories of the Stockton & Darlington 150th Anniversary Celebrations. Great Northern Railway No.990 *Henry Oakley* is seen at Heighington in the parade of locomotives on 31st August 1975. Built in 1898, it can be seen at York's National Railway Museum. Its cab was the first I climbed into when it was preserved in the old museum at York. *Photo, Peter Fitton.*

Plate 169. Here is the real McCoy from the Stockton & Darlington Railway, preserved on a pedestal inside Darlington's station on 31st August 1975. *Locomotion No.1* was in charge of the inaugural locomotive-hauled train in 1825 along that historic line but was not able to participate in the Anniversary Celebrations. Instead, a replica of this famous engine was built and proved to be a great success in the parade. As for the original, seen here, it was moved to Darlington North Road station and relative obscurity together with *Derwent,* seen behind.

Photo, Peter Fitton.

Plate 170. A view of Saltburn station in the early 1970s with the old North Eastern Railway train shed falling into a state of dereliction. Eventually the train shed was demolished and the land between platform 1 and the excursion platform redeveloped into a small shopping centre. However, trains still use the old bay platforms, and the station building with its portico still survives as the focal point of Station Square.

Photo, Author.

of the locomotive, two essential elements appreciated, at least, by the enthusiast's senses. These extra dimensions were demonstrated, to some degree, at the Stockton and Darlington 150 cavalcade to celebrate, as the name suggests, the 150th anniversary of the opening of that pioneer railway. The locomotives on show emphasised, in particular, the developments over that period in the north-east but the visitors came from far and wide and included *Evening Star* and the prototype High Speed Train. In the cavalcade were locomotives rarely seen in steam but perhaps the most impressive entry was the working replica of the historic *Locomotion No.1*, showing, once again, just how much enthusiasts were capable of and how professional they had become.

11. WATERSHED

My memory of 1975 was of a warm summer and so it was when Joyce and I spent our holiday in Scotland. We caught an overnight train to Inverness at Preston on the Friday night, only to find that available space was limited to the corridors! We therefore spent an uncomfortable few hours as far as Perth, during which we got very little sleep. The class 86 had given way to a class 40 at Mossend, near Motherwell, and at Perth we were taken on to Inverness by a pair of class 26s. Here, there was a two-hour wait before resuming the journey, hauled by a class 24 along the Kyle of Lochalsh line as far as Achnasheen, where trains passed at a loop on the otherwise single line. Now we transferred to a one-a-day Highland bus which provided a connecting service from the station to the coastal villages, including Laide, our ultimate destination. The one aspect about travelling in Scotland is the way that the pace of life slows down the further north and west one goes. As early as Perth we had become more relaxed but, at Achnasheen, we just sat around as Alfred, our driver, gathered the mail from the train for delivery to the villages en route. What we did not bargain for was the length of time we would wait on the shores of the beautiful Loch Maree, sometime later. Alfred had agreed to pick up a party of schoolchildren who had been walking in the hills but, unfortunately, there was a two-hour wait before they appeared. We spent the time at the side of the loch, relaxing in the warm sunshine, admiring the grandeur of Slioch, the 3,000-foot mountain at the eastern end of the loch, and watched a black-throated diver making progress across the water. No one seemed to mind the wait. After all, this was Scotland at its glorious best, but if it had been cool or windy I suspect that some of the passengers might have become a little tetchy.

Our first overnight stop was at the Loch Maree Hotel, situated in an idyllic spot on the shores of the loch. Queen Victoria, on a tour of Scotland in 1877, stayed here and we were put up in the room that she occupied. That evening, strolling by the loch, it was pure magic to watch Slioch turn pink and then purple in the light of the setting sun. Back in the hotel I spoke to the proprietrix about our intentions for the following day and that we intended to catch Alfred's bus in the afternoon. Looking a little alarmed she reminded me that it was Sunday tomorrow and the bus did not run. Laide was a further thirty miles and we had two suitcases and some hand luggage. Despite this apparent handicap I decided that, if we set off early enough and I carried the suitcases, we could at least have a stab at reaching Laide by the evening. Within five miles the folly of this plan became all too evident as our pace had already slowed considerably. Some relief was achieved by virtue of roadworks en route. Joyce noticed some thin cable at the roadside and, cutting off a length that appeared to be spare, she rigged up a framework so that I could carry the suitcases on my back. I accept that it must have looked an odd sight and, as we climbed over the mountains to save about ten miles from the coast road, I felt very much like a sherpa, but the rigging had proved useful. However, by the time we were up in the mountains the sun was high in the cloudless sky and, in May, it was very warm. Our stoppages became more frequent and there was discontent in the ranks! At times I was forced to resort to giving Joyce a piggyback for small distances and I realise now that any walkers in the valley below would have been puzzled, even agitated, at the sight of the silhouette on the skyline looking, from a distance, like a two-headed hunchback with hand luggage! By late afternoon we had the village of Poolewe in our sights but there was no chance of making Laide. We attempted to thumb lifts but without response and so decided to look for a place in the village. Having found overnight accommodation we called the lady in Laide, who was very understanding, and, on the next day, Alfred safely delivered us to our destination and the holiday started in earnest.

Better planning would have helped us to avoid these inconveniences and a car would have done likewise. I was now the proud owner of a Lotus Elan Plus 2, an attractive car even now, and it would have been very pleasurable to have driven along some of the quiet Scottish roads but I had a feeling that, if I broke down in some outlandish place, it would have been even more inconvenient than managing without a bus for a day. Of all my cars this was the one with which I truly had a love-hate relationship. I adored driving it but it spent as much time being repaired at garages as it did on the road. During the summer and early autumn everything went well but, from the end of October, this car tested my patience to the limit. The trouble started when the brakes failed as I was approaching traffic lights, but the car was light and there was a helpful gradient to the

Plate 171. Activity at Achnasheen station, a passing point on the single line to Kyle of Lochalsh, as two trains meet. The driver of the Birmingham Railway Carriage & Workshop Co. Type '2', No.26 042, is seen handing the single-line exchange token to the station master as the train arrives. Mail on a trolley awaits transfer onto this train, bound for Inverness. I was a passenger on the adjoining Kyle of Lochalsh train, hauled by Sulzer Type '2', No.24 115 on 24th May 1975.

Photo, Author.

junction so, changing down through the gears, I was able to slow the car down before the lights changed and managed to drive it slowly to the nearest garage without further incident. It was away for a week but within four days of its return the gaskets needed attention. The car not only tried my patience but that of the garage owner too because, unlike the engine compartment in the Vitesse, that in the Lotus was not at all easy to get at. This didn't matter much when the motor bike ran into the back of my parked car but, two days later, when there was a loud clunk from somewhere under the bonnet, just as I was leaving a roundabout, the car returned to the garage for attention to the suspension. The following day, on my way to the garage, I backed out of the driveway into the path of an oncoming Morris 1800. I could tell that the driver wasn't too happy when he exclaimed that this was going to be a police job but, when the cars were disengaged, there was not a mark to be seen on the Morris. There was a rather messy hole in the glass fibre wing of the Lotus, however, so the garage added the job of repairing this to the list.

It may have been a problem with parts but, for one reason or another, the car remained at the garage for seven weeks, so I was delighted when I was able get behind the wheel again. But, one week later, the exhaust pipe fell off! I spent an hour trying to fix it outside Joyce's house and then another piece dropped off. Leaving the car there I returned the following day with some heavy duty tape, sufficient to provide a temporary repair, and drove back home. On the way the brakes failed again. I had driven the car for three days in January and when, in early February, I collected it from the garage I felt sure that all the problems were behind me. Wrong! Almost immediately, a fault with the manifold was noticed and back it went for further repairs. Funnily enough, when walking to the garage to pick up the car I noticed that my shoe was letting in water and, on removing it to inspect the leak, noticed that it, too, was a Lotus! There then followed a period of seven trouble-free days before, first, the rear axle, and then the gaskets (again!) began to give trouble. Enough was enough and I decided to sell the car. Now selling it was not a problem. Like me, the guy just fell in love with it and a sale was agreed, but the car had one final trick up its bonnet. I arranged to drive it to the buyer's house and, while on that final journey along the motorway, the lights started to misbehave. A feature of the Elan was its electrically-operated retractable lights but, out of the blue, one of the lights folded back into its closed position without warning before popping up again. Then the other light did the same thing before both lights retracted. This unpredictable routine at such a late stage was disconcerting, as well as making life difficult on the motorway, but it all ended well and the new owner drove me back without any further problems, apart from my frayed nerves!

At this stage in our lives Joyce and I needed to resolve fundamental differences if our relationship was to become more permanent. In particular, I was keen to have the freedom to work abroad whereas she wanted to be within range of her family and to have a stable life in this country. The extent of my foreign travel to date had been very limited and I was keen to sample the way of life in other countries. I had thought about visiting India, where some English was spoken, but the many advantages that North America had to offer to someone on a limited budget could not be ignored. In order to make the most of this 'Grand Tour' I purchased a Greyhound Ameripass ticket which meant that I could travel anywhere on a Greyhound bus, day or night, for two months. Apart from the cheap travel over long distances I could also save on hotel charges by sleeping as often as possible on these well-equipped coaches. There was a restless spirit in me, perhaps exemplified by Jack Kerouac in his book *On The Road* but I had also been stimulated by the successful television series, 'America', introduced by Alastair Cooke. There was another minor advantage of visiting the USA and that was the opportunity it gave me to submit music tapes to companies I hoped to see in Nashville and Los Angeles. By this time I had virtually stopped writing songs but had made contact with other songwriters with a view to becoming involved in a managerial capacity. I had met Ged Meehan who wrote *The Most Beautiful Drink In The World* for the famous Martini advert, Pamela Carter whose compositions included some intriguing folk and children's songs, and John Parr who had a great pop singing voice and played in a Sheffield band called Mickey's Monkeys. All in all I was quietly confident.

The 22nd May 1976 was the day I had been looking forward to for several months as that was the day I boarded, with eager anticipation, a TWA Boeing 707 at Manchester Airport for New York. The plane touched down at Kennedy Airport at just before 8pm and, after collecting my baggage, I made my way to the bus heading for downtown New York. I stood in a queue by the side of the bus and then a guy walked along the line asking for the fare of four dollars. Everyone duly obliged but when we climbed aboard, the bus driver asked us for four dollars! A good start but I could not help but smile at the cheek of the crook who made a tidy sum of money from the unsuspecting travellers. I then needed to transfer from the terminus in New York to the Greyhound bus station and remember being squeezed into a cab with five others plus cases and rucksacks. The journey lasted five minutes and I found myself having to hand out another five dollars. I knew that New York

was not the place to be if I wanted to acclimatize to the American way of life and so it was with a sense of relief that I boarded a bus to Richmond. It was there in the passenger lounge at the bus station that I had my first experience of the 24-hour lifestyle in the States. The room was warm, there were small televisions attached to each seat and there were comings and goings throughout the three-hour spell there before I opted for the early morning bus to the old colonial town of Williamsburg. We stopped outside the railway station from where it was a short walk into the centre. On my way I was caught up by a man dressed up in period costume. We got talking and I discovered that he was a watchmaker and that he demonstrated his craft to tourists who visited this working museum of a town. As we walked together I absorbed the lovely scents of the magnolia blossoms and reflected on the startling contrast with life in the 'Big Apple' just twelve hours earlier.

During the first seven days I experienced both the hot humidity of the Deep South and the cooler, drier conditions further north as I zig-zagged my way across the States before spending a few days in Nashville. Here I saw Dolly Parton at the Grand Ole Opry and visited some recording companies with the tapes. They listened politely and made some encouraging comments but nothing else and so I moved on across the Mississippi and onto the plains of the Mid-West to El Paso. I spent less than an hour over the border in Mexico and in that time the only conversation I had was with a Mexican who asked me if I wanted to see any naughty women! Time did not permit and I headed back north through New Mexico and Colorado to Wyoming where I camped for the one and only time in my life - in Yellowstone National Park. I had met a Dutchman and two Australians and warmed to the idea of camping, especially as it involved lighting a camp fire, but it was a terrible night. The temperature dipped to somewhere around freezing as I lay awake shivering all night in my 'Parka' jacket under some newspapers! I thought I was going to die of hypothermia. The following morning could not come soon enough when, together, we hired a car to see some of the sights such as the geyser in the park known as Old Faithful and the Mount Rushmore Memorial, featuring the four massive stone-carved heads of former US presidents.

On my travels I noticed many static steam locomotives by the side of the road, rail or in parks such as Holiday Park, near Cheyenne, where I was able to examine the

143

massive proportions of a 'Big Boy' 4-8-8-4, one of twenty-five built for use on the steep gradients between Cheyenne and Ogden. There was still a little of the pioneer atmosphere in Cheyenne, brought to life by an original stagecoach that made its last trip along the Overland Trail in 1868. It stood inside the impressive Union Pacific railway station while a large 4-6-6-4 No.3985 was displayed outside. By way of contrast, two heavy freight trains rolled out of Cheyenne and onto the plains, each hauled by three diesel locomotives. It was very tempting to explore some of the preserved railways in the USA but I needed to make the best use of my bus pass and the next few days found me taking a circuitous journey to Las Vegas via Seattle and Salt Lake City. While changing buses in Butte, Montana, I experienced one of those freak weather conditions that is rarely encountered in Britain. It was a hailstorm but the hailstones were as big as golf balls, raining down with such ferocity that the streets were cleared in seconds, traffic was halted and a window in the bus station was cracked.

Like Blackpool, Las Vegas is at its best at night, when it comes to life. I arrived just after midnight and headed straight for the gaming rooms but won nothing, unlike the lucky punter who stood at a slot machine with a box in his hands as his winnings were spewed out for twenty-five seconds! My lasting impression of this city was of large hotels, gaming rooms, marriage and divorce parlours, funeral and ice-cream parlours and I was glad to be on my way to Flagstaff, for an overnight stay, before savouring the wonderful spectacle of the Grand Canyon. It is preferable to be with someone when visiting this wonder of nature, just to share the experience. I stood alone at the edge of the canyon and marvelled at the shapes and colours of this massive natural phenomenon, wishing that there was more time to spend here but knowing that there was so much else to see. So it was onwards through the sage desert and by mid-morning the bus rolled into Los Angeles, where I booked into a decidedly-shady downtown hotel. Even the characters lurking around the reception area filled me with unease but then it was only three dollars a night! During the next few days there was plenty to keep me amused. I spent a lot of time on Sunset Boulevard enjoying health food drinks such as Pink Cloud (milk, strawberries, banana and honey) and appreciating the company of the 'hosts' I met there. In this city (and others for all I knew) there was an organization called America At Home, allowing visitors

to make contact with individuals or families who would spend some time with you during the day, or in the evening, either at their home or at a meeting place. I met up with some very interesting people including a family whose daughter had won a talent contest, that day, on television at the Burbank studios. There was a party atmosphere at their home in the evening as the girl returned from the studios in a state of elation and then went through her winning act again (based on mime) for my benefit. The following day a vivacious and talented young lady treated me to lunch at the Sources Restaurant on Sunset Strip, from where I could see the white letters on the hillside that spelt 'Hollywood' and, naturally, I devoted some time to touring the Universal Studios (where we were 'attacked' by Jaws) before going on to visit that other fantasy world - Disneyland. This was my kind of America, at least for a few days. The drier heat helped but it was noticeable how the temperature changed to a cooler English climate in San Francisco, where I had an unusual experience.

I was sitting at the only available seat outside a cafe at Fisherman's Wharf, sharing the table with a young man and an older woman. We got talking and eventually the conversation drifted to my family background. I mentioned that my mother had spent her youth in Italy whereupon the woman, whose name was Dianna, made the astonishing statement that she was the daughter of the last king of Italy, Umberto! She then broke into fluent Italian as if to emphasise the point. By this time the young man had disappeared and I had been invited for lunch on board her boat. She made me curious because, on the one hand, she sounded very convincing and, on the other, there was something strange about her and, as the day wore on, I became more sceptical about her claims. Still, she invited me to tea and trusted me with money to buy a list of food items from a local store. On my way back my attention was drawn to a film crew and a crowd across the square. On walking up to find out what was going on I was told that Clint Eastwood was filming a sequel to 'Dirty Harry' and, sure enough, within a few minutes, there he was discussing some aspect of the film sequence with technicians. Dianna chided me for taking so long but, after a drink, we sat down to a nice meal and some deep conversation. When I say it was deep I mean we were talking about Einstein's Theory of Relativity ! Naturally, she did most of the talking and in quite an articulate fashion. I tried to look intelligent (it helps a little) as I

144

listened but, while trying to be of some use in this highbrow conversation, my mind could not help drift to the circumstances of this woman. There was no doubt that she was intelligent but was she a fake, feeding me a pack of lies. These suspicions grew much stronger when we talked a little more about her family life. She told me that she had a son who she did not see but when I asked her if she kept a photograph of him she said "no". I asked her why not and she replied "because Frank wouldn't like it ". Naturally I asked her who Frank was and she replied "Frank Sinatra!". At this point, rightly or wrongly, I became convinced that she was an eccentric wanting to attract attention and I now started to query all her assertions. The friendliness that developed earlier in the day now cooled and, by late evening, I was glad to be back in my hotel, feeling somewhat frustrated that I had not resolved, for definite, what this woman was about. Before I drifted off to sleep I heard the sound of gunfire and got to thinking how normality and the bizarre seemed to co-exist so easily in that country. Perhaps she was telling the truth after all.

Before crossing into Canada I spent a week with the sister of one of my mother's friends. She lived with her husband and four boys in a large wooden shack on a remote hillside in the northern state of Washington. Her husband, Sherman, worked at a sawmill, three of the sons worked with their hands and the youngest was at school. I learned to ride a motor bike and shoot during that week and, while spending one evening with the eldest son, Terry, a quiet Vietnam War veteran, I smoked marijuana for the first time. Like tobacco, marijuana did nothing for me but I never had any great desire to smoke anyway. Within the family only my maternal grandfather had smoked (a pipe) and he died of cancer of the throat. While at this remote outpost I saw humming birds feeding daily, close to the house, and harmless garter snakes slithering across the porch. Kevin told me that there were rattlesnakes on the other side of the hill but I was quite content to stay put. I was very grateful to relax for a week with friendly people but, once again, it was time to move on. The Canadian border was crossed and, after an afternoon in Vancouver, I settled down to three consecutive nights on the bus as it made its way through the Rockies and over the plains to Winnipeg. Skirting around the northern edges of Lake Superior and Huron the bus then headed south for Toronto where, by chance, a working steam locomotive, 6060 was seen at close-quarters on a special train.

Of the natural wonders of America, and there are many,

I would argue that there are few more awe-inspiring sights than Niagara Falls. The sheer volume of water tumbling over the edge, the deafening sound when standing close and the amount of spray generated are all testimonies to a force of huge proportions. I watched this spectacular natural phenomenon during the day and again at night, when it was illuminated by different coloured beams of light. It was with great reluctance that I dragged myself away but a very special day in the United States calendar had now arrived and I wanted to be a part of the action. Not only was it Independence Day but the two-hundredth anniversary of that momentous day in the history of the United States. Leaving Niagara Falls that morning I thought about reaching Boston for the evening but, as time was running out, settled instead for Albany, the capital of New York State. A new spacious plaza had recently been opened boasting a large number of fountains and high-rise office blocks, and that night there was to be a bicentennial concert given by the Albany Symphony Orchestra in the plaza. It attracted large crowds on a warm evening and, afterwards, a spectacular fireworks display rounded off the evening of free entertainment, by which time I was ready to head back to the bus station and continue to Boston. The next day I followed the tourist routes around the city but the highlight for me was a sign outside a graveyard with a warning to the public as follows: "Refrain thine passions thereof, y rubbing of gravestones, y quaffing of alcoholic spirits, y revelling on y lawn and y entering in of thine snarleyyows". So, no messing about in Boston, basically, but I was now back on the road, on my way to Connecticut.

My father had made business trips to the United States, visiting plants in the eastern states, and a contact of his sent an invitation to me to stay for a while. As I happened to be in their vicinity I called him and so began a very pleasant few days at Waterbury, where Walter Cook and his family lived in a luxurious house. It was also an ideal base for visiting New York, Martha's Vineyard and their beach house near Newhaven. During the previous six weeks I had seen evidence of how enterprising and, at least on the surface, how friendly Americans were and Walter's son, John, epitomised this spirit. Studying for a degree, he spent part of his spare time travelling around the world but also found time to run a painting and decorating business which funded his travelling and also his flat in Newport. I stayed with him for two days at the same time as the Queen was calling at Newport on her tour of the USA and Canada (to coincide with the 1976 Olympics). Furthermore, the flat was situated at the edge of a square where the Queen was performing a ceremony so we had a bird's-eye view. A sash window was opened wide enough to allow two of us to peer out and, immediately, we attracted the attention of edgy-looking security officials. Of course, there was no cause for alarm except that, unknown to me, there were no cords for the sash window and, unaware that I was supporting it, moved away, allowing the window to crash down and almost giving the security agents heart failure. Meekly, John opened the window again and gave a gesture that resembled a fawning apology which, in turn, appeared to be accepted by the officials below with a mixture of relief and nervous amusement.

From New England I took another Greyhound bus all along the eastern seaboard to Miami, where cheap flights were available to the Carribean. Soon the mood was set as I relaxed (in so far as that was possible on a plane) on board an Air Jamaica DC9, listening to Typically Tropical's 'Going To Barbados'. Of course, I was bound for Jamaica but, no matter, the song put me in the right frame of mind, which was only disturbed by the taxi ride from Norman Manley International Airport to my hotel in Kingston. In 1976 most taxis there seemed to be British cars of the past - Morris Oxford, Austin Cambridge and Ford Zephyr, none of which were designed for high-speed cornering. For once, sitting in a car was a more alarming experience than flying ! Calm was restored, however, as I showered in my room to the sounds of 'Cool Water' by Marty Robbins before relaxing by the pool. I told Betty, the proprietrix, that I planned to visit Montego Bay the next day but she insisted that I take a taxi to the station as Kingston was not a safe place. Apparently, the economy was in poor shape and there was also a state of emergency that was making life difficult at the moment so, with her words of warning in my mind, I took the taxi in time for the 7am train to Montego Bay. The train was packed and, as far as I could see, I was the only white person. I stood up. I found it easier to appreciate how a coloured individual could feel intimidated in a white community as I looked down the carriage at the sea of non-smiling faces. They did not look like the laid-back sterotypes I expected to see. Perhaps these were some of the very people affected by the current troubles. So I spent most of my time learning a little more about the island as seen from the corridor window. On the

outer edges of Kingston, the shanty towns of corrugated houses and the naked men washing in water channels were evidence of poverty but, once into the open countryside, the natural beauties of Jamaica were a welcome diversion. As the journey of little more than one hundred miles took over six hours there was plenty of time to sample the island's charms. The deeper we penetrated the island the more intense became the appreciation of these charms as banana plantations gave way to lush vegetation, that encroached ever closer to the train, and then the tropical rain forest closed in around us. The most interesting stops were made in the forest clearings where local villagers, some of them balancing large baskets on their heads, would converge on the train and offer fresh tropical fruits to the passengers. I watched to see the reaction of other passengers. No one in my coach bought anything so I too refrained, though I was seriously tempted. The train itself was fairly basic and in the hands of a diesel locomotive, which seemed to sound its horn at everyone known to the driver, as well as the potential hazards along the route.

At Montego Bay I booked into the hotel before strolling down to the beach to admire the shallow, almost turquoise waters, of the Carribean lapping the shoreline. Back in the hotel I chatted to two guys, both deep sea fishermen, and their girlfriends. After a few drinks they invited me to dinner at a club in town. During the evening we all seemed to enjoy the food and drink, the music and dancing, but then something strange happened. I paid a brief call but, on returning to the table, found just one of the girls, Primrose, at her seat. I asked her where the others had gone and, as if it was of no consequence, she replied that they had moved on to another club. I then wondered why she was still at the table and considered the possibility of spending the evening with this attractive Jamaican girl but, still trying to work out this strange situation, I grew wary. I think Primrose understood that I was becoming edgy for she excused herself, but did not return. I don't know if these antics were part of a, possibly, sinister plan but the fun and games continued when I was presented with the bill! I asked to see the manager and discovered, to my surprise, that he was sympathetic. He insisted on taking me back to the hotel as he did not consider it safe to walk back (some island this!). On the way back we looked out for the foursome but, to no avail. It had been an unusual experience, to say the least, and it was with some relief that I boarded the train the next day and savoured the early morning fragrances of the forest, shrouded in layers of mist, as we climbed out of Montego Bay. On my last night in Kingston I sat drinking with four Jamaicans on the terrace, chatting and enjoying the view of the Blue Mountains, then drinking some more and laughing so that we were all quite merry when the proprietrix put in an appearance in her evening dress. It was now my turn to buy a round of drinks, even though my funds were rapidly dwindling, but I was passed caring and, as I walked up to the proprietrix on the way to the bar, I told her that she looked ravishing. She pinched my cheek, affectionately, and said with a broad smile, "why thank you young man". The rest of the evening was a blur but the following morning, when I arrived at the desk to settle my account, I was told that it was on the house. Now I have to say that this is the only time it ever happened to me but it could not have come at a better time. Luckily, much of what I needed to pay for had been pre-booked so travelling was not a problem.

During the next few days I became conscious of stretching to the limit the hospitality of friends I had met in the States. The overnight accommodation they provided allowed me to see Washington and Philadelphia. The journey to the capital was from New York Penn Central station on a Metroliner train, fast and quiet with air conditioning and reclining seats, and all the more impressive as I had yet to experience a ride on the High Speed Train which was just being introduced by British Rail. This was the first of several train trips in the USA, all of them from New York, including an AA train and a D train to the Yankee stadium in the Bronx. Here I saw Pele, almost at the end of his glittering career, play for the New York Cosmos as they beat Dallas Tornados 4-0. There was a great atmosphere inside the stadium as thousands of Italians cheered on their local hero, Seraglio, and vendors mingled with the crowd shouting "Come and getta your ica coola beer". I managed to fulfil another ambition by catching a train from Grand Central station with its huge cathedral-like concourse, the ideal setting for a long-distance journey instead of the local train I took to the outer suburb of Croton-Harmon. It was my last treat before taking the F train from 6th Avenue, out of New York and towards Kennedy Airport. The following day I looked out of the window, as the plane made its descent to Manchester Airport, and noticed how bare the ground appeared after the lush greenery of the eastern States. Admittedly, it had been a prolonged dry summer in England (the driest since 1727 in fact) but the warmth added to the pleasures that I had missed including an ordered way of life, regular sleep and some of my favourite meals. A long-standing desire had now been fulfilled and it was time to satisfy another ambition.

For some years I had been drifting aimlessly, unable to discipline myself to studying at nights for my accountancy exams. If I was to become qualified I would have to return to full-time education and yet I had no clear idea as to what I wanted to do. Then, reading an educational supplement, I noticed an article on property management courses and decided that this was for me. At Oxford Polytechnic there was a practical-based course with the additional benefits of being situated in an historic city, close to the Cotswolds and the Chilterns and only an hour away from London. I was not hopeful of a place because of my low A-Level grades but mature students were being accepted and I certainly came within that category. My doubts were partially overcome when I was chosen for interview but I still needed to make an impression if I was to be sure of gaining a place. While waiting to meet the course tutor I was required to write what I knew about fifty people whose surnames were listed on a form. I remember reading the name 'Rutherford' and thought, initially, of writing down 'Margaret'. I then changed my mind and put down 'Ernest' as I reasoned that it would give a better impression of all-round knowledge. I was happy about all the names but 'Braque', which had me beaten. Believing that it was better to appear positive than to simply leave a blank space I wrote down, impetuously, that 'unless he formed a comedy duo with Brique I hadn't got a clue!' Having submitted the form I began to have second thoughts as to whether it would appear cheeky or arrogant but, by then, it was too late. As I waited outside the tutor's door I heard a loud laugh from inside but could not hear him talking to anyone. Soon he appeared and I was ushered in. Luckily the interview went well and he explained that Braque was one of the artists who created the Cubist movement. In February I was offered a place and a new career beckoned. Together with the worldly experience I had gained from travelling around America I felt that I had reached a watershed in my life and that I had a new sense of direction.

12. THE STUDENT PAUPER

Before returning to student life I spent about three weeks working in accounts departments on a contract basis. The only jobs available through the agency at the time were in Yorkshire but I needed the money and warmed to the idea of travelling along new routes so, in early September 1976, I started to commute to the mining village of Normanton, near Wakefield, on the old Midland main line. Normanton was once an important railway junction with a large shed in steam days but now, like so many railway locations, it was a shadow of its former self and, as I walked up the hill to the office and looked across to the fields of wheat awaiting the combine harvester, I found it difficult to picture the colliery wheel and the pall of smoke drifting skywards from the engine shed. My journey to Normanton had started from Manchester Victoria on the Trans Pennine service to Leeds and then by DMU bound for Sheffield but after a few days I decided to vary the routes so that, returning home one evening, I caught a train at Wakefield Kirkgate and headed south via the scenic Hope Valley line. In doing so I passed through four of the longest tunnels on Britain's railways in one day - at Standedge, Morley, Totley and Cowburn. During my spell at Normanton I also used the Huddersfield-Wakefield line and on the final day returned via Wakefield Westgate to Leeds catching a King's Cross-Leeds express hauled by Deltic No.55 005 *Prince of Wales's Own Regiment of Yorkshire*. This was the first time I had travelled behind one of these hugely impressive machines and I was now keen to have a run behind one at full speed on the East Coast Main Line. I had enjoyed seeing different parts of the country by rail and I was just about to be presented with the ideal opportunity to indulge in that pleasure - the student railcard.

On 23rd September I moved to Oxford and settled in one of the polytechnic's halls of residence at Cotuit Hall, set in very pleasant and secluded surroundings. At the Freshers' Fair I naturally joined the Transport Society and on the following day, aware of the proximity of the Great Western Society's centre at Didcot, took a train there but, as it was closed to the public, there was not much to see. From the station, however, I caught my first glimpse of the new High Speed Trains (HSTs) in action and, standing behind the yellow safety line marked out on the platform, was

immediately impressed as each train bore down on the station at full speed (more than two miles a minute). In a matter of weeks I made use of a special offer, appropriately at £1.25, to travel to Swansea and back on one of the services. Because the coaches were so well insulated, the impression of speed was not quite what I expected but I felt proud of our railway that day because this was not an elite train, it was part of an intensive service that would later spread to many of Britain's main lines.

While spending over two hours at Didcot station admiring the HSTs I also noted a stream of locomotive-hauled trains including six class '50s' (which had recently moved en bloc from the Midland Region to the Western Region), sixteen class '47s' and two class '31s'. During the next few years I would travel behind virtually all the locomotive types that were designed for passenger haulage and the regular Saturday visits I would make to the Cotswolds would provide me with the first opportunity. I would take the train from Oxford to one of the stations on the Worcester line such as Charlbury, Kingham, Moreton-in-the-Marsh or Evesham and either walk to the next station or arrange a circular walk before catching the return train which, at this time, was usually in the hands of a class '47'. During that first autumn term I also made my first forays to London and it was at this time that I saw the last Western hydraulic diesels before their demise after a life span of only fifteen years.

Life in Oxford was fun. Apart from the walks and watching the trains there was the pleasurable round of formal dinners and dances, the occasional Union debate and regular visits to the popular restaurants such as Browns in Woodstock Road where we would sometimes have to queue for up to thirty minutes outside. Life was even more fun when friends were made and in the first few weeks one lad I met, a Pakistani, became a regular snooker opponent. He was full of old-fashioned English phrases but he caused consternation in the games room one evening when, with snooker cue in one hand, he asked those around him if anyone wanted to lick him! Actually I did but only at snooker!

During the Christmas holidays I took another temporary accountancy job, working in a shop in Oldham. The journey from Manchester Victoria was by

DMU and was capable of little variation except via Rochdale, but I busied myself by noting the numbers of class '40s' en route. North Manchester, in particular, was a stronghold for the dwindling numbers of class '40s' and they were seen at Manchester Victoria, Newton Heath depot and on various goods and parcels trains between Manchester and Oldham. In noting the numbers I wondered whether my boyhood interest was returning and I have to admit to being slightly embarrassed about this development. However, my activities fell short of purchasing an Ian Allan trainspotter's book and I reasoned that it was merely idle curiosity that was the cause of the number taking.

Before returning to Oxford I had an important afternoon to spend with a young boy, Christopher, whose father tragically died of a heart attack the previous year at the age of forty. I worked at the same place as his mother on one of my accountancy jobs in Salford and it was late one Monday morning when Margaret walked in, pale and disorientated, to break the news that her husband had died. It is very difficult to offer words of comfort under such circumstances but, from talking to her, I was aware that Christopher's father had promised to take his son to see Manchester United play at Old Trafford but did not live long enough to fulfil that promise. As United were at home on 8th January in the Third Round of the F.A Cup against Walsall I arranged with Margaret to take her son to the match which United won 1-0 but I was able to give him something else which he did not expect, by way of a belated Christmas present. While working for Cancer Relief I had bought a football and arranged for it to be signed by Manchester United players including Bobby Charlton and George Best. The ball was never used and the local branch subsequently ceased operations so here was a golden opportunity to donate it to a good cause and, judging by the look on the boy's face, I knew that the ball had found its rightful owner.

The Transport Society at the polytechnic got into its stride early in 1977 with film shows and visits to Swindon Works and to the T.O.P.S office at Reading, where the movement of wagons was controlled by computer. On my journeys to London, the Cotswolds and home I now noted all the locomotives at the head of my trains and recorded the first class '50' on a Birmingham train from Paddington. They had clearly been displaced from other services by the HSTs as they became regular sights on the Birmingham and Hereford services from Paddington. Early in March, returning to Oxford on the 6.12pm Worcester from Paddington, I was surprised to see two class '50s' at the head of our train. An engineman said he believed that one of the locomotives was returning to Crewe for overhaul but with over 5000 horse power at the front end there was the promise of an exciting run and the distance of sixty-three miles was covered in fifty-five minutes. My visits to London were for a variety of purposes including the theatre (where I was smitten by a young actress, Kate Nelligan, in a National Theatre production, *Tales From The Vienna Woods*), record companies, where I would submit tapes (only to have them rejected), and the various termini which I enjoyed wandering around. At this time King's Cross was my favourite terminus for watching trains as the main expresses were still loco-hauled and, of course, the Deltics continued in charge of the top-line duties. The railcard was also useful when at home for a weekend or on holiday. The journey home from Oxford was either via Crewe or Stoke and at both these centres it was possible to see some of the few remaining examples of the class '24s'. Likewise around the eastern side of Manchester, in particular, these locomotives could be seen with class '25s', '40s' and '76s' (the electric locomotives used on the Woodhead route to Sheffield). It is difficult to say why I developed a growing interest in diesel and electric classes, except that there was still a continuing programme of change on the railways affecting older locomotive types that were now disappearing, together with other aspects and practices of the railway system including lines, semaphore signalling and railway stations, such as Broad Street in London that was clearly being run down. As I took a train along the North London line to Willesden I could not help but notice the weeds growing on the platforms and the paucity of the services suggesting that here was a station at the end of its life.

Although I maintained a keen interest in railways, steam was still my first love and Oxford offered the occasional opportunity to watch the passage of a steam locomotive. One of the saddest moments was the sight of ex-GWR 'Castle' class No.4079 *Pendennis Castle* on its last run before being shipped to Australia. My first year exams started the following day but it didn't stop me standing on the footbridge at Hinksey yard, study notes in one hand and cine camera in the other, to watch *Pendennis Castle* run smoothly past. Sister engine No. 7029 *Clun Castle* was seen at Oxford less than a month later following an Open Day that I attended at Didcot.

As the weather became warmer and flowers could once

Plate 172. In early June 1977 ex-GWR 'Castle' class 4-6-0 No.4079 *Pendennis Castle* left our shores for Australia. On 6th April 1974 it is seen approaching Church Stretton with a southbound train from Shrewsbury. *Photo, Tom Heavyside.*

again be seen at the roadside, so the number of visits into the Cotswolds increased. Many of the walks extended to over twenty miles but a particularly ambitious trek started at Kemble on the Swindon-Gloucester line and finished at Kingham, about thirty miles away. For the longer walks it was important to get the timing right in order to catch the last train back to Oxford. The walk from Kemble started well, under overcast skies, as I made my way through Cirencester and Chedworth to Northleach, but during the afternoon it rained steadily, becoming torrential at times, and for the first time I gave some thought as to whether I would reach Kingham in time. I concluded that it would be touch-and-go so decided on a short cut. I calculated that I could save at least two miles by cutting across fields up to the brow of a hill and then meeting a parallel road that took a more direct course to Kingham. The going was very tough. The rain had turned the ploughed fields into the consistency of a dough and each step I took seemed to gather more of the local clay to my boots. The closer I got to Oxfordshire the more of Gloucestershire I was taking with me - and I could feel myself gaining height! Then one boot was gripped so strongly by the clay that my foot came out and, in the

process of trying to steady myself, I lost balance and the shoeless foot landed firmly in the mud. Far from saving time I was now literally in the thick of it and steadily losing the battle to catch the last train. On finally reaching the road I tried to run but it was only in fits and starts and I was now faced with another problem. It was dark and in the country that means very dark, so I resigned myself to missing the train and at least staying in one piece. Briefly I wondered whether I would be capable of walking an additional twenty miles to Oxford and possibly arriving in broad daylight the following morning, bedraggled and extremely weary. As it happened I only missed the last train by about fifteen minutes but I now had to decide how to proceed. I hovered around the entrance to the nearby Langston Arms Hotel, wiping the excess clay off my boots and estimating how much a taxi would be likely to cost when, on a whim, I rang the doorbell. I was greeted by the proprietrix in her evening dress. Saturday night appeared to be dinner-dance evening and I have no idea what she must have thought when I stood facing her at the door soaking, muddy and tired but when she told me that a single room cost £5 I was happy to take it and to my surprise she allowed me into the hotel. My room

150

had its own shower and bathroom, a television and a teasmaid. It was heaven! I had a thorough wash and even washed the mud from the socks and the boots in the shower but then spent a good fifteen minutes ensuring that everywhere was immaculate as it had been before. Finally I made a cup of tea, watched some television in bed and retired early, sinking into a deep sleep. It had been an unexpected but thoroughly satisfying and comforting end to the day. The following morning I woke up to the sound of birds in the middle of the Oxfordshire countryside, enjoyed a full English breakfast and then went for a leisurely stroll in the sunshine. It had been one of the most memorable of overnight stops and it was with some reluctance that I set off down the road to the station to catch the 11.08am as far as Oxford.

During my first year at college I walked about 270 miles, mainly in the Cotswolds, and, thankfully, only once did I miss the train. By way of contrast to that walk I noted in my diary that 30th April was one of the most enjoyable days for being out in the open air when I pursued a course from Moreton-in-the Marsh via Chipping Campden and Broadway to Evesham. I regard myself as a man of simple pleasures and, for me, there is little to surpass the enjoyment of walking in pleasant countryside on a fine spring day. On that occasion I saw a swallow for the first time that year and heard the first cuckoo and, from the returning train hauled by class '47' No.47 147, spotted the first fox I had ever seen in a field near Charlbury. My diary also records that on the following morning I was up at 5am to take part, with friends, in one of the popular traditions in Oxford - the celebrating of May morning. We gathered at Magdalen Bridge to hear the traditional hymn-singing from Magdalen Tower at dawn before taking part in the revelry in the streets. There was a colourful mixture of floats, Morris Dancers, outrageous costumes, boaters and bonnets while, in the squares and side streets, champagne and breakfasts were served and, on the river, the punts were in demand. I, too, tried my hand at punting, once the exams were out of the way, and found the experience of punting upstream to a riverside pub for lunch to be a very civilised one. On one occasion a group of us were caught in a thunderstorm which, in

Plate 173. A westbound coal train for Fiddlers Ferry passes Hadfield behind the usual combination of a pair of class '76s'. Here we see Nos.76 010 & 76 012 on 22nd July 1976.

Photo, Tom Heavyside.

hindsight, was probably not very bright as the long metal punt pole seemed to stretch half way to the sky and could well have given us an enlightening experience! Now that the hard work and the exams were behind us we could enjoy the highlight of the year when the long days and warmer weather allowed us to get out and enjoy ourselves to the full until on 1st July, the day when Virginia Wade won her Wimbledon Singles title, I discovered that I had passed my first year's exams. Euphoria broke out among the successful students. There was a barbecue, dancing and, most of all, a great sense of relief. Just two more hurdles to jump.

During the summer holidays I returned to contract accountancy but also found time to indulge in some railway travel, my first trip being on 11th July when the 'Royal Scot' express celebrated its fiftieth anniversary. I saw the northbound train passing through Wigan behind class '87' No.87 001, named *Royal Scot* that morning at Euston. Early in September I attended the Derby Railway Works Open Day noting the old steam locomotives on static display as well as new class '56' diesels and the remains of class '44' 'Peak' No.44 003 *Skiddaw*, which I first saw while trainspotting at the newly-opened Manchester Piccadilly station. Then, as D3, it was in tandem with D1 on a parcels train. From Derby I decided to have a look at Toton depot for the first time and here there were four other class '44s', Nos.44 002, 5, 8 and 9 together with a class '20' in faded green livery and, surely, one of the last locomotives in B.R. stock still to be carrying this colour. A week later Joyce and I spent a few days in the Isle of Man and, while touring around the small island, I had the chance to experience the varied railway transport,

from electric tramcars to Ramsay and up Snaefell to steam along the line to Port Erin and Castletown, travelling outwards behind *Kissack* and returning behind *Maitland*.

1977 was quite an eventful year as Joyce and I got engaged in August with parties at her parents' house and at my grandmother's home in Saltburn, where the family gathering included my cousin Clive, on a rare visit from Hong Kong. One person missing from that occasion was my great-uncle Herbert who died a few months earlier at the grand age of ninety. In the same year, Ron Maltby, a cousin of my father became the first of my parents' generation to die. He was a man full of amusing anecdotes including the story of when he and his family were on a caravan site in wet weather, when a neighbour of his on the site became stuck in the mud while attempting to drive out. In his own inimitable style he went over to push the car out of the mud and, as he pushed, the back wheels were just lifted out sufficiently for them to spin round, spraying Ron with a liberal coating of mud. Nothing daunted he continued to push until the car lurched forward and, leaning at a good sixty degrees from perpendicular, promptly fell face down into the mud. As always he took things very calmly and was probably content in the knowledge that he had helped a fellow traveller who, incidentally, drove off unaware of Ron's mishap.

My second year in Oxford, when I shared a house with three friends, followed the format of the first except that there were more theatre visits, more train trips, and less walking. I saw plays in London including the National Theatre's production of *The Country Wife* with Albert Finney and Richard Johnson, and *The Old Country*

Plate 174. Manchester Piccadilly station with a first generation West Coast electric locomotive, class '83' No.83 011, at the head of thirteen coaches comprising the 10.40 am Saturdays-only to Paignton on 6th August 1977. *Photo, Author.*

starring Alec Guinness, while at the Oxford Playhouse it was a pleasure to see John Gielgud, but one of the most enjoyable productions was by a local amateur group, The Fool's Theatre Company, featuring my valuation lecturer. This was the same tutor who once wrote on one of my valuation projects, 'a simply hideous error perhaps unprecedented in its vileness!' Naturally, therefore, I came to have a good laugh at him but 'Salomepantomime', a mime version of Oscar Wilde's *Salome*, turned out to be a very pleasant surprise, not only because of the quality of the acting but also due to the simple yet effective and atmospheric production. That night the company played to an audience of thirteen but as we returned to see later plays of theirs it was gratifying to be a part of larger audiences and, by the following June, they deservedly received a substantial grant and were about to turn professional. The Cambridge Footlights Revue also visited the Playhouse with *Stage Fright,* which featured a young Clive Anderson as director and co-writer among others, and typical lines such as 'you play ball with us and we'll scratch yours' seemed to bear the Anderson trademark. Entertainment was never lacking in this city and if there was nothing at the theatre then alternatives were available - a concert at the Sheldonian Theatre or perhaps chamber music in the Holywell Rooms and, of course, the cinema. There was a trendy little picture house that we used to frequent off the Cowley Road called the Penultimate Picture Palace, a black-and-white building that screened cult movies and films of the great comics such as Chaplin, Laurel and Hardy and The Marx Brothers. It was here that I came to enjoy the humour of Woody Allen and watched most of his early films. His reference to the brain being his second favourite organ is forever etched upon my memory. One did not need to go to the theatre or cinema for a good laugh. There was humour even on an Oxford bus. Luckily it was at night when there were few passengers to see me grinning but it was a simple 'No Smoking' sign that had some of its transferred letters carefully etched out to give a different message from that intended. The original sign stated that "The Executive will press for the highest penalties against all offenders" but, as altered by some mischievous wag now read "The Executive will press his penis against all offenders."

With the benefit of my railcard I travelled further afield. In the autumn I fulfilled an ambition by purchasing a ticket to Newcastle on the 'Flying Scotsman' express hauled by Deltic No.55 005 *Prince of Wales's Own Regiment of Yorkshire*. I noticed the first HSTs on the East Coast Main Line and realised that this was going to be the last year of locomotive haulage for this famous train. I returned as far as York on the 'Aberdonian', hauled by another Deltic No.55 020 *Nimbus* and, from there, took a train to Manchester. Compared with this day out, the trip on the 'Royal Scot' in February behind class '87' No.87 022 from Euston to Preston was something of an anti-climax, especially as it was routed via Northampton, thus adding twenty minutes to the journey time. On 5th May I made a circular trip to Peterborough and Cambridge, primarily to see the last Pullman trains on the East Coast Main Line. From Birmingham I caught a Norwich train behind a class '31' which provided steam heating. Much of this cross-country route was new to me so I sat back and enjoyed the contrasts between the gently rolling countryside of the east Midlands and the flat land east of Peterborough known as the Fens. The service at that time may have been unique in that it travelled briefly along the West Coast Main Line at Nuneaton, the Midland Main Line at Leicester and the East Coast Main Line at Peterborough, where I caught a glimpse of the last southbound 'Yorkshire Pullman' behind Deltic No.55 002 *The Black Watch*. Returning to Peterborough from my first visit to Cambridge, and in very wet conditions, I spent over two hours observing the trains including the 'Talisman', which was now an HST, the last northbound 'Yorkshire Pullman' hauled by class '47' No.47 433, and the final 'Hull Pullman', in the hands of class '47' No.47 410. The class '44' No.44 009, passing through on freight, was the last of these locomotives I saw in service but Deltics were still in charge of some Newcastle and Edinburgh expresses as well as the 'Aberdonian' on which I travelled behind Deltic No.55 007 *Pinza* to London.

There can surely be no city in the world with so many termini as London and during my three years at college I took a train into or out of all of them except Fenchurch Street (for some reason that escapes me). On one visit I decided to call at all the southern termini, starting with a train out of Victoria to Clapham Junction, where trains seemed to stop or pass every few seconds, and they were not all multiple units but included a class '25', '47', '73', '74' and '33s'. From Clapham I took a train to Waterloo and changed there for Charing Cross. Then I shuttled back and forth across the Thames to London Bridge, Cannon Street, London Bridge again and, finally, Holborn Viaduct. From there I walked across to

Liverpool Street, crossing the path of Margaret Thatcher on the way. She was about to climb the steps to the Bank of England while I was about to purchase an awayday return to Stratford, east London. Why ? Well I enjoyed the ambience of stations and I was curious to travel along new lines. Furthermore I could achieve this relatively cheaply and it kept me out of mischief before the theatre performance in the evening.

For obvious reasons Paddington was the most often-used of the London termini but I was not accustomed to catching trains from this station at 6.10am! In order to reach Penzance on a day trip, though, this meant sacrificing a sizeable portion of my night's sleep. The only train providing a connection actually departed from Oxford at 3.58am! Whatever the reason was for a train at this time I was the only passenger until we reached Reading. There was an hour's wait at Paddington before the train left behind class '47' No.47 008, and standing around at that time of the morning in early March was not the ideal preparation for a day out but, as the train warmed up and we sped through Berkshire and Wiltshire, my attention was drawn to the scenery along what, for me, was a new route. Naturally one of the highlights was the famous Devon coastline around Dawlish and Teignmouth and my thoughts turned briefly to that day when, on holiday, I sat in a cafe with my family, mainly watching steam trains passing through Dawlish station back in 1961. I was curious to see how the class '47' would perform on the Devon banks and was surprised that the gradient up Dainton brought the train to crawling pace, certainly

slow enough to admire the primroses that had opened up alongside the track. Another delight was the crossing of Isambard Kingdom Brunel's slim and graceful Royal Albert Bridge, linking Devon and Cornwall at Saltash. I had forgotten about the impressive cathedral at Truro but it made me realise just how fascinating a route this was and I remembered that, when I was a child, one could buy a little booklet showing places of interest to be seen from trains such as the 'Royal Scot', the 'Elizabethan' and the 'Cornish Riviera', the booklet for which would have been useful on this occasion. At Penzance I feel sure that most of the passengers would have remained in the town but I caught the first train out to St. Ives and experienced my first trip along one of the few remaining branch lines in Cornwall. After wandering around the streets and alleyways of this seaside town I returned along the branch line as far as St. Erth, the junction with the main line, and where the palm trees gave the place a tropical feel. From here I boarded the 'Cornish Riviera' for the last ten miles of its journey to Penzance. Like the 'Flying Scotsman' it would soon become an HST but on this occasion the train arrived twenty minutes late behind class '50' No.50 001. There was no nameboard and no destination boards, just the image of photographs or pictures in the railway books of my childhood to remind me that the train bore a famous name. Incidentally, I got back to Oxford at 2am having been up for almost twenty three hours. I was glad it was Sunday morning.

The Transport Society's trip to Bickershaw colliery, near Wigan, to see industrial steam in action, was

Plate 175. One of the 25 kv EMU units built to a standard B.R. design and introduced in 1966 for the Euston, Birmingham, Manchester and Liverpool services, calls at Timperley. This is a class '310' unit No.310 046, a distinctive feature of which were the front 'wrap-around' windows. *Photo, Author.*

Plate 176. A London-Edinburgh service is about to resume its journey from Darlington station on 10th August 1978 behind 'Deltic' No.55 011 *The Royal Northumberland Fusiliers*, shortly before High Speed Trains took over the Edinburgh and Newcastle services.

Photo, Author.

another long day. I have to admit that I had never given industrial locomotives much thought but here we were seeking out one of the last examples. One thing I remember vividly about this trip in the polytechnic van was drifting off to sleep and then waking up to find my colleague overtaking on the right-hand side of a blind bend. Still in the process of coming round I shouted "what the hell are you doing?" to which he replied, over the laughter in the back, "overtaking on a dual carriageway!" I saw the funny side of it eventually and the large saddle tank *Warrior* made a stirring sight as it climbed up the gradient with about two hundred tons of coal behind it and belching out large quantities of smoke. Watching the pit wheels turn I reflected that here was another piece of history drawing to a close - the end of industrial steam and the end of the Lancashire coalfield.

I was still receiving rejections for the music tapes and, at the beginning of 1978, decided to take matters more into my own hands by arranging for Pamela Carter to record her compositions in a studio and for a batch of cassette tapes to be run off and then sold at clubs where she played. I liked her material of childrens' and folk songs so, early in January 1978, we visited a local studio called Smile Recording Studios and, in the space of an afternoon, she sang fourteen songs for an album to be called 'Lifescapes' at her suggestion. Two hundred copies of the tape were produced but few were sold. In time I dare say she would have sold the whole batch but in the meantime she married a descendant of Dick Turpin and became a farmer's wife in Yorkshire. There was something about that year for marriages as my

cousin Clive in Hong Kong married in March, my brother Nigel married towards the end of August in Telford's church at Bridgnorth and Joyce and I tied the knot on 9th September in Stockport. There was no stag night but a meal with my best man, Roger Thornton, an old school friend, in a former Brighton Belle Pullman car in the sleepy hamlet of Rowarth in Derbyshire. The honeymoon was in Scotland but, for once, we were not blessed with good weather and I remember driving along a bleak moorland road in torrential rain and total darkness between Moffatt and St. Mary's Loch where we spent the first night at the Rodono Hotel. Funny though it may seem now, we could not see the front door. I think I lapped the place twice with suitcases before stumbling upon a door at the back. The rooms all bore names of fish. We were in Pike. I was glad that we were not in Chub. Opening the curtains the following morning a lovely view of the loch greeted us and the surroundings looked altogether more appealing. Apart from a brief visit to Edinburgh Waverley station while Joyce looked in some of the shops on Princes Street, railways, appropriately, played no part on our honeymoon, but a few weeks later on a weekend visit to Manchester, I drove over to Strines, near Stockport, to watch 'Royal Scot' class, No.6115 *Scots Guardsman,* in steam, hauling its first passenger train since withdrawal at the beginning of 1966. It only enjoyed a brief fling in steam before being sidelined once again, thus depriving a generation of enthusiasts from seeing it tackle the Settle and Carlisle route where, in the words of Eric Treacy, there was no locomotive more fitting than the 'Royal Scot'. While in that part of Greater Manchester I

155

paid a further visit to Guide Bridge and, once again, saw three of the older classes of locomotives still in action including class '24' No.24 047, class '40' No.40 013 and class '76s' in the nearby sidings.

Joyce and I were now settled in the ground floor flat of a pleasant terraced house in Fairacres Road, off the Iffley Road in Oxford. She found a job quickly with a firm of accountants while I had started my third and final year on the Estate Management course. Life continued as before - a round of theatre visits, concerts, parties, the occasional formal dinner and the walks, but we also embarked on a little entertaining in our new home, mainly for friends from college and relations. We managed some day trips to Norwich, Cambridge, Torquay and, of course, London but also spent a few days exploring the Isle of Wight for the first time. Aware that my railcard had only months to run before it expired, I also continued my visits to railway lines that I had not previously travelled along such as the Waterloo-Exeter main line and the Exmouth and Barnstaple branches. I also regularly walked the short distance to South Hinksey to note the trains and their timings.

For some years I had purchased copies of the current B.R. timetables and I was curious to compare the scheduled passing times with the actual times, to assess punctuality. For instance, in the space of about ninety minutes on 15th December 1978 I recorded nineteen trains including eight freight trains (four coal trains presumably for Didcot Power Station, two freightliners, a bulk cement train and a mixed freight). Of the passenger trains four were late, the poorest timekeeper being the notorious Newcastle-Poole service which was fifteen minutes behind time on this occasion but almost invariably late. I revisited this location on a further ten occasions around Christmas at about the same time between 11.45am and 1.15pm and, of the largely locomotive-hauled trains, it was class '47' haulage that dominated with the occasional class '31' and single sightings of a class '46' No.46 021 on a southbound freight and a class '40' No.40 057 on car wagons. When the new timetable started on 14th May 1979 I paid a further visit to Hinksey at about the same time of day, noting some new trains including the first-ever Liverpool-Paddington and Manchester-Brighton services, both behind class 47s. Interestingly, the Newcastle-Poole train had now become the Manchester-Poole but with no transformation of the poor timekeeping (twenty-six minutes late that day) while class 56s were now in charge of the coal trains.

The trains to and from London, especially the Worcester and Hereford services (by now largely in the hands of class '50s') were, in my experience, regularly on time. With the start of the new timetable I paid a few visits to London where I would inevitably call in on King's Cross. The long-distance trains were now HSTs and the Deltics had now entered the final phase of their working lives, handling the York and Hull services including the 5.05pm 'Hull Executive' which, at that time, was the fastest locomotive-hauled train ever in this country. On my final visit to this terminus, at the end of June, I decided on a return trip to Peterborough but the York train I caught was in the hands of class '47' No.47 426. I was in luck, though, on the return journey as this had Deltic No.55 007 *Pinza* at the front end and, as a bonus, the locomotive rostered for the 'Hull Executive' was sister engine No.55 008 *The Green Howards*, the only member of the class I had not previously seen. When visiting London I would usually return on the 6pm Hereford, invariably a class '50' duty. It was on this service that I once suffered some embarrassment when I crossed my legs only to knock over a loose-fitting table support, causing newspapers and magazines of fellow passengers to slide down into the central corridor. Thankfully this incident took place early in the journey, before teas and coffees had arrived! This non-stop service to Oxford was, in fact, the fastest train of the day between the two cities and a week before my finals I was treated to a truly exhilarating run, to rival the performance of the 'Hull Executive'. Class '50' No.50 023 *Howe* was required on this occasion to make two unscheduled stops at Reading and Didcot and reached its first port of call in just twenty three minutes, at a remarkable average speed of 93mph. Three minutes were spent here together with a brief stop at Didcot but still we arrived in Oxford in fifty-seven minutes!

In 1979 Paddington celebrated its 125th anniversary and, to mark the occasion, a special train behind ex-GWR 'King' class No.6000 *King George V* ran to Didcot. It was due to return to Paddington but developed axle-box trouble and the return journey was taken over by one of the ubiquitous class '47s'. Thirty minutes after the 'King' departed from Paddington I caught the Weston-Super-Mare HST which overhauled the steam train well before reaching Didcot! Also on display at Paddington was a 'Hall' No.5900 *Hinderton Hall* which, two days later, took a special train to Birmingham. I filmed it at Heyford as it struggled up the gradient, after a signal check, with eleven coaches, causing heavy delays to following service trains. I wondered how it would perform on Hatton bank!

The culmination of three years' work came on 29th June 1979 when the results were posted on the notice board, but not until 5.45pm, prolonging a day full of tension. However, all ended well when our names appeared in the list of examination passes and the sense of relief was clearly visible on everyone's faces. It had been one of the most important moments of my life and in the evening Joyce and I called on friends Jon and Rob at Cotuit Hall, where I had spent my first year, and attended the end-of-year barbecue. We ate, drank champagne and danced before making our final farewells and disappearing into the darkness, like in a movie. Friends and colleagues over the past three years would now be preparing to return to their respective homes and begin their working lives. Very soon all would be eerily quiet again and in a matter of two short weeks it would be our turn as well, having accepted a post with a firm of Chartered Surveyors in Liverpool.

The three years I had spent at Oxford had been the happiest of my life. I had worked sufficiently hard to

Plate 177. The changing scene at King's Cross as Deltic No.55 011 *The Royal Northumberland Fusiliers*, is ready to depart with the 2.05pm to York while the High Speed Train will form the next Newcastle service on 21st June 1979. *Photo, Author.*

gain a degree and enjoyed myself into the bargain. There had always been stimulating and amusing company, lovely countryside anytime I cared to venture out, plenty of entertainment to enjoy on a shoestring, and London had been accessible yet always at arm's length. Oxford would be a hard act to follow.

Plate 178. On the 125th anniversary of the opening of Paddington station ex-GWR 'King' class 4-6-0 No.6000 *King George V*, departs Paddington with the 'Paddington 125 Special' to Didcot at 11.15am on 1st March 1979. The author caught a High Speed Train at 11.45am and still reached Didcot, 53 miles away, before the steam train.

Photo, Peter Fitton.

13. LIVER BUDS

On returning to the north we lived, initially, with Joyce's parents in Stockport. I commuted daily into Liverpool knowing that I had two weeks in which to find suitable accommodation, before starting work for my new employers. It was a frustrating business and we were forced to find a cheap hotel near the city centre, at first. Luckily, by the end of the first week we found a clean and modern flat off Smithdown Road at an acceptable rent and, by the second week, we were able to feel a little more settled.

My first trips into Liverpool by train enabled me to grasp quickly the range of motive power on view at Lime Street station. On the first day I was surprised to see one of the Glasgow-Edinburgh push-pull class '47s' No.47 707 *Holyrood* (possibly running-in after overhaul at Crewe) and, during the next two weeks, noted a class '40' and class '46' as well as the more usual class '47s'. There was also the full range of WCML electric locomotive classes. However, I was not prepared for the sight that greeted me late in July as I returned to Lime Street after another unsuccessful day of house hunting. On arrival in the morning I noted the only green class '40', No.40 106, but surely it was unprecedented to see a Deltic, No.55 017 *The Durham Light Infantry*. There was sufficient interest from enthusiasts and railwaymen alike to suggest that this was the first such visit or, at least, a recent innovation. It had arrived on a Newcastle-Liverpool service and was to return on the 5.05pm to Newcastle. Though it meant over an hour's wait I decided to travel on the train as far as Manchester. One of the features of the train services here, at this time, was the simultaneous departures of several London and either York or Newcastle trains. So it was at 5.05pm when a London express, behind class '86' No.86 007, left as we pulled out of the terminus. The electric engine drew quickly ahead of us but, as we plunged into the tunnels, the Deltic pulled out all the stops and made a sensational climb, catching up the London express just as we burst out of the tunnels at Edge Hill. By milepost two I was timing our speed at 65mph and we briefly topped 80mph before slowing down for the first stop at St. Helens Junction, where we arrived with three minutes to spare. Despite a signals check on Chat Moss and a dead stand, we drew to a halt at Victoria station five minutes before departure time. On a route not renowned for fast running this had seemed an impressive performance and my appetite had been whetted. I tried to get out to Lime Street at least one lunchtime a week to record the motive power on view. Throughout 1979 most of the Newcastle and York services were in the hands of class '47s' but Deltics were occasionally seen as well as class '45s', '46s' and even class '40s'. Standing at the outer end of the platform, looking towards the high cutting and the tunnels, it was easy to imagine an earlier steam age. Although this was now a diesel and electric era there was still a tinge of excitement when the simultaneous departures were made.

The satisfaction I felt at having some form of qualification was quickly tempered on discovering that my starting salary would be less than I was earning nearly five years previously, and there had been inflation in the meantime! We could not afford a car and had no television but made our own fun at home, read books and, after work, went out to the theatre where, on Monday nights, it was possible to get two tickets for the price of one in the rear circle. In fact, we had a regular routine on theatre night of meeting at the Pier Head after work, catching the Birkenhead ferry across the Mersey (good fun on stormy nights) and calling at the bus station cafe, next to the ferry terminal, for an egg and chips and a cup of coffee. Yes, we knew how to live! We would then return to Liverpool and get to the Playhouse Theatre in plenty of time for the performance. It was here where we first saw a Willy Russell play, *One For The Road*, still one of his funniest as far as I'm concerned. There were regular visits to the Philharmonic Hall to see the Royal Liverpool Philharmonic Orchestra perform a range of orchestral works (a young Simon Rattle was assistant conductor there for a time), and there was a good selection of travelling plays, operas and 'pop' concerts at the Empire or Royal Court Theatre.

Although the flat was comfortable we knew that this was not a part of Liverpool in which we wanted to live and, in any event, we wanted to buy our own house instead of paying rent to the landlord for the privilege of having a roof over our heads. We kept our eyes peeled for suitable locations and showed interest in one or two properties but we knew immediately, when we inspected the house on Belgrave Road, St. Michael's Hamlet, that we had found a suitable home that was spacious, in a suitable environment and convenient for commuting. In fact, the four-bedroomed terraced house was just two hundred yards from St. Michael's station and a similar distance to the main Aigburth Road into the centre. It backed on to a conservation area and was situated near shops, restaurants and the large expanse of Sefton Park. As the price was within our range we acted quickly and, by May 1980, we moved into the first house that we could truly call our own. From that month I started commuting from St. Michael's station, which had recently been re-opened with the completion of the new underground loop line that connected the old Central station, Exchange station (renamed Moorfields) and Lime Street with the Wirral, Southport and Garston lines. Initially, services were run by the ageing electric trains dating from the nineteen-thirties but, soon, these were replaced by new trains drafted in from the Southern Region. Until we left the flat, however, I continued to use the historic Edge Hill station, then undergoing extensive restoration to its original condition (as far as possible), because that year was its 150th anniversary. Indeed, it was and still is the oldest station in the world in continuous use. It handled only local services including the Wigan diesel multiple units that I caught every day into the city, except for one occasion in the winter when, surprisingly, the usual stock was replaced by a class '40' No.40 078 and six Mark 1 coaches.

Liverpool was the place to be in 1980 for railway enthusiasts as the 150th Anniversary Celebrations, to mark the opening of the Liverpool-Manchester Railway, were taking place. Edge Hill station was, historically, a most important structure but a series of events was planned with the highlight being the locomotive cavalcade at Rainhill in May. Things got off to an excellent start when I managed to buy a return ticket to Manchester Victoria behind ex-LNER 'A3' *Flying Scotsman*. This was my first main-line trip behind a preserved steam locomotive and, as far as I am aware, the first steam departure from Lime Street station since that last BR train on 11th August 1968. Large crowds were present to watch the famous engine and its train of ten coaches depart into the gloom of the tunnels and cuttings, shrouded in smoke and steam. The journey itself was uneventful but, as we picked up speed across Chat Moss on the way back, the smoke drifting down to the undulating telegraph wires, I thought of those childhood journeys behind similar locomotives on the East Coast Main Line when I would hear that familiar three-cylinder exhaust beat. Passing through Olive Mount Cutting on the approach to Edge Hill I reflected on my good fortune to be travelling behind one of the world's most famous locomotives on one of the world's most historic lines and at a budget price. That's the way to sell tickets!

Most of the celebrations took place in the summer and, on 24th May, I caught a train to Rainhill to see the Cavalcade, featuring replicas of three of the contestants in the original Rainhill Trials. This time, however, the history books were re-written as it was *Sans Pareil* which ran under its own steam and not *Rocket*, which suffered a derailment and did not run on that day. *Novelty* was carried on a low loader. Naturally, there was greater emphasis on the locomotives of the

Plate 179. In 1979 the Deltics started to appear in Liverpool on services from Newcastle and York, having been displaced from most of the London-Newcastle services by the High Speed Trains. On 16th October 1981 Deltic No.55 002 *The King's Own Yorkshire Light Infantry* is seen waiting to take charge of the 14.05 to Newcastle.

Photo, Gerry Bent.

Plate 180. One of the class '507' units No.507 032, arrives at Aigburth station, soon after introduction of this class on the Garston-Liverpool-Southport services in the early 1980s.

Photo, D.J.Sweeney.

Plate 181. At this time there were regular, simultaneous departures at five past the hour of trains for Euston and for the north-east. On 9th January 1980, class '47' No.47 436 is seen heading into the tunnels with the 1.05pm to York, side-by-side with an unidentified class '86' on the 1.05pm to Euston.

Photo, Author.

Plate 182. From time to time all the types of West Coast electric locomotives could be seen at Lime Street. At rest alongside platform 1 are two of the first generation types in the form of class '82' No.82 007 and class '83' No.83 001, on 23rd January 1980. *Photo, Author.*

Plate 183. On a wet 29th January 1980 the twin Napier engines of Deltic No.55 019 *Royal Highland Fusiliers,* erupt into action in getting the 1.05p.m to York away from platform 5 at Lime Street as a DMU for Wigan North Western prepares to depart from the adjacent platform.

Photo, Author.

constituent parts of the LMS and its antecedents such as *Lion* and *Hardwicke*, but engines from around the country appeared, while the latest in motive power was represented by the Advanced Passenger Train, due to appear in service later that year. Another major aspect of that year's celebrations was the Grand Exposition held at Liverpool Road station, Manchester, where I took the opportunity of a short ride (oozing history) in a replica Liverpool and Manchester Railway 3rd class wagon behind *Lion* within the confines of the world's oldest station (though, unlike Edge Hill, not in continuous use). There was a feast of steam in Liverpool that year and few more impressive sights than ex-LMS 'Coronation' Pacific *Duchess of Hamilton* on, first, the 'Anniversary Express' and, then, on a train commemorating one hundred and fifty years of the Travelling Post Office. The locomotive looked quite majestic as it stood at platform seven (the London platform), thus renewing its aquaintance with the city that was its base for many years.

My enjoyment of trains and railways in general extended well beyond the celebrations that year. As well as visiting Lime Street station regularly I paid visits to various parts of the country where I had not hitherto been and began to time trains more often. As we returned to Manchester to visit our parents every month the 6.05pm York express was often timed, the fastest journey being a net time of 34 minutes and 28 seconds for the 30.5 miles behind class '47' No.47 402. This was marginally faster than the Deltic run the previous year. Perhaps the most exhilarating run at this time was from Crewe to Lime Street behind class '87' No.87 004 *Britannia* on a train from Birmingham. It was late

leaving Crewe at 10.20pm and, after spending a minute at Runcorn and five minutes in the tunnels beyond Edge Hill, drew to a standstill at 10.52pm, a remarkable net time of around 26 minutes for this 35.5 mile section of track (an average of in excess of 80 mph). Lunchtime visits became even more interesting with the start of the new timetable when an arrival from Barrow and a departure for Edinburgh supplemented the London, Birmingham and north-east departures in the space of a lunch hour. Even on house inspections north of the city I would sometimes see a container train crossing the dock road, on its way to the Seaforth container terminal, behind a class '40' or '47'.

The opening of the Tyne and Wear Metro in 1980 opened a new chapter in suburban rail travel while other lines were living on borrowed time. With this in mind I visited the branch line to Clayton West and also travelled to Hull to catch a ferry across the Humber to New Holland Pier, before the opening of the fabulous Humber Road Bridge. The signs at New Holland Pier were still in the dark blue Eastern Region colours but the rest of the station was in a neglected condition. Nevertheless it was interesting to travel new routes, especially in an area that I knew little about. As a child I had visited Cleethorpes in August and remember a line of excursion trains at the terminus but, on this occasion, a couple of DMUs seemed indicative of the times. Before leaving the town I wandered around the centre and noticed a travel agent with the curiously self-defeating title of Spurn World Travel! Another trip I made at the same time was to Basingstoke on business.

Class 50s had now been drafted into this region to breathe new life into the Waterloo-Exeter service and

Plate 184. 1980 was a special year for railway enthusiasts on Merseyside as the 150th Anniversary of the opening of the Liverpool & Manchester Railway was commemorated by a number of events, one of the first of which was a Liverpool-Manchester special train hauled by ex-LNER 'A3' Pacific No.4472 *Flying Scotsman*. It was the first steam-hauled train to be seen at Lime Street since the last steam special in 1968 and, in this splendid picture, we see it entering Lime Street station from the sandstone tunnels and cuttings on its return run on 12th March 1980.

Photo, Peter Fitton.

my train was hauled by class 50 No.50 018 *Resolution*. The return journey was also interesting as it was the first time I had travelled on a push-pull service with diesel locomotives (apart from the HSTs), the locomotive in question being class 33 No.33 115 and a 4TC set from Salisbury. What I remember most of that day, however, was sitting in a department store in Basingstoke with a cup of coffee and trying to open one of those three-cornered mini packets of milk, just sufficient to provide a white coffee. Having removed the seal over the aperture I made the fatal mistake of squeezing the packet, only to be at the receiving end of a jet of milk that squirted into my face and then dripped down my jacket. Hoping that this moment of unintentional slapstick had gone unnoticed, I wiped my eyes and focused on my surroundings, only to find that everyone

else in the cafeteria was facing opposite to me and, no doubt, a few of them enjoyed the entertainment at my expense!

Returning now to my trip behind 'Flying Scotsman' in March, I should have mentioned that the day ended on an even higher note when I was presented with a ticket for the League Cup Final at Wembley, the following Saturday. A colleague of Joyce's happened to be a season ticket holder at Everton (his wife, however, was a committed Liverpool fan - hardly a recipe for marital harmony) and was able to obtain a ticket for Wembley. As the finalists were Nottingham Forest and Wolves, however, the ticket was of no interest to him but, in characteristic generosity, he passed it on to me and I thoroughly enjoyed the spectacle of Wolves beating Nottingham Forest 1-0 (scored by Andy Gray) to take their first trophy since the Cup Final of 1960. Perhaps Nottingham Forest had more important games on their mind as they went on to retain the European Cup. Liverpool, needless to say, ended their league campaign with yet another Championship trophy, taking their tally of league titles to four out of the last five. For Liverpool, though, the Shankly era was drawing to a close and, in September 1981, he died, less than a year after another Liverpool legend had his life cut short by an assassin's bullet in New York. That morning, in December, we heard the news of John Lennon's death on the *Today* programme and, of course, the placards in the city centre were full of the dramatic headlines. At lunchtime I walked down to Matthew Street, site of the Cavern Club, where a group of people had gathered to lay flowers below the memorial to the Beatles.

In one way or another Liverpool seemed to pass through troubled times. Unemployment was high in the area and a large rally of over one hundred thousand people assembled in the city in the November to hear speakers denounce Government policies. Some people cite unemployment and others social deprivation as the cause of the riots that gave Liverpool an unjustifiably bad name. Rioting began in Brixton, earlier in the year, and manifested itself in Bristol the previous year but the three nights of violence, firstly around the Upper Parliament Street area of Toxteth and, later, in Dingle seemed to attract a disproportionate amount of press attention. Unfortunately, a policeman was killed in the clashes and several buildings were destroyed but the rioting was very localized and, although we lived about one mile away from the troubled area, there was no hint of any disturbance to the normal routine except that a badminton match near the Dingle was cancelled as a precaution. Margaret Thatcher visited the city the following week to survey the damage and to speak at

Plate 185. A variety of motive power could be seen at Lime Street in charge of the north-eastern services at the time. Apart from Deltics and class '47s' there was also the occasional appearance of class '40s', '45's and '46s'. On 20th February 1980, class '40' No.40 117 is seen awaiting departure from platform 5 with the 1.05pm to York while class '85' No.85 016, is about to move away from the station precincts prior to taking up its next turn of duty.

Photo, Author.

Plate 186. Class '84' No.84 003, stands at platform 6 at Lime Street in between empty stock duties. On the right is class '47' No,47 542 at the head of the 9.28am from Newcastle on 14th March 1980. *Photo, Author.*

163

the Town Hall and, whether as a result of this visit or not, a package of incentives and plans was put in place to help revitalize derelict areas which would, in time, bring in substantial income from tourism. It would be some years before journalists could refer to riots without mentioning Liverpool but, for us, it was a storm in a teacup and, at the end of 1981, following a disco in the city centre, the queues for taxis after midnight were so long that we decided to walk the three miles to St. Michael's Hamlet, through Toxteth and Dingle, and both districts were as peaceful as wayside villages!

We continued to enjoy a variety of live entertainment including new productions by Willy Russell (*Educating Rita*) and Alan Bleasdale (*Having A Ball*). I may be prejudiced but it seems a shame that plays produced regionally do not receive national attention until they are given a 'run' on the London stage. I recall reading an article in one of the Sunday colour magazines which referred to the critical acclaim given to *Educating Rita*, following its appearance in London, and wondered,

maybe naively, why this attention had not been given to the play when it opened in Liverpool. 1981 was also a memorable Grand National year when Bob Champion rode Aldaniti to a famous victory as we watched from near the second fence. It was our first visit to this great sporting occasion and we came away with smiles on our faces as my parents won £20 and I won the office sweep.

Our holiday in Switzerland that year was our first abroad for several years and gave me a chance to sample its railways. We purchased a Swiss Travel Pass which enabled us to travel anywhere in the country for four days. I was very impressed by the punctuality and cleanliness. During those few days only one train was late and that was due to engineering works. Standards of comfort were nothing out of the ordinary but the trains were smooth, quiet and clean and we were able to see for ourselves that guards stood no nonsense from anyone resting his or her legs on a seat. More than anything else the views must surely be amongst the

Plate 187. The climax of the year's events took place, appropriately, at Rainhill where a cavalcade of motive power from down the ages took part, over three days, in front of masses of people seated in grandstands. In a twist of fate, however, it was *Sans Pareil* that was the only one of the three replicas of the original contestants of the Rainhill Trials to travel under its own steam on the first day. On 24th May 1980, *Sans Pareil* runs past the stands at Rainhill whilst the replica of *Rocket* was unable to take part on that day because of a derailment.

Photo, Peter Fitton.

Plate 188. Another of the replicas of the original Rainhill Trials contestants, *Novelty*, passes spectators, in steam but on a low loader.

Photo, Peter Fitton.

finest in the world to see from a train. Our first journey started from Interlaken West on the 8.15 am to Hamburg as far as Berne. Allowing time for sightseeing, we called at Zurich and Lucerne before returning to Interlaken by the remarkable mountain route via Meiringen and Brienz. As can be imagined, the gradients through the Bernese Oberland are very steep and, at the point where our train reached the steepest sections, it stopped in order to engage cogs before proceeding up into the mountains. I would have thought that, given the splendid views from the train, even the locals would have found it hard to read their books or newspapers without regular interruptions to look out of the window! The journey the next day, however, was the most remarkable of all as we were taken 11,000 feet up into the mountains (literally!). From Interlaken Ost, via the mountain villages of Lauterbrunnen and Wengen, we reached Kleine Scheidegg, from where there were stunning views of Eiger's north face, Monsch, Jungfrau and Wetterhorn. As if this were not enough, the railway then continued through the Eiger to reach the summit at Jungfraujoch, not far below the tops of these Alpine

peaks. Any railway trip was bound to be an anti-climax after the previous two days but the unspectacular agricultural countryside on the way to Geneva was not unwelcome. It helped one appreciate the spectacular scenery of the Bernese Oberland, to which we returned on the last of the four days covered by the pass. The trip was into Italy but, once again, we were treated to some superb views as the train made its way through the Kanderstag valley, then high above the Rhone valley before plunging into the Simplon Tunnel towards Italy. It had been a truly memorable holiday and I fully expected to return to Liverpool on a late-running train, by way of contrast, but instead arrived in Lime Street a very creditable ten minutes early behind class '87' No.87 018 *Lord Nelson*.

There were other trips from home to places of railway interest such as the Sunday diversions from Manchester Piccadilly along the Woodhead route to Sheffield. Regular passenger services along the full extent of this line had already been withdrawn and this was the last time I would use the route. The electric locomotives, which had now become class '76', were still handling

165

freights but they were nearing the end of their working lives. The last time I saw the class in action was in the same year when Nos.76 006 and 76 024 passed through Dinting on a coal train for Fiddlers Ferry power station. Returning to Piccadilly the same day I travelled on the old Glossop electric trains, knowing that they, too, were living on borrowed time and that, when they were replaced, the old divide that had existed at Manchester London Road, and later Piccadilly, would come to an end. How different it seemed from the days when, under a single roof, one could see possibly an 'A3' Pacific or 'B1' at the former LNER side of the station, and a 'Royal Scot' or Stanier class '5' on the LMS side. As a child I had had a very brief glimpse of the old era with steam but, when the Glossop and Hadfield lines were converted to 25Kv power supply, the last vestige of the old division passed with it and there remained just two trains here that still broke the mould of uniformity. One was the 'Manchester Pullman', by then the only daily (Monday to Friday) Pullman service in Britain, and very distinctive in silvery-grey. The other was the 'Harwich Boat Train', still steam heated and, within its formation, a Gresley-designed restaurant car. Each time we spent a weekend in Stockport with Joyce's parents I would catch a train to Piccadilly, partly to shop in Manchester but also to note the railway activity, and the 'Harwich

Boat Train' became a regular source of interest. While the usual motive power was a class '45' it was possible to see other types in charge, including classes '37', '40', '46' and '47'. The determining factor in the choice of locomotive was whether it could provide steam heating, at least in the winter months, when the sight of the steam rising from the carriages in the cold air appeared as a time warp in an otherwise modern station.

1981 also saw the passing of the Deltics after little more than twenty years in service. They continued to make forays into Liverpool to the end of the year and I had my last trip along this route with a Deltic on 4th November as far as St. Helens Junction, behind No.55 022 *Royal Scots Grey,* which was also the last of its class I would see at Lime Street on 17th December when it departed with the 1.05pm to York. The decline of the Deltics had seemed sudden as, only three years earlier, they were still in charge of many of the top-link expresses. Now they were chiefly employed on services to York and Hull from King's Cross and it was while I was travelling around some east Yorkshire lines that I took the opportunity of a return trip from York to Selby behind Deltics both ways. The journey back to York behind No.55 017 *The Durham Light Infantry* was my very last behind this class and, a few weeks later, on 2nd January, the Deltics ran in service for the last time.

Plate 189. 'The Great Railway Exposition' was held at the former Liverpool & Manchester Railway terminus at Liverpool Road, Manchester, from 2nd August-14th September 1980 and a variety of locomotives was on display. Former Midland Railway compound 4-4-0 No.1000 is seen resplendent in its company livery on 5th September. *Photo, D.J.Sweeney.*

Plate 190. Drawing a smoke screen across the spectators, *Lion*, the world's oldest original steam locomotive in working order, and built for the Liverpool & Manchester Railway in 1838, appears to be in fine form and immaculate condition on 24th May 1980. *Photo, Peter Fitton.*

Another era had passed and much was being swept away in the name of modernization which, of course, was to be welcomed if it meant sustaining railways as a continuing and viable means of transport but, at the same time, I found myself gripped by a feeling of nostalgia for the old order, whether it was in the form of locomotives, trains, signalling, track layout or railway practices.

I had now completed over two years in residential property management and was about to transfer to the commercial side, specializing in industrial premises and offices. I had seen many rented houses owned by a variety of landlords, some of whom were sympathetic to their tenants and others who were remote (in some cases, tax exiles) and interested, primarily, in vacant possession. Acting for landlords was often difficult as there was a natural tendency to support a tenant's grievance, which was usually justified. To answer complaints of damp I once opened up floorboards to find water up to a depth of several inches and, on one inspection, I was in an upper room when part of the chimney collapsed, sliding down the roof and crashing into the back yard. These were situations brought on by neglect but one house stood out above all others. This was partly because the tenant had contributed to its

appalling state and had never written to complain of the condition. It was the rampant vegetation outside that made me suspicious so I arranged an appointment to inspect the house. On entering I was immediately confronted with a huge hole in the hall where rot had eaten away at the floor. Turning right into the lounge I noticed bare wires hanging down from the ceiling and out of sockets while, in the kitchen, the natural light had been totally obscured by a sycamore tree, towering over the property. Finally, upstairs, the vegetation I noticed from outside was, in fact, ivy and this had spread through a gap in the window and was now lying, in large quantities, on a bed! It was a case for immediate action and the move away from residential management came as a relief. I had now qualified as a Chartered Surveyor, thus fulfilling one of three long-standing ambitions, the others being to write a book and to make a success in the music industry. The pages of the railway manuscript were still languishing at home while I made one last attempt to break through into the tough world of 'pop' music.

Being in full employment meant that I could not devote as much time to my music interests as before but, while watching England beat Hungary 1-0 in November 1981, and thus qualify for the World Cup Finals in 1982,

167

I came up with an idea. I rang John Parr and suggested that we record a soulful version of *Abide With Me* to coincide with both the FA Cup and the World Cup, thus capitalizing on two major footballing events. John had, by now, entered into a publishing contract with Carlin Music, which was good news, but he was interested in the idea in principle. A friend of his, Mick Charlesworth, had a recording studio at the back of his house in Hathersage, near Sheffield, and a session was booked for 9th February. The first session lasted eleven hours during which the keyboard, drums and guitar tracks were laid down together with a reference vocal from John. That night I took with me a rough mix for evaluation over the next few days. I then contacted the Grenoside Male Voice Choir in Sheffield to discuss the demonstration record and a further session was arranged so that the choir could add their contribution. They duly completed this in just two hours leaving John to add his lead vocal and guitar. Finally, the mixing process was undertaken so that it was after midnight when I came away with two versions of *Abide With Me* that I felt

happy with. It had been hard work but very satisfying and it was with considerable optimism that I arranged visits to record companies and wrote to disc jockeys and the sports department at the BBC. A representative at John's music publishers thought it was a great idea and well recorded, but February had not ended when the first rejection came from CBS. At the beginning of March I travelled to London to see Polydor and Phonogram. I wrote to both companies well in advance agreeing a time and date to meet their respective A&R men but neither was available on the day. Magnet Records enjoyed the tape but said that it would need to go to their senior A&R guy. Within three weeks I received rejections from Polydor, Magnet, Stiff and Spartan Records. Further letters expressing disinterest were received in early April, by which time it was abundantly clear that time had run out as far as the FA Cup was concerned. I realised then how important it was to live in London, in order to make any progress and, for the time being, abandoned further attempts to market the song. I had hoped to try again for the

Plate 191. Ex-LMSR 'Coronation' class 4-6-2 No.46229 *Duchess of Hamilton* storms through Olive Mount Cutting, one of the principal engineering features of the original Liverpool & Manchester Railway, with the 'Anniversary Special' on 14th September 1980. The train stopped at Eccles station so that VIPs could transfer to a train hauled by *Lion* and composed of replica Liverpool & Manchester Railway coaching stock for the short trip to Liverpool Road station, Manchester. Olive Mount Junction signalbox in the background controlled the junction with the line to Bootle. *Photo, Peter Fitton.*

Christmas market but the final straw came when, in a matter of weeks, another version of *Abide With Me*, by the Inspirational Choir, was released, making the Top 30. It clearly bore similarities to the style of our version and I was convinced that the idea had been partially copied as a result of leaving the tapes at the recording companies. Naturally I felt that our recording had a lot more to offer, not least because of the strength of John's voice, but there was nothing I could do except to reflect that this was a sordid business. When Joyce heard the other version she was in tears, probably at the thought of another creative venture falling by the wayside, but I still own the rights to the production and still have the master tapes so if anyone out there is interested?

Still smarting from the disappointment of this failure I was beginning to think that 1982 was going to be a depressing year. After all, there were three million unemployed, there were railway strikes causing disruption and then Argentina invaded the Falkland Islands. We listened to the radio that morning on 3rd April as the Government debated the crisis and made the decision to send in the Navy. It was the first time that Parliament had sat on a Saturday since the Suez crisis in 1956 and it was the first time I had listened to a live debate of such importance. It was impossible not to be stirred by the arguments and feel a sense of patriotism, once the decision had been made. Naturally, these initial reactions were tempered somewhat when the first news came through of casualties but it brought about an Argentine surrender just over two months later. I reasoned that the victory would send a message to others to think twice before attempting invasions but subsequent events show this to be optimistic reasoning. While wars were relatively infrequent we were well and truly living in an age of terrorism around the world. The previous year Reagan had been shot, Sadat had been murdered and even the Pope was the subject of an assassination attempt. It seemed to me that the peacemakers of this world lived more dangerously than the terrorists. The Pope recovered and returned to his gruelling schedule of visits around the globe and, in 1982, he received a rapturous welcome in Britain. Liverpool was on his itinerary and, by coincidence, his route was planned to pass along the Aigburth Road, at the top of our street. There was some atmosphere on 30th May as tens of thousands of people lined the streets into the city centre to watch the Pope pass by in his purpose-built vehicle (which, incidentally, was later acquired by the Commercial Vehicle Museum at Leyland, south of Preston) on the way to the two great cathedrals at either end of Hope Street.

At the time of the Pope's visit Mum and Dad were temporarily staying with us. They had sold their house in Sale and, following my father's retirement from full-time employment, had chosen to live in a bungalow in the countryside near Craven Arms in Shropshire. Curiously, my mother's dog, Timmy, died of a heart attack just days before the move. With my parents in Shropshire I expected to enjoy regular trips behind class '33s' that were now handling many of the Crewe-Cardiff services. However, fate or, more appropriately, good fortune intervened as I received my first company car. It was an Austin Metro that was destined to have quite an impact on my rail travel but there were still journeys that I wanted to make for my own enjoyment. A good example was the 'Round Robin' to Glasgow and Edinburgh from Manchester. In my view, this circular day trip can hold its own against most railway journeys in Britain. There is plenty of contrast, from the Lancashire mills and Glasgow or Edinburgh tenements, to the mountain scenery of the Lake District and the coastal attractions of the North Sea. There are the splendours of Durham Cathedral and York Minster as well as a small selection of castles. Finally, one must not forget the railway engineering highlights such as the steep banks to Shap and Beattock, the bridges over the Tweed and Tyne, and the imposing stations of Edinburgh and York. Other moments to savour on this occasion were the first-class haddock and chips I

Plate 192. Steam heating of the Harwich Boat Train at Manchester Piccadilly on 31st December 1981. The locomotive providing the heating on the day was class '45' No.45 010.

Photo, Author.

169

devoured in the restaurant at Glasgow's Queen Street station and overhearing Japanese tourists praising enthusiastically the High Speed Train that took us from Edinburgh to York. I'm sure that the Settle and Carlisle line would feature on many lists of favourite railway journeys and I thoroughly enjoyed mine while on a Glasgow train, just two weeks before through services by express trains were withdrawn. Later in the year I had the pleasure of travelling on the 'Cumbrian Mountain Pullman' along this route behind Gresley 'A4' *Sir Nigel Gresley*. The rugged scenery, gradients and often inhospitable weather seem to be ideal for bringing out the best in steam locomotives and I can honestly say that it is difficult to imagine becoming tired of this route. I would have preferred a 'Jubilee' or 'Scot' at the front end, for the sake of authenticity, but this, my first run behind an 'A4' Pacific, was a great experience. As an added bonus, the train was later hauled by an ex-Southern Railway 'West Country' Pacific, No34092 *City of Wells,* between Hellifield and Carnforth, the first time I had travelled behind any Southern locomotive.

My parents' bungalow was about two miles from Craven Arms station, itself a good location to see steam specials in the capable hands of the likes of 'Coronation' No.46229 *Duchess of Hamilton* and 'Merchant Navy' No.35028 *Clan Line*. Like the Settle and Carlisle, this line had interesting scenery, gradients and plenty of semaphore signals to provide good photographic opportunities and, courtesy of No.6000

King George V' and a below par ex-Southern Railway No.850 *Lord Nelson*, I also had the chance to view the route from the train. The nearest steam centre to Liverpool was the Steamport complex in Southport, based at the former Lancashire and Yorkshire depot, just a short walk from the BR station. When Joyce went shopping in Southport I would visit the shed. That was almost always the arrangement and, yet, for all the times I visited Steamport I don't recall seeing an engine in steam! Not that it mattered that much because I enjoyed the atmosphere. It took me back to the days of Trafford Park shed, especially when I walked up and down the rows of locomotives, although there were almost as many buses and trams at Steamport. The depot was never going to be a great tourist attraction but I, for one, was sad when the whole complex was later sold for redevelopment.

Despite the set-back to my musical ambitions, life was good to us. We were earning more, the house had been decorated to our tastes and the car gave us more flexibility to visit people and places. One product of these changes was the marked increase in visits to the theatre and concerts, not just in Liverpool but around the country. At the Playhouse Theatre the latest production from the pen of Willy Russell, *Blood Brothers*, starred Barbara Dickson while, just around the corner at the Empire, Oscar Wilde's *The Importance of Being Ernest* was performed by a strong cast led by Judi Dench. At the Philharmonic Hall we were treated to a succession of great pianists such as Alfred Brendel, Sir

Plate 193. Last of the Pullmans, the unique silver-liveried 'Manchester Pullman' is seen at Crewe behind class '86' No.86 242, on 1st April 1977.

Photo, G.Bent.

Clifford Curzon and Radu Lupu but few soloists seemed to give so much of themselves as the violinist, Kyung-Wha Chung, about whom one music critic wrote of her performance, "her playing so often reaches an exalted level that she seems to be creating a legend in her own lifetime". I feel fortunate to have wide musical tastes and it gave me great pleasure to introduce classical music to a colleague of mine at work who was, at least, willing to give it a try. I invited him to a concert that I thought would suit him. It featured Mozart's Symphony no.33, Beethoven's Piano Concerto no.3 and Debussy's *La Mer*. Mike admitted afterwards to being pleasantly surprised and, remarkably, converted from being an avid Radio 1 fan to a regular Radio 3 listener, which was far more than I could ever claim! As children, we were taken quite often to the Free Trade Hall to see the Halle Orchestra but, in 1983, we made what was, by then, a rare visit to see a performance of Berlioz's *Symphonie Fantastique*, a spectacular and rousing work requiring physical fitness as well as passionate commitment on behalf of the musicians. The female percussionist put her heart and soul into it but her individual performance suffered a momentary blip when, at the beginning of a strong downward stroke, the drum stick flew out of her hand and shot, like a meteorite, into the upper side circle at about row E! There was a brief look of horror on her face but she quickly recovered her composure and continued with a replacement stick that was close at hand. However, at the end of the evening's concert, it was clear from expressions and overheard conversations what the main topic of interest was among the departing throng in the foyer!

Early in 1983 I watched live ballet for the first time at Joyce's request. She had been having regular ballet lessons for the fun of it and now wanted to see one of the visiting ballet companies. So we watched a performance of *Giselle* by the Northern Ballet Theatre at the Theatre Royal, St. Helens, and I enjoyed it, to the extent that we attended further productions by the London Festival Ballet, Sadlers Wells Ballet Company and the less traditional styles of Ballet Rambert and Wayne Sleep. I had always found opera difficult to comprehend, but Liverpool was visited by the Scottish and Welsh National Opera Companies on tour and I was particularly struck by the fast flowing production of Janacek's *The Cunning Little Vixen* performed by the Welsh company. Although I knew little about opera I was intrigued to see whether a performance in one of the world's great opera houses would make any difference. The opportunity arose when we decided on a holiday by the side of Lake Como in Italy. Milan and its famous opera house, La Scala, were within easy reach so I decided to try and book tickets but, in a moment of mad impulse, I picked up the phone and rang them. It was a brief conversation that went like this : "Buongiorno !" "Buongiorno" "Parla inglese ?" "Non" "Arrividerci" Luckily, there was a Linguistics Department at Liverpool University and, thanks to the

Plate 194. The 'Ffestiniog Pullman' was a special train organized for a trip to Blaenau Ffestiniog on 6th June 1982. Originating at Northwich it travelled via Altrincham, Manchester and Stockport to Crewe where it is seen behind green liveried class '40' No.40 106, prior to resuming the journey as far as Llandudno Junction. A second trip was run the following week.
Photo, Author.

171

help of a Mr. Davey in that department, I was able to compose suitable letters and receive translations of replies from the Opera House. Everything went smoothly and we enjoyed a memorable performance of Mozart's *Cosi Fan Tutte.*

I believe that comedy makes a very valuable, therapeutic contribution to life and, with Liverpool's established reputation for producing great comedians, you would expect Liverpudlians to be in the rudest of health. I'll never forget a Ken Dodd show up the coast in Southport when we sat behind a couple who were clearly there at the wife's insistence because her husband showed, by his expression and behaviour, that he was there under sufferance. However, his resistance was broken when two punch lines were delivered in quick succession and his shoulders moved involuntarily. Soon he was laughing with the rest of the audience. It was a lesson in how a master comedian could handle an audience and we were able to witness the same techniques at the Guild Hall in Preston, where we had the privilege of seeing one of the greatest entertainers of the twentieth century, Bob Hope, still possessing a wonderful comic sense of timing but, in his eighties, passed his peak.

Life was as hectic as it was enjoyable and I tried to keep fit by swimming, playing badminton, and running,which I did twice a week around the circumference of Sefton Park - over two miles. Perhaps I had been inspired by Seb Coe and Steve Ovett, whose great rivalry was at its peak in the early 1980s and marked this period as arguably the greatest in middle

distance running. We made our only visit to an athletics meeting in 1982 to Crystal Palace where Coe, Cram, Elliott and Cook broke the world record for the 4 x 800 metres. To these regular physical routines I also flirted with windsurfing and succeeded in climbing all the Welsh 'Munros', the fourteen peaks over 3000 feet. While driving down to Wales to climb the Carnedd range I was about ten miles from my destination when the radio programme was interrupted for a weather warning, advising that winds of storm 11 were expected off the Irish Sea. Luckily, I had plenty of food and drink with me as well as weatherproofs and warm clothing but, that day, I was given a clear demonstration of how powerful were the forces of nature. The Welsh 'Munros' are grouped into three ranges separated by two U-shaped valleys, facing out to the sea. The early part of the climb was achieved below the clear skies that had tempted me to make the ascent but, with the steepest section accomplished, I looked down into the valley to see moist air blown in from the sea and forming cloud, that would have a significant effect on visibility later on. It was only when I gained the plateau of this range that the winds whipped up into, possibly, the most fearsome that I had ever encountered outdoors. At one point I was almost scooped up, losing my hat in the process. Then I was thrown against a rock and the Thermos flask was broken, a strap on the rucksack snapped and some chocolate was sucked out by the wind. I managed to hide behind a boulder where I tried to regain my strength and composure, while carrying out repairs to the back pack. This was probably the most dangerous time for me as, having climbed the steepest section to the plateau, I simply could not resist the temptation of the remaining distance to the summit. Without anything to drink, and showing questionable judgment, I pressed on, taking regular rests and, on one or two occasions, actually resorted to making minimal progress on my hands and knees. I reached the peaks of Foel Fras and Foel Grach and now, with the wind behind me, I was able to make short work of the return from the plateau. Once off the tops I found that the wind had relented but the poor visibility added to my overall journey time to such an extent that it was almost dark when I left the mountainside.

It was at times like this that I understood the pleasures of watching sport instead of participating, and few things gave me as much pleasure as seeing Wolves beat Liverpool 1-0 at Anfield in 1984. It had been their first win there since 1950 and, by remarkably good fortune (my only visit to Anfield), I was there to witness the triumph. Liverpool fans seemed very good-natured in defeat but, perhaps they had reason to feel relaxed. At the end of the season the sting in the tail for Wolves was their relegation from Division 1 (now the Premier League) to which, at the time of writing, they have yet to return. For Liverpool another Championship was theirs, the third in a row, and the seventh in nine seasons! They also added the European Cup to their trophies that year. They reigned supreme in this period but not even Everton fans could feel too unhappy as they won the FA Cup in 1984 and, later the same year,

when I was invited to Goodison Park by a business friend, I was able to see Everton beat Stoke City 4-0, thereby stretching their unbeaten run to a record of ten consecutive victories, on the way to a Championship title in 1985.

On the subject of unbeaten runs, my grandmother had now reached her 90th birthday but she had left Saltburn. Our Christmas holidays there came to an end in 1976 and the last time Joyce and I visited 25 Emerald Street had been in 1981. It was a year or so later when my grandmother opened the door to two men, who advised her that they were from the Water Board to check the pipes, as they believed that there was a fault. She let them in and one walked through to the kitchen while the other went upstairs. It was when she heard footsteps in her front bedroom that she became suspicious and, in a frightened state, called round to a neighbour. By the time the police arrived, the bogus officials had disappeared, together with items of jewellery and money. She had lived in this large house for nearly forty years and by herself for the last twenty years, but now her spirit was broken and she would spend the rest of her life with members of her family in Yorkshire. Her 90th birthday was spent in Clifford, where she was living with my uncle, but not in Springfield Cottage. My uncle's employer had died quite young and the large house and gardens in Old Mill Lane were sold and then redeveloped as a housing estate. Consequently, he was forced to move to a small house near the centre of the village.

Plate 196. Impressions of 'Big Bertha' at Haworth by former Somerset & Dorset Railway class '7F' 2-8-0, No.13809, in LMS livery on 1st May 1983 during a Somerset & Dorset weekend on the Keighley & Worth Valley Railway.

Photo, Author.

Although it was becoming more difficult to pursue my interest in railways I still found time for the occasional, imaginative and reasonably-priced 'Round Robin', such as the trip to South Wales via the Lickey Incline, Cardiff and Swansea, returning along the Central Wales line to Shrewsbury. While on holiday near Oban we travelled along the spectacular route from Oban to Glasgow Queen Street behind class '37s', and also between Fort William and Mallaig behind ex-LMS Stanier class '5', 5407. This line has subsequently proved to be the most consistently successful 'main-line' route for steam but, on that day, there was a lot of upheaval. Our train was held up for two hours at Glenfinnan as we waited for the passage of a three-coach train hauled by former North British Railway 'J36' 0-6-0 *Maude.* Then our locomotive took four attempts to surmount a gradient near Arisaig, adding to the obvious frustrations of passengers on the service train which, just a few miles from its starting point, was already three hours late! Early in April of the same year I heard the sound of an engine whistle from home for the first time. As a regular reader of the latest railway journals, I guessed that they were the miniature locomotives undergoing crew-training around the circuit of the proposed International Garden Festival site that was situated just the other side of St. Michael's station from us. Over the period of the next six months this brilliant exhibition gave us a lot of pleasure and, on most evenings in the summer, we would walk the four hundred yards or more to the site and, as season ticket holders, wander round different sections or just picnic in one of the variety of splendid gardens such as the Chinese (complete with pagoda), Japanese, Indian, Turkish, Dutch and, of course, English gardens. Naturally, I rode behind all the locomotives, provided by the Ravenglass and Eskdale Railway and the Romney, Hythe and Dymchurch Railway including *River Irt, Samson* and *Black Prince.* In October, though, the short-lived railway closed with the Festival. 1984 was quite a year for Liverpool because the city was also one of the venues for the Tall Ships Race. I can't pretend to be a great fan of sailing boats but I don't think anyone could have failed to be impressed by the sheer scale and number of these beautiful ships as they completed their voyages from Newfoundland and Denmark. On the Saturday night there was a carnival atmosphere when they set sail from the Mersey, watched by thousands from various viewing points along both sides of the river. The traffic jams that night were so horrendous that we left the car in Blundellsands and caught the train home.

Liverpool was still beset by industrial action, one strike actually closing the Mersey Tunnel for the first time in its history, but the Garden Festival, the Tall Ships Race and the opening of a new shopping centre at Cavern Walk (featuring a New Cavern Club) were evidence of a revitalized city in the spotlight. We even had an earthquake, measuring five on the Richter scale. I happened to be in the bathroom at the time and, although my stomach rumbles before breakfast, I knew immediately that this was something more profound! On the news that day it was described as the strongest earth tremor in Britain for one hundred years but, luckily, we suffered no damage. On the subject of the earth moving, we discovered in June that Joyce was expecting a baby. She was thirty-six, and we had been hoping for a small family, so we looked forward to a change in our lifestyle that would mean devoting much of our time to someone else other than ourselves. Naturally, our families were very pleased about the news although Joyce's grandmother was confused and asked Joyce who the father was! When she found out it was me she added "and I always thought he was a nice young man!" It seemed that the time was ripe for new generations as Nigel's wife, Lynda, gave birth to a daughter, Joanna, and cousin Clive's wife, Lynne, later gave birth to a daughter, Kelly, in Hong Kong. At the time we did not realise how big a change would take place but, in the November, I accepted an offer of a job near Preston and, from then, time began to run out for us on Merseyside.

As in Oxford, we had enjoyed the years spent in Liverpool. There had been so much to do in the city, the people were friendly and humorous, and there was a buzz about the place. Those who want to portray the city in a poor light may refer to the strikes, riots, unemployment and dereliction which have affected most large centres of dense population from time to time. I like to think of Liverpool as a city with one of the world's finest waterfronts, two great contrasting cathedrals, tourist attractions converted from derelict buildings and with a great tradition of entertaining the world with its home-grown stars of comedy, the stage and music, not to mention football. I don't imagine that I will ever tire of returning to Liverpool.

14. AGE OF MATURITY

I recall that books on parenthood advise against embarking on major undertakings around the time of the birth of a child and during its first few weeks. Unfortunately, my new job meant that we would have to change house as well and, during the transitional period of long-distance commuting, Helen was born at the Oxford Street Maternity Hospital, Liverpool in February 1985. With these major changes taking place there was little time to pursue my interest in railways which, itself, had lost some of its vigour. The company car, my parents' move to Shropshire and now a new addition to the family were all factors in this process. Futhermore, I had now travelled on most of the passenger lines between the Midlands and Scotland so any further exploration of the railway network would entail longer journeys, which I was not prepared to undertake. My continued interest in railway practices was now confined mainly to the north west so that, for instance, in 1984, a Saturday afternoon found me on a return trip between Stockport and Manchester on the last loco-hauled Swansea service behind a class '86' No.86 258, before it became a High Speed Train. Then, on the following Monday, I was at Liverpool Lime Street during my lunch break, to watch the first HST leave for Plymouth, waved off by various railway officials in bowler hats. During the same year I travelled for the last time behind class '40s', '45s' and '81s', all of which were well on the way to being withdrawn from service. My trip behind class '45', No.45 132, on the 8.05am Liverpool-Newcastle, was also the last time I travelled on the expresses between Liverpool and Manchester Victoria. Like most express services between these cities, the trains now use Piccadilly station. On that last trip I saw the remains of another class '45' that had recently run into the back of a goods train near Eccles. 1985 saw my last trips behind class '33s' (along the Crewe-Cardiff line, where they were replaced by class '37s') and class '50s' (on our last Oxford reunion with college friends). The class '50' No.50 029 *Renown* took us from Charlbury to Oxford on the 8.40am Hereford-London, then named 'The Cathedrals Express', evoking the name of one of the last Western Region steam-hauled expresses. Ominously, the return journey was by HST on a service named 'The Cotswold and Malvern Express'. Steadily, the era of loco-hauled trains was in decline in many parts of the country but, along the WCML, the HSTs had made little impact. This line was to have been the stronghold of the new Advanced Passenger Train which, in 1985, could still be seen on non-timetabled runs from Preston but, unfortunately, they did not see active service.

Attempts were clearly being made to reduce train times and even Crewe station was closed for several weeks for track re-alignment to permit higher speeds to be achieved by through trains. By way of an aside, I found it difficult to pass through Crewe at this time without smiling because of the presence of a large boarding at the north end, advertising the production of vodka in Warrington, proclaiming 'The Russian buggers are coming!' Presumably, the inclusion of a small bugging device in the picture made the advert acceptable to the censor! Returning to train speeds on the WCML the class '86s' (which were now twenty years old) and '87s' seemed to be coping well from my observations and, on a number of occasions during that period, I found myself arriving in London several minutes early from Preston. In fact, it was only on the odd occasion when I needed to be in London on time that I was let down ! I made a last effort to drum up support for the *Abide With Me* project and arranged appointments in London. I was forced to cancel my first visit because the train was over two hours late in Preston. On the second trip I caught a late-running train but then was delayed over two hours owing to signal failure while, at the third attempt at a punctual arrival, I arrived one hour late for my appointment, hardly the ideal preparation for attempting a promotion. In the event, the tapes were turned down again but there was a postscript to this story.

Shortly before the *Abide With Me* project, John Parr had signed a publishing contract with Carlin Music Corporation. This opened the door to new opportunities including co-producing some songs with the American performer, Meat Loaf, in 1983. Early in 1984 he signed a contract with Atlantic Records in the USA and, later the same year, his first single, *Naughty Naughty*, was released over there reaching no.23 in the charts. At the beginning of 1985 the record received its first airplay in England, on Paul Gambaccini's Top 100 US programme and, a few days later, a package that was delivered to our home turned out to be a complimentary copy of his first album, on which I received a credit for

had declined as a shopping area, due to the retail shift towards the Square, but this is what happens when the fortunes of town centres are left to market forces. It seems so much more sensible for councils to own their buildings as, in the long run, this would give them better control over planning, transport and highways, and the environment, and reduce the risk of fragmentation that lessens the appeal of a town centre. Once my grandmother had left Saltburn, the old ties had virtually been severed and, in 1987, she returned there for the last time to be buried with my grandfather, who had died thirty-five years earlier to the day. I was glad that she had lived long enough to see Helen and, on one of our last visits, she was still in sufficiently good health to sing Russian tunes to her. With her passing went the last of that generation and, already, several of my parents' generation had died, including my father's brother and my father-in-law. It was a stark reminder of my own mortality which I preferred not to dwell on and, luckily, having a young child meant that my thoughts were usually focused outwards than inwards. It took some time before the novelty of having a child wore off. During the first two years of her life I took over a thousand photographs and it seemed as if everyone who was sent a Christmas card, in that first year, also received several pictures of her. Looking back, I now realise how boring it must have been for others but, at that stage, I found it very difficult to be objective.

There were the usual landmarks of a young child that a parent looks forward to such as her first tentative steps, her first words and her interaction with other children and, while I did not exactly look forward to her first day at Primary School, it was not the emotional strain that I expected. The contrast between her first day and that of her father's could not have been greater! She was very excited about going to school, getting her bag ready the previous night without being told (which is more than can be said for her now!) and thoroughly enjoying the experience. Most of all, it has been her personality and sense of humour, evident throughout her childhood, that has made parenthood so much fun. She was still only two when, climbing into our bed to get comfortable one morning, she borrowed phrases from *Goldilocks and the Three Bears* to explain that Daddy was too hot, Mummy too lumpy but Baby was just right! On another occasion, while putting her to bed, I began to whistle. She said "stop whistling Daddy!" I replied "whistling makes me happy. You do like to see your Daddy happy, don't you ?" "Yes" she said "but not

that happy!" One of the amusing aspects of a young child's development (as seen from an adult's perspective) is its sense of reasoning. One night, after shopping at the local supermarket, Helen spotted a full moon and then, as we stepped out of the car at home with our shopping, she looked up and saw it again, exclaiming "there's another moon!" On being told that it was the same moon she replied "it can't have been, the other one was outside Asda!"

Since leaving Liverpool, visits to the theatre and concerts had become a rarity and, apart from the occasional main-line steam special, trips to preserved steam railways tended to be fitted in if we happened to be in the area. Holidays, for example, were an ideal time to visit these locations, especially those that had not been seen before. The North Norfolk Railway was just such a line, conveniently situated near to our holiday cottage ! I was surprised to discover that it was not on the flat but over two hundred feet above sea level, with brief views out to the North Sea. The same holiday gave me a chance to see the locomotives preserved at Bressingham Gardens, near Diss. I must be honest and express the view that the large engines did not look right in this location but, on the other hand, one has to be thankful that there is someone out there willing to put time and money into restoring them. The highlight for me was my first glimpse of *Royal Scot* but the huge *Duchess of Sutherland* or *Oliver Cromwell* would, alone, have made the visit worthwhile. The two tank engines on view, Stanier 3-cylinder 2-6-4 tank, No.42500, and Whitelegg 4-4-2 tank *Thundersley* were both representatives of classes I had not seen before so, all in all, it had been a satisfying day. While on holiday in Somerset we stopped, overnight, at a guest house in Blue Anchor, and a stroll down to the station the following morning gave us plenty of time to await the arrival of GWR Prairie tank, No.5572, bringing back memories of the same location, so many years before. Similarly, we managed to see the Bluebell Railway, the Swanage Railway and the North Yorkshire Moors Railway during the course of holidays. Although it didn't really matter which locomotive I travelled behind, it was, nevertheless, nice to be hauled by something new and with a class of engine indigenous to the area, such as the Great Central 'Director' on the Great Central Railway at Loughborough, the LSWR 'T9' at Swanage or even BR 2-10-0 No.92220 *Evening Star* on the West Somerset Railway.

When everything went well, though, there was little to

Plate 199. To commemorate the centenary of the opening of the Forth Bridge ex-LNER 'A4' Pacific No.60009 *Osprey*, alias *Union of South Africa*, took an Edinburgh Waverley-Perth train across the bridge on 4th March 1990. *Photo, Peter Fitton.*

surpass a day on the main line, behind a steam locomotive in fine form. Particularly memorable at this time were the performances of 'Castle' class No.5080 *Defiant* and 'King' class No.6024 *King Edward I* on a series of Tyseley-Stratford runs in 1990. With thirteen coaches, the 'Castle', unsurprisingly, found the two miles at 1 in 75 to Wilmcote and the ten miles at 1 in 150 to Earlswood taxing but the 'King' reeled off the twenty-two miles in thirty-one minutes, an exhilarating run. Later in the year, I travelled for the first time behind the last express locomotive to be built, BR class '8P' No.71000 *Duke of Gloucester*, from Crewe to Holyhead. It was a competent and smooth performance but there was nothing spectacular, and it felt as if the engine was being restrained for much of the time. The true potential of this remarkable loco was better demonstrated on the Settle and Carlisle line and, later, up Shap. This was surely the greatest success story in locomotive restoration, not only restoring it to its former glory, but correcting the original faults to produce a superior performer. In terms of atmosphere, however, I found little to compare with a run behind a

Gresley 'A4' from one of my favourite stations, Edinburgh Waverley, across the Forth Bridge to Perth and back. The occasion was the centenary of the opening of the Forth Bridge. All the ingredients were there including a Haymarket Pacific, 60009 *Union of South Africa* (renamed *Osprey* for this trip), working from its former home town, across arguably the most famous railway bridge in the world, to Perth, where the locomotive was a regular visitor in its twilight years on the Glasgow-Aberdeen expresses.

By 1988 we had moved again, this time to Lytham, primarily for the convenience of Joyce and Helen. The house was situated close to the Green, fronting the Ribble estuary, but it was also less than half-a-mile from the shops in the town centre and Helen's primary school. Everything fell into place and this distinctive town has remained our home ever since but, within months of moving, I was offered a good job, based initially in Rochdale. This meant a daily drive of over an hour each way, but the journey was relatively trouble-free compared with the daily crawl into and out of city centres. On the first day, I travelled in by train, which

179

Plate 200. The changing face of motive power as the old and new meet at Blackburn station. Pacer unit No. 142 043, which has just arrived with the service for Blackpool South from Colne, stands alongside one of the first generation DMUs of class '104', built by the Birmingham Railway Carriage & Workshop Co.
Photo, Author.

Plate 201. The shape of things to come. The TGVs have revolutionized railway travel in France and it was a memorable experience to use the service from Paris to Nice in 1992. TG847 stands at Gare de Lyon, Paris while my daughter, Helen, poses next to the train.
Photo, Author.

Plate 202. Almost shades of the 1960s as ex-LMSR 'Jubilee' class 4-6-0 No.45596 *Bahamas* stops for water at Garsdale with a clear road ahead prior to restarting the 'Cumbrian Mountain Express' on 13th April 1991.
Photo, Author.

Plate 203. Steam action at Burrs, near Bury, with ex-BR class '4' 2-6-0 No.76079 (masquerading as former sister engine 76031) in charge of the 8.00am demonstration freight with ex-Great Eastern Railway 'N7' 0-6-2 tank, No.69621, banking at the rear on 27th July 1991.   *Photo, Tom Heavyside.*

took twice as long as the average car journey, although it was necessary to change trains at Preston and Manchester Victoria. In the process I had my first rides on both Pacers and Sprinters, which had largely replaced the DMUs. The Sprinters, in particular, were a significant development as the more luxurious versions were making further inroads into the stocks of locomotive-hauled trains. They had taken over from the class '37s' along the Welsh Marches route and had even replaced the class '47s' on the Liverpool-Newcastle and York services. This took some getting used to when thinking of the locomotive-hauled services of the past with ten or more coaches, including a restaurant or buffet car. Admittedly, when I had a chance to ride on one of the '158s' from Craven Arms to Shrewsbury, I found it comfortable and quiet but, from the narrow perspective of a trainspotter, it seemed that only the very serious enthusiast would still get any pleasure from this, once much-loved, past time.

The nineteen-eighties, the decade that witnessed the

breaking down of barriers in Europe through Glasnost, also witnessed a transformation on the railways, with a massive reduction of locomotives, in favour of multiple units from High Speed Trains to Pacers and, blurring the old distinction between trams and trains, came the new breed of super trams that returned to city centres. It was not all doom and gloom for locomotives though and when, in 1990, I had my first run behind a new class 90, the train arrived no less than twenty minutes early in London. Impressive though this was, it did not matter to me as I was in no hurry but, when time was important, guess what? Admittedly, the weather conditions were poor in the February, when we decided on a visit to Amsterdam for a few days, but this was the occasion when BR blamed the delays on the wrong kind of snow! In Preston and the North the weather had been fine but, still, our Glasgow-Poole train arrived one hour late. I'm sure it has nothing to do with Poole but, in my experience, almost every train I've encountered for that destination has been late. BR did their best to cope with the weather-related problems further south by providing relief trains from Birmingham to London and from Liverpool Street to Harwich, so that we were able to board the Stena Line ship with little time to spare. For Helen it was all part of the excitement on this, her first trip abroad and, just trying out the bunk bed in our cabin for the first time, made the holiday worthwhile for her. Although Amsterdam's canals were frozen, the scenes were picturesque, reminding me of Christmas cards as skaters made progress along the waterways. It had been a relaxing few days except for one heart-stopping moment when Helen tripped up while approaching a large Rembrandt in the Rijksmuseum and almost put her hand through it! On returning to England the snow was still causing problems in East Anglia and the Home Counties but, after another fine run behind a class '90', we arrived on time in Preston.

The following year we took a holiday on the Italian Riviera by coach and train and, once again, BR managed to make things difficult by announcing that all Inter-City trains to London on that day had been cancelled. Consequently, our train was an EMU, stopping at all stations, causing us a lot of aggravation as we arrived at the coach terminal with just five minutes in hand. This was all forgotten on the second day when we boarded TGV847 to Nice at Gare de Lyon station in Paris. There followed a fantastic run to Lyon and then down the Rhone valley to Avignon, Marseilles and Toulon, reaching Nice three minutes ahead of time. On the return journey, heavy storms and flash floods delayed the arrival in Paris by one hour but also brought chaos to the roads of the capital. We were booked to check in to our hotel at 11pm but finally arrived at 2am. The pleasures of travel! In between these setbacks was a memorable holiday during which, exactly five hundred years after the momentous journey of Columbus to America, we made our own modest discovery, locating the flat where my mother had spent her childhood in Genoa, Columbus's birthplace.

In the early nineteen-nineties I travelled for the first time behind *Britannia* to Holyhead, *Duchess of Hamilton*, *Princess Margaret Rose* and *Bahamas* along the Settle and Carlisle route, and *Blue Peter* in Scotland. During this period I also visited twelve different steam railways and paid annual visits to the East Lancashire Railway, Worth Valley Railway, North Yorkshire Moors Railway and the Severn Valley Railway, enjoying the variety of scenery that these lines provided and the steam action. An LSWR 'T9' ambling through the

Dorset countryside near Swanage, a 'West Country' Pacific drawing to a halt at the pretty station of Four Marks and Medstead, an NER 'Q7' storming the bank towards Goathland or GWR Prairie tank setting off with its chocolate-and-cream coaches from the picturesque setting at Highley, are all well-remembered images from this time. I have already said that I liked to see locomotives working in the areas they were designed for but, the 'importing' of visiting engines has its attractions, as it gives the enthusiast a chance to see types that may otherwise be seen only rarely. The visit of Holden's Great Eastern Railway 0-6-2 tank No.69621 to the East Lancashire Railway was a case in point, during the summer of 1991. It seemed at home on the line to Rawtenstall and, watching the steam pump in action while the engine awaited the 'right of way' was an interesting and novel experience.

Unless I was actually travelling by steam train I felt disinclined to drive too far simply to take photographs but, in 1993 and 1994, I made two visits to North Wales to see, first of all, the first grouping of three Stanier Pacifics in preservation and, then, to see three more locomotives in action, namely, *Duke of Gloucester*, *Princess Margaret Rose* and *Sir Nigel Gresley*. Both trips were simply too good to miss and, while Llandudno Junction was popular with photographers, I found that Penmaenmawr offered a quieter location to film the trains at speed. The second occasion was of special significance as it marked the end of British Railways as an operating entity and the beginning of a more complex regime of different operating companies. I feel sure that the new division of responsibilities contributed to the confusion and delay on the night of 1st October 1994 when our steam-hauled excursion, behind LNER 'A2' Pacific No.60532 *Blue Peter*, came to an abrupt halt at Durham. I think I have a love-hate relationship with this engine as, in the space of two years, I made three separate trips behind it, the first of which also ended prematurely. That was from Edinburgh to Aberdeen, a route on which *Blue Peter* spent much of its life when in BR stock. Unfortunately, owing to problems with the coaching stock, the train was forced to start at Dalmeny, where it left an hour late, and then, climbing out of Dunfermline from a standing start, the 'A2' lost adhesion on the icy rails and had to wait for assistance. The time lost was substantially added to when it lost its path on a single-line section, causing it to arrive in Perth three hours late. It was decided to abandon any attempt to reach Aberdeen, in order to ensure that passengers got home that night! A second attempt was made the following August but, this time, from Stirling, and it was a success. Apart from some good work by the locomotive on the punishing grades, I caught my first view of the Tay Bridge (although we did not cross it), visited Aberdeen for the first time, the only city of any size on the mainland in which I had not previously set foot, and my faith was restored. So, when I received details of the proposed journey by *Blue Peter* from Edinburgh to York, I was tempted once again.

The prospect of travelling south from Edinburgh, behind an LNER Pacific, was very much on my list of 'wants' and, as the trip started in York and involved a reasonable stopover in the Scottish capital, I thought it would also appeal to Joyce and Helen. Everything did, in fact, go well until we re-started from Durham on the return journey. Barely yards out of the station *Blue Peter* suffered severe wheel slip to such an extent that the con rods were shattered, bringing the journey behind steam to a premature end. From the locomotive owners' point of view this was an unfortunate incident as the damage was clearly going to be costly to repair, but there then followed a confused sequence of events that may well have had something to do with the apportioning of responsibilities in the new privatised era. First of all, passengers requiring certain connections were required to detrain and walk back along the viaduct to the station. Then the plan was changed and, in the rain that was now adding to the misery, they were asked to climb aboard once more. There then followed a long wait, during which delays were caused to other trains, and it was three hours later when we finally got under way again by an Inter City service to York. From there we drove home, which we reached at 1am, but there were other passengers with much further to go, including some who were making another steam trip the next day in the south of England! Incidents like this test the patience and loyalty of all but the committed railway enthusiast and, even now, when I mention *Blue Peter*, Joyce and Helen react as if I'd uttered a curse. Only a Santa special on the Lakeside Railway that year helped to mend bridges, as far as Helen was concerned, but Joyce, I think, will take some persuading to try main-line steam again. Me? I bounced back with a London-Exeter special behind 'Merchant Navy' class No.35028 *Clan Line*, even though I got my car clamped in the process!

Throughout the years that Mum and Dad lived near Craven Arms I was frequently treated to the sight of passing steam specials on the 'North and West' route and, even on the Central Wales line, which was visible from the bungalow, less than half-a-mile away. Sunnybank, as my parents' home was known, reminded me of my great aunt's bungalow at Cynwyd in that trains could be seen on a similar frequency with hills in the background. DMUs manned the service at first, until replaced by Sprinters in the 1990s but, despite there being a weight restriction on the line, an occasional special train was seen (including the Royal Train), usually hauled by a class '37' or '47'. The bungalow stood in a large garden which, with the vegetable plot, amounted to nearly an acre, surrounded by farmland. It was a splendid, safe haven in which Helen and her cousins could play, while the lawns at the front and back were large enough for putting and even pitch and putt. Mum and Dad worked hard to maintain the borders and lawns and, especially in autumn, we would give them some help in removing the masses of pine needles that fell from the dozen or so Scots Pines, and pick the fruit from the apple, pear and plum trees. When the sun was shining and there was no wind it was idyllic. It was a holiday home where we could relax, with views of typical English countryside - hills and valleys, and fields bordered by trees and hedgerows. But, by 1994, it all came to an end when they moved to a flat near us, in Lytham.

It had seemed a long time since those first visits to a bare bungalow to help with the decorating. I can still remember Nigel, standing at a window with no curtains during a thunderstorm, when I crept up to the door and quickly flashed the light switch on and off, provoking the response "bloody hell, that was close!", before he guessed what had happened. The house and its garden fulfilled its potential when the children were born and, for several years, there was rarely any need to look for holidays elsewhere. As a base it was ideal for venturing into Wales, for climbing the Shropshire hills and for the occasional longer trip to the Welsh coast or South Wales where, in 1992, we paid a visit to the last of the Garden Festivals at Ebbw Vale. On that same day we called at Aberfan and to the Memorial Garden, situated on the site of the school buried under the slag heap, more than twenty five years earlier. Another generation of children played in the park nearby while Helen spent a few minutes on the swings. In 1993, an outing with a difference was made to Wem Moss, in north Shropshire, to see an adder! I had read in the local Wildlife Trust guide book about an adder population in this location

Plate 205. Recalling the sight (and conjuring up in the imagination, the sound) of an ex-LMSR 'Princess' 4-6-2 seen from the top of Ingleborough. Here is No.46203 *Princess Margaret Rose* at Ais Gill Summit on a 'Cumbrian Mountain Express of 29th August 1994

Photo, Peter Fitton.

Plate 206. A particularly pleasurable steam trip was behind ex-LMSR 'Coronation' Pacific No.46229 *Duchess of Hamilton* up Shap bank to Carlisle in 1995. Here is the locomotive a year later in charge of 'The Caledonian' at Carlisle on 19th September 1996, recalling memories of the fast London-Glasgow service with which these locomotives were associated. 'The Caledonian' of old, however, was a non-stop train.

Photo, Peter Fitton.

At the time of writing main line steam trains pass near or through Preston, on the way to the Settle and Carlisle line, or along the West Coast Main Line up to Shap and Carlisle. A short visit to Leyland station or to Brock, north of Preston, is all that is required to catch a glimpse of these trains, and there have been some fine sights of express engines from each region but, to date, the most thrilling spectacle was that of two Stanier class '5s' thrashing up the gradient and sweeping through Oxenholme station at the head of a heavy train. As I stood on the station with many others, enthusiasts and passengers, I could hear the pulsating beat of the engines at least a mile further south and, as the train pounded by, I found it easy to appreciate just why the steam locomotive is such a captivating beast. There was a similar experience some years ago when we climbed Ingleborough. Near to the summit I caught the sound of a powerful locomotive working hard as it headed up the gradient towards Ribblehead and Ais Gill. There was no noticeable slowing in the rhythmic beat until the train approached the Ribblehead viaduct, by which time there was a splendid view, from the top, of *Princess Elizabeth* as it made its way, cautiously, across the magnificent structure. I mentioned earlier that I had wanted to travel along the East Coast Main Line from Edinburgh, behind an LNER Pacific and, similarly, I had a longstanding wish to ride behind a Pacific up Shap and Beattock. This wish was largely fulfilled when two steam specials, both hauled by *Duchess of Hamilton*, accomplished the task, the locomotive in fine fettle making light work of the formidable gradients.

In the thirty years and more since the end of BR steam I have had the pleasure of travelling behind almost all the surviving types of express locomotives on the main line but there are still endless opportunities for enjoying steam and railways in general. It's nice to come across something new, whether it be a locomotive or a route, but there is still a pleasure to be derived from seeing the same regular engine, as often happens on the preserved steam railways. Apart from those lines and engines I have yet to see, there are the projects in the pipeline or coming to fruition, such as the building of a new LNER 'A1' *Tornado*, the relaying of the Welsh Highland Railway and, a non-steam project, the relaying of tracks in Wensleydale, to improve transport links in the Dale. I believe that, in the long-term, the main line steam market will change and that the trains marketed for enthusiasts alone will diminish.

On the other hand, I think that the tourist routes such as Fort William-Mallaig and the luxury trains, such as the VSOE, are likely to remain popular. I hope that there will be more short-haul specials in tourist locations such as Blackpool and Stratford, and I'm sure that the Settle and Carlisle will continue in popularity for many years to come with, one day, the chance to ride behind a 'Royal Scot'.

I probably live closer to a railway now than ever before, just over four hundred yards but, when I look at the Pacers and Sprinters picking their way through the farmland between Kirkham and Lytham, I find it hard to imagine that 'Royal Scots' and 'Jubilees' were once regular sights here. When I hear the sound of the train in Lytham, sometimes it is the old clickety-clack of the Sprinter and, at other times, the more tram-like rhythm of a Pacer but, at least, the sounds continue and I can still claim that the train's quite like an old familiar friend.

Plate 207. That old familiar friend. Sprinters and Pacers share the services between Blackpool South and Colne and on 10th June 1989 a three-car Sprinter, class 150/2 No.150 216, is seen passing Royal Lytham St. Annes Golf Course on its way to Blackpool.
Photo, Peter Fitton.

15. POSTSCRIPT

Of the railways and stations of my past much has either disappeared or drastically altered. Saltburn station still exists in a much-reduced form: the train shed, excursion platform and run-round loop have all gone together with the sidings. Happily the main station building with its portico still stands at one end of Station Square even though it ceases to perform a railway function other than indicate where trains can be found. The route from Saltburn to Darlington bears little resemblance to that of steam days when heavy industry dominated the scene. Although a rationalized iron and steel industry still generates railway traffic and the chemical industry has expanded since my childhood the docks at Middlesbrough have disappeared along with stations such as Cargo Fleet.

The journey to Saltburn has also undergone substantial changes. The Metrolink services from Brooklands offer a direct service into Victoria station (largely unrecognisable from the huge rambling station it once was) but the cross-country services to the north-east now leave from Piccadilly and travel via Guide Bridge to reach the old route at Stalybridge. Leeds City was modernised in the nineteen-sixties while the Harrogate-Ripon section of the route was a casualty of the Beeching era. At Darlington the diesel trains to Saltburn don't use the bay platforms any longer as the service runs to and from Bishop Auckland, entailing the use of through platforms.

South of Manchester, too, little has been left unaltered. The old LNWR line that I could just see from the cherry tree has, like the tree, disappeared. The line through Broadheath has, in fact, been obliterated by redevelopment while the former CLC trackbed remains in situ for possible future use as a freight line serving the industrial complex at Partington. The route to Chester remains largely intact although the termini at both ends of the line play no part in current services. Manchester Central, like Exchange station, was deemed surplus to requirements and closed in 1969 but its large roof is still a familiar site in Manchester where it lives on as the G-Mex Centre. Northgate station in Chester was demolished and trains re-routed into what used to be

Plate 208. Looking along the 'through' platform at Saltburn to the former Zetland Hotel on 18th August 2003. It is interesting to compare this picture with **Plate 60,** taken in steam days.

Photo, Author.

Plate 209. Only the buildings and chimney in the left background offer any clues as to the location, west of Manchester Victoria station, as ex-LMS Stanier class '5' No.45407 and Deltic No.55019 *Royal Highland Fusilier* take charge of 'The Dalesman' on 10th September 1999. The photograph, taken from the old Manchester Exchange platform 3, gives a view of the MEN arena, which sits above the station, dominating the horizon. The train will now proceed via Bolton and Hellifield to Clapham.

Photo, Tony Oldfield.

called Chester General. While the Chester trains still use Altrincham station they begin their journey at Manchester Piccadilly and, instead of using the MSJ&AR, call at Stockport and the CLC line westwards to Skelton Junction.

Cynwyd is the one holiday destination of my childhood that cannot be accomplished throughout by rail. The line from Llangollen closed in 1964 and while sections have been re-opened as a tourist operation it appears most unlikely that this will extend to Cynwyd. The station building could still be seen in the early nineteen-seventies when I paid a visit by car. It was in a dilapidated condition but ten years later, when I next visited the village, it had disappeared. Although I regret its passing there is little room for nostalgia for, if railways are to attract customers back they must change and adapt.

As I see it the two most important requirements that railway services should achieve for passengers are convenience and reliability. On long-distance routes trains need to cut timings in order to compete with the airlines but I believe that most passengers would trade a small increase in journey time for a more reliable service. Personally, I would like to see more 'parkway'-type stations, away from the city centres, that offer generous amounts of parking space. In the same way that shoppers enjoy the out-of-town retail experience I believe travellers would appreciate the convenience of avoiding the congested city centres. All stations should receive regular attention from purveyors of food, drink and magazines etc and there should be good, clear communications with accurate information to passengers waiting for a delayed train. For passenger safety and security there should be sophisticated swivel-type cameras coupled with tannoys that show those guilty of anti-social behaviour that they are being watched.

Personally I regret the passing of British Rail as a seperate entity though I appreciate that vast sums have been invested since then. My main gripe is that the train-operating companies have less control over railway infrastructure. Competing railway companies such as those that existed before nationalization seem to make more sense than the present arrangement. Committed railway men and women are needed; personnel that want to spend their working life in the railway industry, confident that their morale won't be sapped and who will gain a thorough understanding for what the public want and receive backing from their employers in seeking to achieve that target. Maybe then I will return more often.

Plate 210. The new face of railways as Metrolink tram No.1001 undergoes crew-training on 21st January 1992. It is seen passing one of Manchester's best-known landmarks, the Midland Hotel, while to the left of the picture stands the former Manchester Central station, now serving as the G-Mex Centre. *Photo, D.J.Sweeney.*

Wheel Arrangement

To virtually all railway enthusiasts the description of wheel arrangements is second nature, especially as locomotive descriptions are often explained by reference to the wheels. However, the system adopted may not make much sense to the layman. It is, in fact, based on the 'Whyte' wheel arrangement which indicates the total number of wheels on each section of the locomotive beginning with the small bogie wheels at the front (if applicable) the driving wheels in the centre and the small trailing wheels (again if applicable). So, for instance, the 'Big Boy' locomotive has four small bogie wheels at the front, followed by two groups of eight driving wheels in the centre, and four trailing wheels (though not visible in this shot) below the cab. The wheels carrying the tender at the rear do not count towards the wheel arrangement. The smallest locomotives are the tank engines with four driving wheels only and they would be described as 0-4-0s as they would have no bogie wheels and no trailing wheels.

Plate 211. The massive form of No.4004, a 'Big-Boy' 4-8-8-4 freight locomotive, is seen here at Holiday Park, Cheyenne, on 3rd June 1976. It was one of twenty-five built in 1941 for use on the Union Pacific's heavily-graded line between Cheyenne and Ogden in Utah. It was withdrawn in 1958. *Photo, Author.*

Railway Companies and their Chief Mechanical Engineers

To those of you who are not familiar with the evolution of railway companies and their chief mechanical engineers I hope the notes below are of some use. In the text the type of locomotive is often described by reference to its designer and this is because these men were closely linked with, and often had a profound influence on locomotive development. What follows is a selective list of railway companies (mainly those mentioned in the book) and their chief mechanical engineers.

Post-Grouping Companies (1923-48)
Great Western Railway (GWR)

Probably the best-known railway company (affectionately known as 'God's Wonderful Railway) it absorbed other, mainly smaller companies and retained its title at the Grouping (of the railways into four companies) until nationalisation in 1948. Most of its locomotives were built at Swindon Works.

Its designers include William Dean (1877-1902), G.J.Churchward (1902-21), Charles B.Collett (1921-41) and F.W.Hawksworth (1941-47).

London, Midland and Scottish Railway (LMS)

With a railway network that stretched from London to Wick and Thurso this huge company absorbed many smaller but still sizeable constituents including the Midland Railway, the Lancashire and Yorkshire Railway, the London and North Western Railway, the Caledonian Railway and the Highland Railway. (The Lancashire & Yorkshire and London & North Western Railways had already amalgamated in 1922).

Its designers were George Hughes (1923-25), Sir Henry Fowler (1925-31), Sir William Stanier (1932-41), C.E.Fairburn (1944-45) and H.G.Ivatt (1945-47).

London and North Eastern Railway. (LNER)

Formed in 1923 this company's territory also stretched from London to the north of Scotland, having absorbed constituent companies such as the Great Northern Railway, the North Eastern Railway, the Great Eastern Railway, the Great Central Railway and the North British Railway.

Its designers were Sir Nigel Gresley (1923-41), E.Thompson (1941-46) and A.H.Peppercorn (1946-47).

Southern Railway. (SR)

This fourth and remaining company formed in 1923 absorbed the London and South Western Railway, the London, Brighton and South Coast Railway and the South Eastern and Chatham Railway among others.

There were two chief designers: R.E.L.Maunsell (1923-37) and O.V.Bulleid (1937-47).

Some Pre-Grouping Companies
Lancashire and Yorkshire Railway (L&YR)

Its locomotives were built and repaired at Horwich Works near Bolton and its best-known designers were W. Barton Wright (1876-86), John A.F. Aspinall (1886-99) and George Hughes (1904-22).

London and North Western Railway (L&NWR)

The main locomotive works was at Crewe and the designers familiar to railway enthusiasts include John Ramsbottom (1857-71), Francis William Webb (1871-1903), George Whale (1903-9) and Charles John Bowen-Cooke (1909-20).

Midland Railway (MR)

The principal locomotive works at Derby also provided locomotives for the Somerset and Dorset Joint Railway. Its designers were Matthew Kirtley (1844-73), S.W.Johnson (1876-1903), R.M.Deeley (1903-9) and Henry Fowler (1909-23).

Great Northern Railway (GNR)

Its railway works was situated at Doncaster and its designers were A.Sturrock (1850-66), Patrick Stirling (1866-95), H.A.Ivatt (1896-1911) and H.N.Gresley (1911-22).

North Eastern Railway (NER)

The locomotive works was located at Darlington and its locomotive designers included T.W.Worsdell (1885-90), Wilson Worsdell (1890-1910) and Sir Vincent Raven (1910-22).

Great Eastern Railway (GER)

Its locomotives were built at Stratford, East London, and familiar designers included T.W. Worsdell (1881-85), J.Holden (1885-1907), S.D.Holden (1908-12) and A.J.Hill (1912-22).

Manchester, Sheffield and Lincolnshire Railway (MS&LR)

It provided locomotives for the Cheshire Lines Committee and its best-known designers include Charles Sacre (1859-86), T.Parker (1886-93) and H.Pollitt (1893-97).

Great Central Railway (GCR)

The MS&LR changed its name to the Great Central Railway as its network spread to London. The main railway works was at Gorton, Manchester, and its principal designers were H.Pollitt (1897-1900) and J.G. Robinson (1900-22).

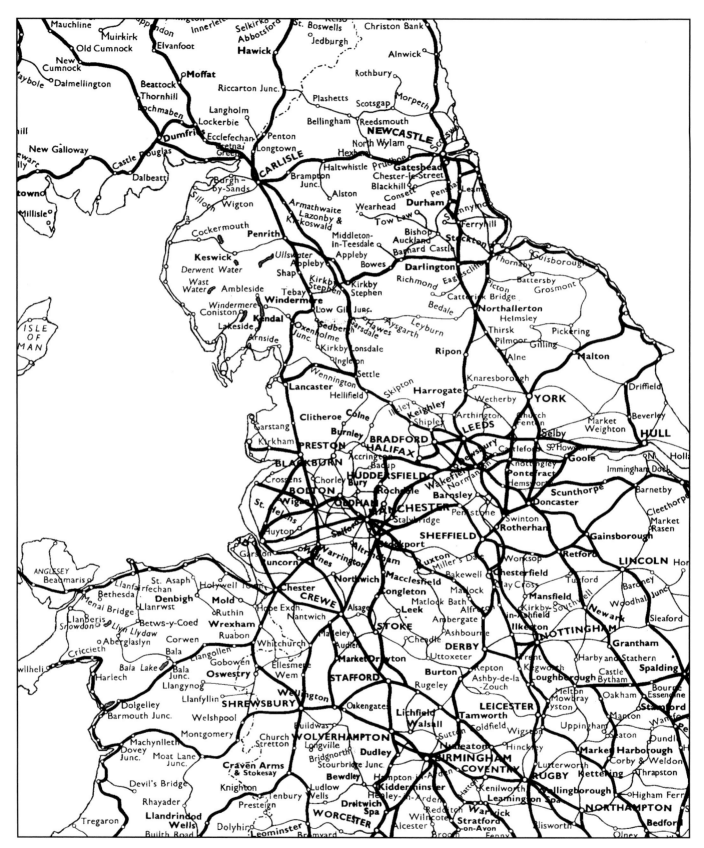

Railways in the Midlands, North of England and North Wales, early B.R. era.